The First Last Man

THE FIRST LAST MAN

Mary Shelley and the Postapocalyptic Imagination

Eileen M. Hunt

PENN

UNIVERSITY OF PENNSYLVANIA PRESS

PHILADELPHIA

Published by
University of Pennsylvania Press
Philadelphia, Pennsylvania 19104-4112
www pennpress.org

Printed in the United States of America on acid-free paper
10 9 8 7 6 5 4 3 2 1

A Cataloging-in-Publication record is available
from the Library of Congress
Hardback ISBN 9780812254020
eBook ISBN 9780812298611

CONTENTS

PREFACE

Mary Shelley Created "Frankenstein," and Then a Pandemic

The world teeters in collective anxiety in the midst of a pandemic. A novel and lethal plague spreads its tentacles around the Earth. It ravages human populations and simultaneously undermines their interconnected economic and political systems. An elite group of political leaders gathers to ask: *what should be done in the face of a worldwide public health crisis?*

This story line should sound familiar. But I am not summarizing the news headlines about Covid-19. I am recalling the plot of a great work of literature. It is Mary Shelley's futuristic novel about a global plague, *The Last Man* (1826).

Shelley saw that the disaster of a pandemic would be driven by politics. This politics would be deeply personal yet international in scope. The spiraling health crisis would be caused by what people and their leaders had done and failed to do on the global stage—in trade, war, and the interpersonal bargains, pacts, and conflicts that precede them.

As we heed scientists' warnings that we are entering "the age of pandemics" we can benefit from reading *The Last Man* as the first major modern postapocalyptic novel about a planetary epidemic that threatens to make the human species extinct.[1] In her second great work of science fiction after *Frankenstein* (1818), Shelley—the child of two philosophers—gave her readers an existential mindset for collectively dealing with the threat of a global man-made disaster.

The Last Man is set in the year 2100. A highly contagious disease attends the novel's driving conflicts. Like the coronavirus, the novel's plague spreads by a combination of airborne particles and contact with carriers. In both cases, it has been incubated, exacerbated, and left unchecked by destructive human behavior.

The Last Man has been so influential that you are already familiar with its basic plot even if you have not read it yet. It presents the history of the ostensible sole survivor of a global plague. Much like *Frankenstein*, *The Last Man* repeatedly has been remade in the science fiction and horror genres—from the works of Edgar Allan Poe to countless zombie apocalypse movies inspired by the 1964 film *The Last Man on Earth*. The latter starred none other than the king of horror, Vincent Price. He played the last human left alive on the planet after a virulent contagion turned other people into vampires.

In Shelley's novel, it is a man named Lionel Verney who finds himself in this extreme and precarious position. In her allegorical reworking of biblical narratives of the fall and rebirth of humankind, Verney is a humble shepherd boy who marries into the royal family at Windsor Castle. He quickly ascends to the top of the diplomatic leadership ranks. He serves as a trusted adviser to lords, ministers, and legislators as the plague breaks out in Constantinople then creeps toward London.

After Verney leads a failed expedition of plague survivors from the crumbled republic of England to the vacant coast of Italy, he is left alone in Rome to contemplate the future. He climbs to the top of the dome of St. Peter's Basilica and carves the year—2100—in the stone. From that sublime vantage, he surveys the remains of human civilization. He summons the hope that there must be other survivors somewhere on the planet. In the final frame, Verney departs on an epic sea journey to discover them. For companions, he brings some signs of his humanity: his mutt, and the works of Homer and Shakespeare.[2] Although Verney is not certain that he will find fellow humans, he discerns a deeper obligation to himself and the whole planet to act upon that hope.

In other words, Verney realizes that even if he is the last man on Earth, he must live as though he is not. He must sustain humanity by acting upon his profound sense of the interconnectedness of his fate with other forms of life—human or not.

Shelley completed *The Last Man* when she was a twenty-eight-year-old widow. She was grieving the loss of her husband, the poet Percy Bysshe Shelley, and three of their children. Her first baby girl was born prematurely and survived less than two weeks, the next daughter died of dysentery and fever, and her firstborn son died of malaria. Then her young husband drowned in a sailing accident at the peak of his career. Writing *The Last Man* was her attempt to reconcile herself to the tragedies of life without losing hope in humanity itself.

Shelley located the human roots of her fictional plague in a centuries-long war between Greece and Turkey. Scientists think that the spread of the new coronavirus grew from a toxic mix of economic, political, and environmental factors surrounding the largely unregulated market for wild animal meat in China and beyond. It has since percolated into an irresponsible game of blame among nations, whose leaders spread rumors that the coronavirus is a foreign bioweapon or even deny the seriousness of the public health crisis within their own borders. As with the coronavirus outbreak, travelers in *The Last Man* disperse the deadly disease across continents, infecting their own families and communities.

Much like *Frankenstein*, Shelley's first novel, *The Last Man* proves to be a work of political science fiction. *Frankenstein* shows how a scientist's abandonment of his artificially made Creature brings ripple effects of suffering to them and the community. The teenage Shelley may have identified with Victor Frankenstein's so-called monster, for her birth had killed her own mother, Mary Wollstonecraft, via a surgically transmitted infection.

Similarly, *The Last Man* originates in the author's experience of devastating personal loss. After Shelley suffered a mental crisis about whether she could live after the loss of almost everyone she loved, she wrote a cosmopolitan answer to this existential question. The unexpectedly hopeful ending of *The Last Man* suggests that all disasters—however threatening to particular individuals or countries—are ultimately about humanity's responsibility to the world as a whole.

Wise beyond her years, Shelley reminds us through the heroic voice of Verney that we should always act upon hope for retaining what makes us loving, humane, and connected to others, even in the face of total catastrophe.

Reading the storylines about the escalating coronavirus outbreaks around the world, we have felt worry—even fear—especially for ourselves and our loved ones. But like Shelley and her avatar Verney, we should summon the strength to look beyond that fear with an attitude of hope and collective problem-solving. Only then might we humanely work together to fight the spread of Covid-19 and future contagions, instead of contributing to a chain of international epidemiological disasters.

The First Last Man

INTRODUCTION

Contagions of Misfortune

Plague as a Metaphor for Disaster

Beyond her nightmarish vision of Frankenstein's Creature, Mary Shelley's other dark and complex legacies for politics, literature, and the arts include the overlapping ideas of the "last man," the "last woman," and the "invisible girl." After losing a premature infant, two toddlers, and a young niece to genetic or infectious diseases, a foster child to an unknown illness, and her husband the poet Percy Bysshe Shelley to drowning, the twenty-four-year-old widow buried herself in the intensive study of three Greek tragedies about plague, infection, and love: Sophocles's *Oedipus Rex* (429 B.C.E.) and *Philoctetes* (409 B.C.E.), and Euripides's *Alcestis* (438 B.C.E.). Her transcriptions and translations of Sophocles informed her authorship of the first major modern pandemic novel about the near-extinction of the human species through war, disease, and corruption, *The Last Man* (1826), and *Alcestis* shaped her Gothic romance about resurrected love, "The Invisible Girl" (1832–33).

Shelley's novel *The Last Man* yielded the iconic image of a heroic survivor who narrates the history of an apocalyptic disaster in order to save humanity—if not as a species, then at least as the practice of compassion or humaneness. In visual and musical arts from 1826 to the present, this postapocalyptic figure has transmogrified from the "last man" into the globally familiar filmic images of the "invisible man" and the "final girl."[1] By reading her work against the background of epidemic literature from ancient Greece to Covid-19, I reveal how Shelley shaped the classics of science fiction (sf), and existentialist and dystopian writing from H. G. Wells, M. P. Shiel, and George Orwell to Octavia Butler, Margaret Atwood, and Emily St. John Mandel. It is this Shelleyan literary tradition that has generated modern postapocalyptic political thought, which uses writing and other art to reflect upon the vital existential and ethical question: what is to be done *after* a massive, human-made disaster?

The Plagues upon the House of Shelley

What is a plague? How do they spiral into wider disasters? And why do people suffer from these contagions of disease and other grave misfortunes?

Mary Wollstonecraft Godwin Shelley (1797–1851) spent her troubled adulthood preoccupied with this trio of life-and-death questions. As the daughter of leading Enlightenment philosophers—the women's rights advocate Mary Wollstonecraft and the anarchist William Godwin—she learned from a young age how to think about the problems of human existence through the lens of futuristic, or as yet unrealized, ideas. Shelley also learned how to deal with death from the very onset of life, when her mother succumbed to a childbirth-related infection eleven days after she was born.[2]

Beginning with her earliest preserved writings, the journals that begin with her 1814 elopement with a married poet to war-ravaged France, the teenage Shelley examined the concept of plague through a prism of personal, literary, political, scientific, religious, and philosophical perspectives.[3] Over the next eight years, her collaborative intellectual partnership with Percy exposed her to a wide range of Western plague literature, from the ancient classics of the Hebrew Bible, Homer, Sophocles, Thucydides, Lucretius, and Ovid to the modern texts of Villani, Boccaccio, Daniel Defoe, Charles Brockden Brown, and John Wilson.[4] From the study of these myths, prophets, poets, playwrights, historians, novelists, and political thinkers, she discerned three dominant interpretations of the meaning of pestilence in the Western intellectual tradition. First, science and medicine had treated plagues as natural afflictions.[5] Secondly, poetry and drama had represented them as curses and scourges. Thirdly, religion and politics had borne them as burdens of conflict and fate.

Between 1815 and 1822, Shelley endured the death of five children she bore, fostered, or cared for, and then suffered a hemorrhaging miscarriage that nearly took her life just a month before her husband's drowning.[6] Amid this series of losses, Shelley developed her own double-sided view of plague. Plagues could be both *literal diseases* that spread death and debilitation throughout a population and figurative *contagions of misfortune*, or human-made disasters spurred by emotional, social, and political conflict. Like the chain of deaths that took five children from her familial circle, disasters were a concatenation of bad or unfortunate events produced in part by human choices and actions: both what people had done and what they had failed to do. Personal misfortune seemed—or even felt—contagious because it often grew to affect others. Shelley observed in her writing, private and public, how people made bad situations worse by turning the misfortune of their own lives into wider social and political catastrophes.

Based on the elopement journal that she co-kept with Percy, Shelley's first publication was *History of a Six-Weeks' Tour through a part of France, Switzerland, and Holland* (1817). The book began with a stark political premise: the worst of the figurative plagues upon humanity were war and other human-made disasters spurred by pride and other selfish passions. "War," she wrote with a maturity beyond her twenty years, was a "plague, which, in his pride, man inflicts upon his fellow."[7] Whether interpersonal or international in scope, war and other human conflicts had devastating emotional and social consequences. Among them, she wrote in her "Journal of Sorrow" (c. 1822–26), were "misery," "utter solitude," "suffering," "despair," "hopeless[ness]," to be "Poor," and, worst of all, to live "without loving & being loved."[8] Lovelessness was a desolate state that could even bring on the "desire" for "death" itself.[9]

As a grieving mother, Shelley knew that literal plagues could be the immediate cause of these figurative plagues upon humanity. Yet in her published work and in her private manuscripts, she would keep circling back to reflect on "Strife" as the root cause of all contagions of misfortune, beginning in the family and extending to international politics.[10] In the collection of Mary Shelley's papers at the Bodleian Library at Oxford, there is a manuscript from Shelley's time in Italy, with the provocative title "Principal causes of Misery."[11] "Strife" was at the core of the list.[12]

I have done the first systematic examination of the paper, watermarking, and handwriting of "Principal causes of Misery" in comparison with other Bodleian Shelley manuscripts. I observed that this unsigned, undated, and previously unattributed document is on paper with a nineteenth-century Italian triple fleur-de-lis watermark and a signature countermark for Fratelli Galdieri.[13] Given that there are no Italian papers in the Bodleian Shelley manuscripts prior to 1818, the manuscript's terminus a quo—or earliest possible date of writing—must be after the Shelleys moved to Italy in March of that year.[14] I concluded that the document is quite possibly in the recently widowed Shelley's grieving hand and part of a correspondence with one of her close friends in Italy in 1822–23.[15] I have surmised that this friend was most likely an Anglo-Irish aristocrat who had dressed as a man to become a medical doctor: Lady Mount Cashell, also known as Margaret King (Moore) and "Mrs. Mason."[16]

In 1786–87, Margaret King's governess in Mitchelstown, Ireland was Shelley's mother Mary Wollstonecraft.[17] King maintained close ties to the Godwin family after her childhood mentor's death in 1797. She even adopted the same name—"Mrs. Mason"—as the fictional governess in Wollstonecraft's *Original Stories from Real Life* (1788). This was a popular work of children's educational literature based on the author's service to the King family in Ireland.[18] To cement her identification with Wollstonecraft as a mother-teacher figure, Lady Mount Cashell penned her own book on children's health and education, *Advice to Young Mothers on the Physical Education of Children* (1823), while a senior member of the social and literary circle of the Shelleys in Pisa.[19]

"Principal causes of Misery" reflects many of the "mental health" themes of Shelley's correspondence with "Mrs. Mason" in the year after Percy's death.[20] It appears to be a kind of philosophical chain letter. It echoes their personal letters on the widow's ill "health"—especially her tendency to "fret" and feel "melancholy," instead of focusing her mind on securing her "means of subsistence" through writing a new novel.[21] On the second page of "Principal causes of Misery," the writer asks the unidentified correspondent to add to a "black list" of causes of human misery on the first page of the folded paper.[22]

Shelley packed "Principal causes of Misery" among her papers when she left Italy for England in July 1823.[23] Regardless of who composed it, she kept it for a reason. Its contents suggest that it served as a reminder of how she had survived her first, and worst, year of widowhood, when she fought the desire to "end" her life and hence her "miseries" without her beloved husband (Figure 1).[24]

Principal causes
of
Misery

—

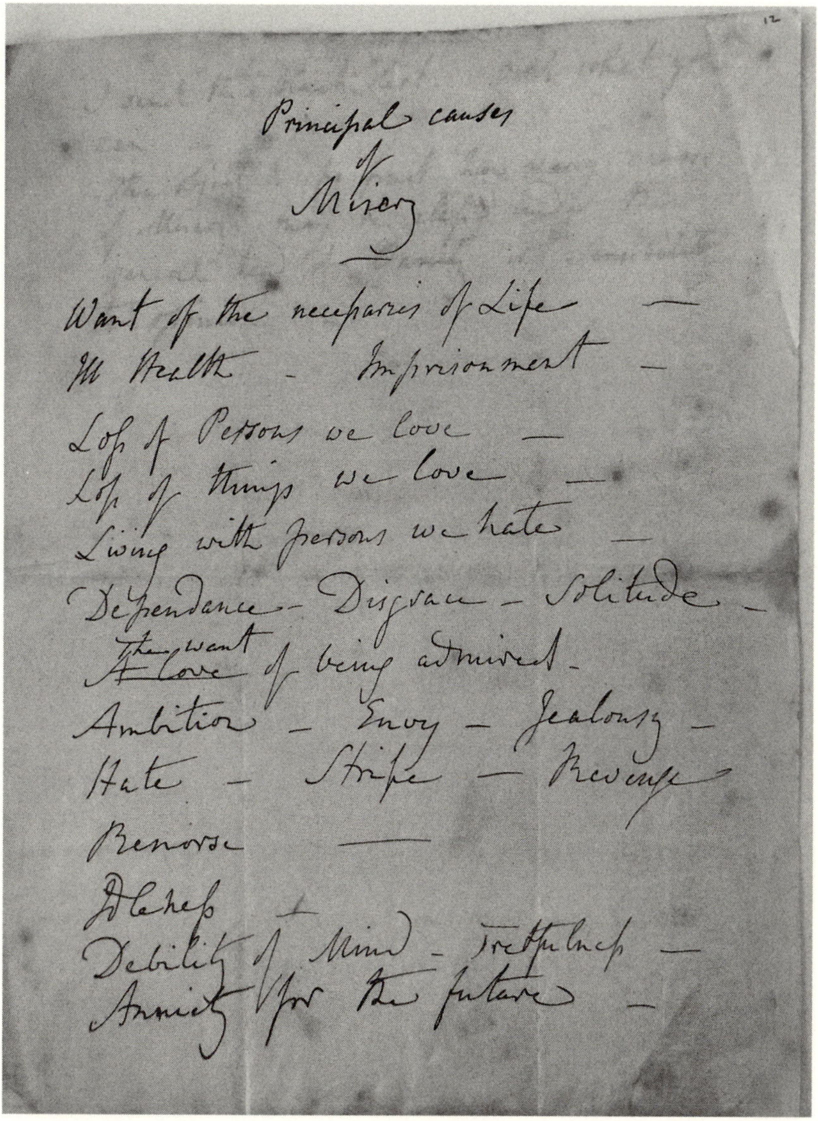

Principal causes
of
Misery

Want of the necessaries of Life —
Ill Health — Imprisonment —
Loss of Persons we love —
Loss of things we love —
Living with persons we hate —
Dependance — Disgrace — Solitude —
The want of being admired —
Ambition — Envy — Jealousy —
Hate — Strife — Revenge
Remorse —
Idleness
Debility of Mind — Fretfulness —
Anxiety for the future —

Figure 1. "Principal causes of Misery." MS. Abinger c. 65, fol. 12, Bodleian Library. Reproduced courtesy of the Bodleian Library, Oxford University.

Want of the necessaries of Life —
Ill Health - Imprisonment —
Loss of Persons we love —
Loss of things we love —
Living with persons we hate —
Dependence __ Disgrace __ Solitude —

The want
~~A love~~ of being admired -
Ambition - Envy - Jealousy _
Hate - Strife — Revenge
Remorse ——
Idleness —
Debility of Mind - Fretfulness—
Anxiety for the future—

This abstract yet analytical list places "Hate—Strife—Revenge" at the core of twenty-one principal causes of misery, which begin with extreme physical and social deprivations such as "Want of the necessaries of Life," "Loss of Persons we love," "Imprisonment," and "Solitude" and conclude with psychological ailments such as "Debility of Mind," "Fretfulness," and "Anxiety for the future."[25] But before we can fully appreciate the contents of this "black list" and its thematic ties to her journals and the plot of her plague novel, we need to examine another list that she wrote in a homemade booklet made of mourning stationery. Its blackened edges signify her years of deepest grief as a widow from 1822 to 1824.[26]

A Widowed Woman Writer

From September to May of her first year of widowhood, Shelley used woven Italian mourning stationery—with the paper's edges dusted with black ink—when writing to a select few friends who shared her grief: Maria Gisborne, Jane Williams, and Edward Trelawny.[27] Like Lady Mount Cashell, Gisborne was another mother figure and mentor to Shelley who had been friends with Wollstonecraft. Gisborne was the first recipient of a black-edged letter in September 1822, two months after the sailing accident that killed Percy.[28] The following winter, the only man to receive black-edged letters from Shelley was Percy's friend Edward Trelawny.[29] Not only had he saved her dead husband's blackened heart from the funeral pyre on the beach in Tuscany, but he also had salvaged the poet's translation of the *Symposium* from the hull of the wrecked ship.[30] Shelley sent the most ink-dusted letters to her "best girl" Jane Williams, who had lost her husband Edward in the sinking of the *Don Juan*.[31] The women expressed their bond as widows with their reciprocal use of mourning stationery through May of 1823.

In a homemade booklet made from black-edged paper, Shelley wrote down the title of her pandemic novel. She cut, notched, and folded the sheets so that they could be held together by a string. On the top left corner of a surviving page, she scribbled "Last Man" at the beginning of a list of books (Figure 2). This black-edged bifolium preserved in her papers at the Bodleian is undated, so we can only infer the terminus a quo of Shelley's writing on it (Figure 3). This would be September 1822, when she first used similar mourning stationery to correspond with Maria Gisborne.

"Last Man" appears in a cluster of Shelley's works that she may have wanted to claim as her own: "Valperga" and "Nontonpaw." Her historical ro-

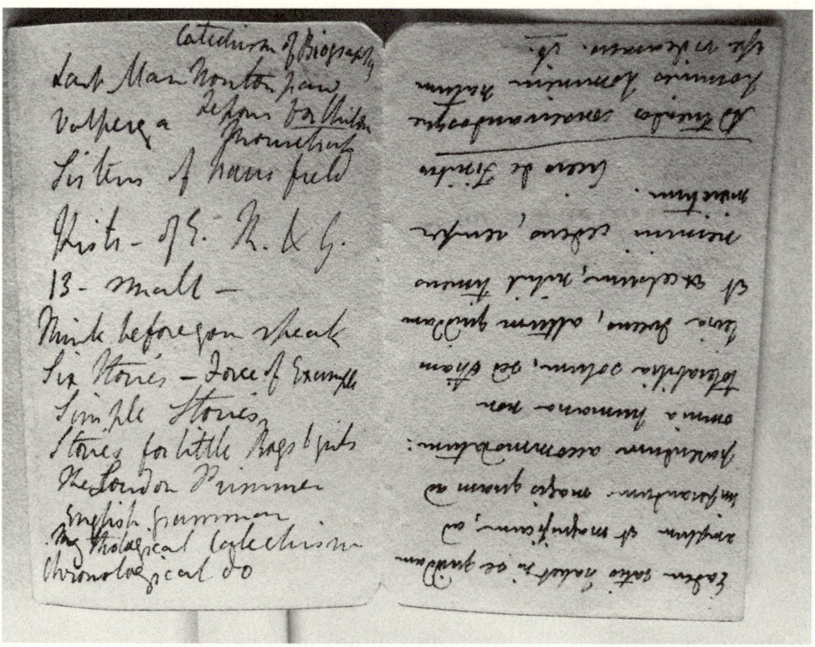

Figure 2. List of books in homemade booklet, with "Last Man" visible at upper left. MS. Abinger c. 65, fol. 10, Bodleian Library. Reproduced courtesy of the Bodleian Library, Oxford University.

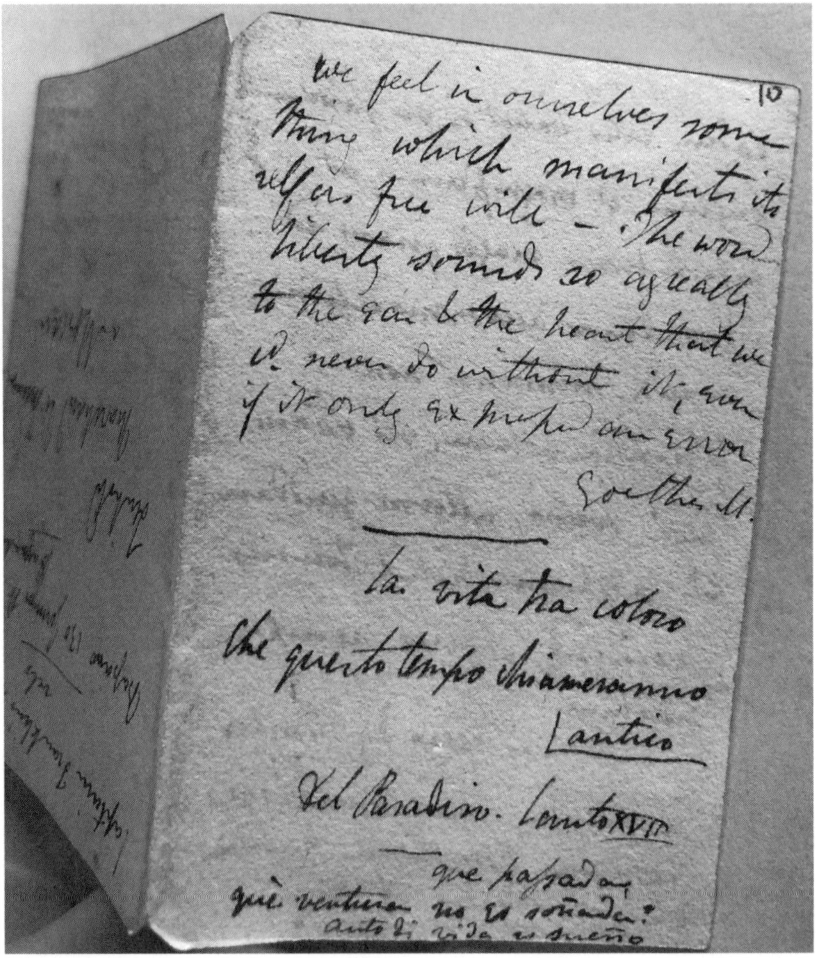

Figure 3. Homemade booklet, reverse side, with black edge visible at top. MS. Abinger c. 65, fol. 10, Bodleian Library. Reproduced courtesy of the Bodleian Library, Oxford University.

mance *Valperga* had been published as "by the author of *Frankenstein*" by her father in mid-February 1823.[32] An adult's version of her humorous children's story of *Nongtongpaw*—an Englishman who can't speak French—had been published anonymously in 1808, and reissued in 1823, also by her father.[33] Around these titles she wrote a list of children's books by other authors, initially crammed into the right margin and then extending vertically down the rest of the page. Beneath "Valperga" she wrote the title of her friend

Lady Mount Cashell's two-volume novel *The Sisters of Nansfield* (1824). Her handwriting suggests that she added to this black-edged list of book titles over time, from as early as September 1822 through at least 1824–25, if "Last Man" refers to an idea for a book title that Shelley wanted to publish.

In 1823–24, her first and saddest year of living in London as a widow, Shelley had reasons to be concerned about cultivating her public identity as an author. Both her first memoir *History of a Six-Weeks Tour* and her first novel *Frankenstein* had been published anonymously, and were rumored to be by her husband.[34] Jules Saladin's unauthorized yet influential French edition of *Frankenstein* appeared in Paris in 1821 with a misspelling of her name ("Shelly") and misattribution of her identity (the "niece" of Godwin) on the title page.[35] Her full and correct name ("Mary Wollstonecraft Shelley") would not appear on the title page until Godwin issued, without her oversight, the second edition of *Frankenstein* around the time she returned to London in August of 1823.[36]

The manuscript of Shelley's second novel, *Mathilda* (c. 1819–20), had been embargoed by the all-controlling Godwin, who thought that the provocative father-daughter incest plot should not be made public for fear of damaging the family reputation beyond repair. Consequently, this milestone of gothic and feminist literature would not be published until 1959.[37] Since 1821, Godwin had edited the manuscript for *Valperga*, the romance that she sent him from Italy. He published the revised historical novel, as "by the author of *Frankenstein*," in London in mid-February of 1823. Shelley would not have learned of the publication of *Valperga* until she received, a few weeks later, Godwin's letter about "editing" and "printing" it.[38]

The most intriguing notation on Shelley's black-edged booklet is her inclusion of "Nontonpaw" next to "Last Man." *Mounseer Nongtongpaw* was a children's book published by her father Godwin in London in 1808. When she was ten, Shelley composed a now-lost incipit to this text.[39] Inspired by a popular late 1790s song, her piece of juvenilia satirized the inability of English people to speak and understand French. Godwin solicited from an unknown poet a revision of his daughter's "scribble" on the laughable figure of John Bull.[40] The published story mocks Bull as "Mounseer Nongtongpaw" because he keeps mispronouncing "Je vous n'entends pas." The proud father produced the lavishly illustrated revision of *Nongtongpaw* for the Juvenile Library series that he founded with his second wife Mary Jane Clairmont.[41] Despite its appearance in Shelley's booklet, on a handwritten list with two of her other works, *Nongtongpaw* remained unpublished under her name and would not be formally attributed to her until 1980. The attribution continues to be contested, but the rediscovery of her writing of "Nontonpaw" next to "Last Man" and "Valperga" suggests her authorship of the original "scribble" for the children's book.[42]

The bespoke black-edged form of Shelley's booklet allowed me to push back, from 1824 to 1822, the earliest possible dating (terminus a quo) of her conception of *The Last Man*.[43] Previously, scholars had assumed that she began the novel in the spring of 1824 due to her mournful comparison of herself to the "solitary being" of "The last man!" in her "Journal of Sorrow" on 14 May.[44] The editors of her *Journals* had dated the scrap of paper with her book titles to December 1824 due to her meditation on its same Cicero passage in her "Journal of Sorrow" on the third of that month.[45] But neither of these proposed dates relied upon the distinctive material properties of the black-edged scrap of mourning paper itself.[46]

According to their study of a large sample of her papers through the year 1823, the editors of the *Bodleian Shelley Manuscripts* contended that Shelley used black-edged mourning paper only for correspondence between September 1822 and May 1823 before she fulfilled her father's wish that she return to England with her sole surviving child.[47] Following their lead, I compared Shelley's manuscripts held at the Bodleian, focusing on the period 1822–28. This survey suggested that this black-edged bifolium quite possibly contains her earliest use of "Last Man" as a title for her fourth novel. She wrote down the capitalized phrase "Last Man" sometime between September 1822, when she first wrote to Gisborne on black-edged paper, and mid-to-late 1824, when she had briefly resumed using mourning stationery again in her correspondence with other close friends in grief over the loss of Percy, Leigh Hunt, and his wife Marianne.[48]

Shelley seems to have jotted down some notes in this booklet when she returned to England as a widow and independent woman writer in 1823. Her list of children's books, including "Nontonpaw," might have been a packing or purchasing list with an eye toward her young son's education. On the reverse side, she noted "Captain Franklin's Travels," a book about Arctic exploration published in London in 1823.[49] She also recorded the address of a "Harness" maker at "130 Jermyn Street" in London: John Dodd, who was active in 1823, according to *Kent's Directory* of merchants and traders.[50]

The final item written on the reverse side of the black-edged bifolium was the address of her stepsister Claire Claremont, who was working as a governess and music teacher in Moscow in autumn 1825.[51] Given the preponderance of items in this booklet dating from 1823 to 1824—which is also the period of her most frequent use of mourning stationery—Shelley most likely conceived the "Last Man" as a concept or title for her roman à clef during this timeframe. Certainly by autumn 1825, when she had submitted the manuscript for publication and received mail from her stepsister at her new address in Moscow, Shelley had settled on the title for her autobiographical and allegorical plague novel.[52] In a letter dated 15 November 1825 to her literary agent Charles Ollier, she reported that the first two volumes of her fourth novel were in press and its "title is to be simply 'The Last Man, a Romance, by the Author of Frankenstein.'"[53]

Shelley's Postapocalyptic Political Philosophy

In early 1823, Shelley wrote an unfinished biography of her late husband and her life with him, which she described in her "Journal of Sorrow" as "romantic beyond romance."[54] She preserved these fragments alongside "Principal causes of Misery" and her black-edged booklet in the Italian papers that she took to London that summer.[55] Though under-studied in her corpus, these deeply personal manuscripts shaped the characters, plot, and driving themes of her second great work of speculative and gothic fiction after *Frankenstein*.[56]

Even as it dramatizes the "romance" of her life with Percy, *The Last Man* follows the stark logic of "Principal causes of Misery." The roman à clef illustrates how plagues, both literal and figurative, spread due to the deprivation of the things that make life worth living—above all, love. Shelley's speculative fiction about the near extinction of the human species trains the mind's eye to consider how *the want* of conditions for love brings to humanity the worst miseries it can suffer. Her war-and-plague novel suggests that strife or conflict causes the want of love, which in turn exacerbates other human wants, such as peace, health, and happiness. Shelley thus gave a relational and emotional response to the problem of human strife that resonates with feminist political philosophy today. As the leading feminist theorist of gender Judith Butler has argued in the aftermath of Covid-19, a "world in which such viral threat and destruction is possible" raises the very "question of life": "what does it mean to live as a living creature, a creature among creatures, a life among living processes, under conditions such as these?"[57] Shelley might have asked, with a sharper edge: can life retain meaning when human strife drains it of love?

The Last Man addresses this existential and political question with the rise of a "PLAGUE" during a war between Greece and Turkey in Constantinople in the year 2092.[58] The Greeks' military strategy is to besiege their Turkish enemies behind the city walls during "intolerable heat."[59] It succeeds but at the cost of causing "famine," "scarcity," and "bad quality" of food, "suffering," "waste and riot," the "scourge of disease," and then a lethal "epidemic" that threatens to wipe out the human species.[60] Akin to Octavia Butler, her twenty-first-century ecofeminist successor in sf and plague literature, Shelley grasped that humans and their technology can and do shape and potentially destroy the whole environment through artifice.[61] Even disasters that appeared purely natural, such as extreme weather, were artificially made more miserable and deadly by human intervention and conflict.[62]

Through her double-sided—literal and figurative—view of the miseries that beset human beings due to want and conflict, Shelley came to see that all plagues provoked existential questions about the meaning of human life in the face of the "inevitability" yet "indeterminacy" of mortality.[63] For this reason, the widowed Shelley should be seen as a philosophical precursor to the modern field of "political existentialism," as defined by Israeli political scientist Uriel Abulof.[64] "Political existentialism," Abulof wrote in *Mortality and the Morality of Nations* (2015), understands "humans as meaning-seeking and meaning-making animals. It deciphers the political play and interplay of the distinctive human traits of mortality, morality, liberty and language."[65] Especially in her devoted study of Ancient Greek (1814–39) and in her diaristic masterpiece the "Journal of Sorrow" (which she filled between the death of Percy in 1822 and the January 1826 publication of *The Last Man*), Shelley embodied the spirit of political existentialism. As a political and existential thinker, Shelley sought meaning—for herself and for humanity itself—through the use of her prodigious gifts for reading, writing, interpretation, translation, and editing. Following in the footsteps of her philosopher parents, she used these literary gifts to reflect on the ties between morality and liberty in the shadow of the ever-present specter of death.

Abulof placed "awareness" of "mortality" at the center of his conception of political existentialism.[66] Humans know that death "is bound to happen," he writes, "but its exact timing is unknown, unless we choose to bring it on."[67] When she wrote her "Journal of Sorrow," Shelley put down on paper the moral struggle and quest for liberation that attends this existential consciousness of the threat of death, especially in times of crisis. Although she began the fourth volume of her journals with a poetic epigraph in which she wished her life "could not / End too soon," she resisted the pull of suicide in order to care for her three-year-old son Percy Florence.[68] By daring to fill the "white pages" of her journal with her darkest thoughts, the widow found meaning in exercising her freedom to find love in life again—a real reason for being—both as a mother and a writer.[69] As a writer, she self-consciously strove to be "a philosopher," or lover of wisdom, in the stoic mode of Cicero.[70]

On the same black-edged scrap of Italian mourning paper that she wrote the title "Last Man," Shelley copied the following quote from Cicero's *De Finibus Bonorum et Malorum* (Of Ends Good and Bad, 45 B.C.E.):

> Eadam ratio habet in se quiddam
> amplum atque magnificum ad
> imperandum magis quam ad
> parendum accomodatum:
> omnia humana non
> tolerabilia solum, sed etiam
> levia ducens, altum quiddam
> et excelsum, nihil timens
> nemini cedens, semper
> invictum[71]

In 1987, the editors of the five volumes of Shelley's *Journals*, Paula R. Feldman and Diana Scott-Kilvert, noted that Shelley copied down the same Latin passage in her 3 December 1824 entry.[72] They also noted that the Loeb edition of *De Finibus* gives this translation: "Further, reason possesses an intrinsic element of dignity and grandeur, suited rather to require obedience than to render it, esteeming all the accidents of human fortunes not merely as endurable but also as unimportant; a quality of loftiness and elevation, fearing nothing, submitting to no one; ever unsubdued."[73]

Without providing a full translation of this passage in her "Journal of Sorrow," Shelley paraphrased its meaning as she offered a meta-reflection in her journal on the experience of pondering the original Latin: "I endeavour to rouse my fortitude and calm my mind by high and philosophic thoughts—and my studies aid this endeavor—I have pondered for hours on Cicero's description of that power of virtue in the human mind wh renders man's frail being superior to fortune—"[74]

In a Platonic and Ciceronian dialogical style, she went on to ask: "What should I fear—to whom cede—by what be conquered—?"[75] "Little truly have

I to fear—," she answered herself. "One only misfortune can touch me—that must be the last—for I should sink under it—."[76] This bad end or *last misfortune* would be her "unhappiness" due to the social "negligence" of others.[77] If she could not find a way to happiness in society again, death would seem to be the only end left for her.

On 14 May 1824, she had confessed to her journal that she felt trapped in a "prison-room" of isolation and despair, for even her closest friends had left her in solitude to feel intolerable grief.[78] This entry ran parallel to the "Principal causes of Misery" manuscript that she brought from Italy, which listed "Imprisonment" on the second line. Six months later, on 3 December 1824, she noted with even grimmer irony the ties between social imprisonment and psychological isolation: "At the age of seven & twenty in the busy metropolis of native England I find myself alone."[79] Still she scribbled with poetic insistence, as she reflected on *De Finibus*, "cannot I yet forego the hope of loving & being loved—the failure of this sweet nourishment fills my heart with gall my soul with sorrow." She concluded her stark meditation on the pains of solitude by asking, "Is this my comentary on the philosophy of Cicero"?[80] Just by invoking the Roman philosopher's name, she seemed to regain a stoic resolve borne of reading *De Finibus*: "I will endeavour to remain unconquered by hard & bitter fortune."[81] But with "tears" in her eyes, the daughter of Wollstonecraft and Godwin still doubted her ability for "philosophizing."[82] With a Socratic self-skepticism, she ended the entry, "Shall I ever be a philosopher?"[83]

Perhaps without realizing the paradox, Shelley proved to be a philosopher that mid-winter day. In the skeptical style of Plato and stoic mode of Cicero, she used writing and reflection to cast doubt on what she thought she knew, in order to find out what she should be able to learn in the future. What she foresaw was the necessity of "loving & being loved" for the sustenance of not only her life and humanity, but also the health and happiness of "my fellow creatures."[84] Struggling against "mysanthropy" and a sense of being "disjoined" from others, she wanted a good or happy ending to her life. Such an ending, she projected, would mean feeling connected to the whole human "species" through the "sweet nourishment" of love.[85] If the "Loss of Persons we love" and the "Loss of things we love" were among the "Principal causes of Misery," it followed that the *regaining* of love could reorient humanity toward happiness. She infused this hopeful, pacific, and cosmopolitan theme into *The Last Man*, which she devoted much of the following year—1825—to bringing to publication.

As she filled the five extant volumes of her journals, from 1814 to 1844, Shelley kept returning to consider—with an ever-deepening maturity—a series of questions that we now associate with the modern existentialist tradition, and particularly with the author of *La Peste* (1947), Albert Camus.[86] Like Camus after her, Shelley used writing and storytelling to dare to ask things that were thought to be taboo. And like Camus, she dared to push her existential, life-and-death questions on pestilence to the point of asking: With all of its horrors, should life be lived at all? And if it should be lived, could life be lived well, whether alone or in community with others, while overshadowed by the plagues of war, disease, and consciousness of mortality?[87]

Ancient Greek literature proved to be a source and solace for Shelley in her existential ruminations about the meaning of life in the shadow of death and conflict. From her study of Ancient Greek since 1814, and her participation in both established and nonconformist Reformed Christian churches in England and Scotland, she knew the original meaning of apocalypse (ἀποκάλυψις): a "revelation," "unveiling," or "uncovering."[88] As with the ancient Athenian playwright Sophocles—whose *Oedipus Rex* she translated in full—Shelley was more interested in what is revealed *by* and *after* a series of man-made disasters than in speculating any final or absolute end to the consequences of human faults and failures.[89] This made her, like Sophocles, a *postapocalyptic* political thinker: a writer who used the darkness of the imagination to uncover the wisdom of how *not* to live after the witnessing or endurance of a seeming catastrophe.

Tellingly, it was *after* her husband's untimely drowning in July 1822 that Shelley immersed herself in the intensive study of three Ancient Greek plays—Sophocles's plague tragedy *Oedipus Rex* and war tragedy *Philoctetes* and Euripides's dark comedy about resurrected love, *Alcestis*.[90] In her journals and other unpublished notebooks and papers between 1814 and 1839, she recorded her ongoing reading, transcription, and translation of these and other Attic dramas, including Sophocles's *Oedipus at Colonus* (401 B.C.E.) and *Antigone* (441 B.C.E.) and Aeschylus's *Seven Against Thebes* (467 B.C.E.).[91] Reading these playwrights informed her treatment of tragedy and romance in her private writing concerning what she called the "strange drama" of her own life.[92] It also drove her authorship of two further "threshold texts" for the evolution of "modern political science fiction"—or politically oriented sf—after her first and most famous novel *Frankenstein; or, the Modern Prometheus* (1818).[93] These works are the first major modern pandemic novel to speculate the near-extinction of the human species through war, disease, and corruption—*The Last Man* (1826)—and a gothic romance about the resurrection of love against all odds—"The Invisible Girl" (1832–33).[94]

After the waking nightmare that gave the teenage Shelley the "hideous" vision of Frankenstein's Creature, she as a young woman gave three more complex and creative gifts to literature and political thought. These are the interconnected ideas of the "last man," the "last woman," and the "invisible girl."[95] Shelley's "lived experience" of plagues—real and metaphorical—led her to bequeath the ideas of the *last (wo)man* and *invisible girl* to her artistic contemporaries and successors.[96] As her roman à clef, based on her own journals, *The Last Man* incarnated in the modern novel the iconic image of a heroic narrator who lives through the seeming end of the world to write down their story of survival for the benefit of others who too may evade destruction. As a grieving widow and mother, she had *implicitly* identified with the solitude and misfortune of the "Last Man" at least since she wrote down the title for her roman à clef on the same black-edged slip of mourning paper where she had copied her favorite quote from Cicero's *De Finibus*. By May of 1824, Shelley *explicitly* identified with the "solitary being" of "The last man!" in her "Journal of Sorrow" as she was in the thick of composing her pandemic novel.[97]

On 15 May 1824, an eerie and tragic irony befell Shelley. The very next day after she had compared herself to the "last man" with all her companions "extinct" before her, she received the news that her friend Lord Byron had also died young, near the field of war in Greece.[98] The loss of this towering public figure and literary collaborator only reinforced her self-image as the last (wo)man of the second generation of British Romanticism, as expressed in her "Journal of Sorrow" since her first year of widowhood.

The Last (Wo)man

Between September of 1822 and the end of 1825—when she conceived, composed, and proofed her plague novel—Shelley consistently rooted the concept for *The Last Man* in her personal manuscripts and her memories of the lives and deaths of Percy Bysshe Shelley, their children, and Lord Byron. She did not want posterity to miss that she, Mary Wollstonecraft Godwin Shelley, was not merely the author, but the living mind from whence the unprecedented plot had been drawn. When she wrote the quasi-autobiographical preface for the novel, she had the unnamed woman narrator relate in her first-person voice how she discovered and reassembled the fragments of a prophecy found in a cave near Naples on 8 December 1818.[99] This prophecy, she implies, is the story of the "Last Man" to survive a near-extinction event for the human species in the late twenty-first century.

Although the prophecy of the "Last Man" at the core of her pandemic novel is fictional, Shelley had in fact visited the cave of the ancient Sibyl of Baiae on 8 December 1818 with Percy and her stepsister Claire Clairmont. She recorded this journey in her second journal book, less than two months after death of her second infant daughter Clara.[100] By rooting her pandemic novel's title and preface in her private manuscripts and journals of "misfortune" and "sorrow," Shelley left open the possibility of interpreting the narrator of her global plague tragedy on two levels at once: as a historical woman, the famous author Mary Shelley, as well as her fictional male avatar, the self-described "LAST MAN" Lionel Verney.[101]

The classics of modern political science fiction, especially in its dystopian and feminist postapocalyptic strands, have rebooted this last (wo)man plotline with men, women, and nonbinary people as the surviving protagonists. In the milestones of dystopian literature by men—H. G. Wells's *The War of the Worlds* (1897), M. P. Shiel's *The Purple Cloud* (1901), George Orwell's *Nineteen Eighty-Four* (1949), and Richard Matheson's *I Am Legend* (1954)—we find men survivors in search of, or surprised by, women with whom to survive.[102] In the classics of feminist postapocalyptic fiction—Joanna Russ's *The Female Man* (1975), Margaret Atwood's *The Handmaid's Tale* series (1985–2019) and *MaddAddam* series (2003–13), Octavia Butler's *Clay's Ark* (1984) and *Parable* series (1993–98), and Emily St. John Mandel's *Station Eleven* (2014) and *Sea of Tranquility* (2022)—we find women (or sometimes cross-species or gender-hybrid) survivors in search of women, men, and other creatures with whom to rebuild community.[103]

Soon after the 1826 publication of her allegorical plague novel, Shelley's postapocalyptic figure of the "last man" became associated with her own notoriously tragic life story, especially her youthful losses of family, friends, and literary collaborators. Thus, it should not be surprising that her idea of the "last man" almost immediately transformed into the idea of the "last woman" in popular media of the period. Just a month after *The Last Man*'s publication in January 1826, a reviewer cruelly asked why the author, who had outlived her husband, did not simply call her novel (and herself) "The Last woman."[104]

None other than Godwin rose to the occasion to defend the author. In early March of 1826, he penned an advertisement for *The Last Man*, which is

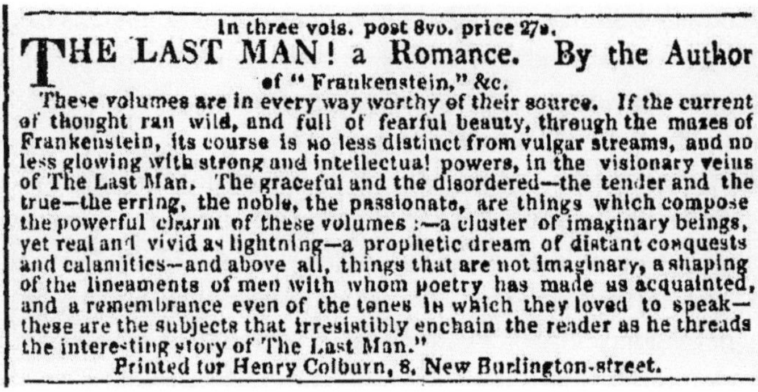

In three vols. post 8vo. price 27s.

THE LAST MAN! a Romance. By the Author of "Frankenstein," &c.

These volumes are in every way worthy of their source. If the current of thought ran wild, and full of fearful beauty, through the mazes of Frankenstein, its course is no less distinct from vulgar streams, and no less glowing with strong and intellectual powers, in the visionary veins of The Last Man. The graceful and the disordered—the tender and the true—the erring, the noble, the passionate, are things which compose the powerful charm of these volumes :—a cluster of imaginary beings, yet real and vivid as lightning—a prophetic dream of distant conquests and calamities—and above all, things that are not imaginary, a shaping of the lineaments of men with whom poetry has made us acquainted, and a remembrance even of the tones in which they loved to speak—these are the subjects that irresistibly enchain the reader as he threads the interesting story of The Last Man."

Printed for Henry Colburn, 8, New Burlington-street.

Figure 4. "THE LAST MAN! a Romance." Advertisement in *The Morning Chronicle* (London), 24 March 1826, 1. Reproduced courtesy of British Library Newspapers database.

preserved in the Abinger collection of his papers at the Bodleian. Although the Abinger catalogue identifies it as a copy of a "review" of the novel, the comparison of Godwin's dated manuscript with digitized newspapers of the period reveals it to be a manuscript copy (perhaps a fair copy) of an advertisement placed in the *Morning Chronicle* on 24 March 1826.[105] On 17 March 1826, Godwin made an appointment to see Shelley's publisher, Henry Colburn.[106] Colburn may have placed the anonymous advertisement in the *Morning Chronicle*, or Godwin did it himself as he had done for a self-authored advertisement for one of his own books that month.[107] Regardless, it appeared on the front page of the paper a week after the men met (Figure 4).

What is poignant about Godwin's advertisement is not only its humble anonymity but also its poetic insight into the autobiographical basis for the "fearful beauty" of the "Romance" at the heart of the "passionate" story of "THE LAST MAN!"[108] It praises the author of *Frankenstein* for "shaping of the lineaments of men with whom poetry has made us acquainted, and a remembrance of the tones in which they loved to speak."[109] The "prophetic" novel did not simply spin an "interesting story of The Last Man," which Godwin knew was already a popular poetic trope in early nineteenth-century French and British Romantic literature.[110] What made this version of the story of the "Last Man" a great work of literature were its "subjects"—the great Romantic poets now dead, Percy Shelley and Lord Byron, and implicitly Godwin's daughter, the last of this young yet epoch-making circle of artists still alive.[111] Shelley's novel combined the "real" and the "imaginary" into something "visionary": she captured the speech and mannerisms of the great British Romantics after they had passed, bringing them back to life, as it were, to use their personas and poetry to envision the "wild" possibility of reanimating humanity after apocalypse.[112]

Godwin preserved a handwritten copy of the advertisement, noting the date of its publication in the *Morning Chronicle*, a London newspaper that had prominently advertised "*The Last Man!*" as a "Romance" several times since early January.[113] During the week it appeared, Shelley visited with her father. One wonders if they discussed over dinner the reception of the novel, including this anonymous advertisement that conspicuously countered the growing public sarcasm about her being "The Last woman."[114]

But even Godwin could not immunize his daughter and her latest innovative contribution to the genre of the "scientific romance" against the public onslaught of small-mindedness and poor taste.[115] In May 1826, the Glasgow-based satirical cartoonist William Heath issued an intentionally offensive depiction of "The Last Woman" as a Black woman slave (Figure 5).

The first known work of visual art based on Shelley's *The Last Man* employed the novel's postapocalyptic setting to make an overtly racist and misogynist point: if an international war or other global disaster wiped out all but one woman, men of all nations and races would fight to the death to

Figure 5. William Heath, "The Last Woman." *The Northern Looking Glass*, n.s., vol. 1, no. 1 (Glasgow: May 1826), 2. Reproduced courtesy of the British Library.

possess her no matter if she were an African slave. Heath could be read as mocking men as much as women, and whites as much as people of color, but either way, the artist crudely exploited gender and race stereotypes perpetuated by British imperial politics of the Georgian era. In the editorial commentary on the cartoon—emphatically titled "*THE LAST WOMAN!*"—"the artist" drew a telling parallel between the Black woman and the widowed author of *The Last Man*.[116] Heath wanted to draw "the likeness" of the "'*all-engrossing*' Mrs. Shelley," perhaps to hint at her unorthodox past among the poetic and atheistic "lords of creation" of British Romanticism, Percy Shelley and Lord Byron.[117] But he refrained from directly caricaturing Shelley because it would have caused a "row."[118] Instead, he depicted the absolutely final woman on Earth as one who would otherwise be "the last to *go off*" the marriage market.[119] The commentary salaciously implied that the reverse was true in the case of "Mrs. S": for she was early to *go on* the market when she eloped with a married man at age sixteen.[120]

In Heath's satirical cartoon of Shelley's *The Last Man*, the double-edged quality of the humor meant that women—especially Black women—got the last laugh. The image suggested that in some future anarchistic state of war like Shelley's twenty-first-century plague novel, men would fight to the death over women, leaving a single Black woman to survive to potentially start life anew on the planet. In an ironic reversal, she would be alone and freed from the twin chains of slavery and patriarchy. If she had seen Heath's caricature, Shelley might have smirked, for she had written a story that was widely recognized as an allegory for the rising struggle against chattel slavery. In a March 1824 letter to Trelawny, she said she was "pleased" that Foreign Secretary George Canning "paid a compliment to *Frankenstein*" as the British parliament debated legislation for the "amelioration of the state of the slaves in some parts of the West Indies."[121]

In Heath's dystopian cartoon, the hidden (and likely unintended) utopia is not so different from the aporetic ending of Shelley's pandemic novel: Lionel Verney, the male avatar for the female author, is *the last to go off* in search of other survivors with whom to remake the human condition and hopefully restore peace on Earth. Octavia Butler's *Parable* series (1993–98) would make explicit the feminist point of this postapocalyptic plotline. Butler envisioned a teenage Black woman survivor, Lauren Olamina, leading the way out of the crime- and plague-ridden, burning city of Los Angeles into a brighter postapocalyptic future on the anarchistic frontier of northern California in the early 2020s.

Back in early 1826, the public's gendered reception of the title of her pandemic novel seems to have provoked Shelley to develop yet another version of the last (wo)man trope—a surviving man and woman who live, as a pair, to tell the tale of enduring a common chain of tragedies. Although she had her analogue Verney—the titular "LAST MAN"—set out to search for a "saved pair of lovers," she did not bring this postapocalyptic trope fully to life until she wrote her gothic romance "The Invisible Girl."[122] Published for a largely female audience in the mass-marketed annual Christmas anthology *The Keepsake* (1832–33), the story unspools the mystery of how the orphan Rosina appears to rise from the dead to reunite with her betrothed, who was haunted both by his father's blocking of their marriage and by an uncanny sense of the girl's lasting presence in a seaside tower near his family estate in Wales.[123] This romantic ghost story contains an allusion to the ancient Greek mythological furies or fates, the "Eumenides," which calls to mind Euripides's tragedy by the same name.[124] But since she partly transcribed and translated his *Alcestis* after 1825, it seems more likely that Shelley paid homage to Euripides's archetypal tale of romantic resurrection in writing "The Invisible Girl."[125] His darkly comic play dramatizes the ancient Greek myth about the bride Alcestis who gives up her life to save her new husband and then, with the help of Hercules, unexpectedly returns from Hades to reunite with him.

J. C. Edwards's 1832 engraving for "The Invisible Girl" reinforces Shelley's poetic association of invisibility with the solitude of being a woman reader-writer who has lost the intellectual and romantic companion to whom she had communicated her innermost thoughts (Figure 6). Painted *before* she is disconnected from her betrothed, this artwork later decorates the tower where Rosina rediscovers her lover Henry. He adorns the painting with the inscription, "The Invisible Girl," as a testament to her death-defying will to regain visibility among the living. Both in the restored painting in the story and in the story's actual frontispiece, Shelley's "Invisible Girl" is the original fictional *last(ing) woman*: she outlasts loneliness and despair by raising herself from the appearance of death to find love in life again.

Shelley's journals illuminate the gradual evolution of a psychological parallel between herself and the 1832 illustration. The opening entry in her "Journal of Sorrow," dated 2 October 1822, was Shelley's first diaristic writing since Percy's death in early July of that year. As she began to fill the "white paper" of this new volume, she reflected with irony on how "gifted I had been in being united to one whom I could unveil myself, & who could understand

Figure 6. William Buxall and J. C. Edwards, "Rosina." Frontispiece to Mary Shelley's "The Invisible Girl," in *The Keepsake* for 1833 (London: Longman et al., 1832), 211, and reproduced on the web in "Mary Shelley's Gothic Tales in the *Keepsake*: A Digital Scholarly Edition Created by Caroline Winter" (2019). Reproduced courtesy of Caroline Winter.

me," only to be left to feel unseen and unknowable, except by herself in her "Literary labours."[126] In this melancholic light, the 1832 illustration's historical analogue is not the almost-suicidal widow who composed "The Journal of Sorrow," but rather the woman who eventually made peace with her life and all its hardships during her thirties and early forties. This is when Shelley gained strength and serenity from raising her only surviving child into his young adulthood. By crafting her editorial commentaries on Percy's *Poetical Works* (1839) and *Essays, Letters from Abroad, Translations, and Fragments* (1840), she imbued his poetry and other writing with new layers of insights from her lived experience as a woman, writer, translator, wife, widow, and mother. By meditating on her personal experiences of loss in the slower-paced, fifth, and final volume of her journals, she came to accept her personal history as more than tragedy: for its darkness was the source of her "imagination," which gave the world *Frankenstein, The Last Man,* "The Invisible Girl," and her other fertile works of fiction and nonfiction.[127]

Through her journaling and editing, the once reclusive widow made her life visible again, on her own terms, both for herself and for the public. From her ringlets and sleeve puffs to her scholarly posture and slight smile, the restored portrait of Rosina as "The Invisible Girl" even bears a striking likeness to the unknown sitter in an 1831 painting by Samuel John Stump. Some have said this writer is the thirty-four-year-old Mary Shelley, who had just published the third edition of *Frankenstein* (Figure 7).

The 1831 edition of *Frankenstein* was a literary milestone because the author, for the first time, had complete editorial control over its contents. The first anonymous edition of 1818 featured an anonymous preface by Percy, recounting the night of ghost stories that inspired the novel, and foregrounding its Godwinian premise that people are not born monsters but rather are made evil by the conflicts and injustices they suffer in society.[128] The preface, alongside the book's dedication to Godwin, soon led reviewers to suspect that the politically radical and atheistic poet was the author of the book.[129] Not to be outdone by Percy, Godwin produced the second edition of 1823 with his daughter's name on the cover but without her oversight.[130] Writing the autobiographical preface to the third edition of 1831 finally gave "the author of *Frankenstein*" the opportunity to tell her story of the novel's conception, as she tartly put it, "in my own mind."[131] While she was once the invisible girl behind *Frankenstein*'s creation, it was always her book made in the dark recesses of her "imagination"—and she, at last, had made that fact visible.[132]

Figure 7. Samuel John Stump, unknown woman (1831) in the Mary Shelley portrait collection at the National Portrait Gallery, London. Reproduced courtesy of the National Portrait Gallery, London.

The reprinting of Shelley's "Invisible Girl" story in her *Tales and Stories* (1891) meant that it informed the peak decade of Victorian gothic and sf literature, led by her readers Bram Stoker and H. G. Wells.[133] The year 1897 alone saw the invention of two of the leading monsters of modern English literature after Frankenstein's Creature, with the publication of Stoker's *Dracula* and Wells's *Invisible Man*. Shelley's gothic prototypes of the "invisible girl" and the "last man" as lone (and lonely) survivors of disaster seem to have filtered into the now globally familiar idea of the "invisible man." Traces of "invisible" and "last" men kept reappearing in milestone works of fiction and film, from the 1933 Universal Monster movie adaptation of Wells's *Invisible Man* directed by James Whale, to the Black existentialist novels of Richard Wright and Ralph Ellison.[134]

The parallel concept of the "last woman," rooted in Shelley's life story, contributed to iconic artistic images of the "last" or "final girl" who survives a man-made disaster on her own: from Muriel Spark's desert island novel *Robinson* (1958) and Lorraine Hansberry's Broadway play *A Raisin in the Sun* (1959), to the Universal Monster movie-inspired *Scream* horror-satire film series (1996–2022) and the 2020 feminist reboot of the 1930s *Invisible Man* movie franchise.[135] Regardless of their gender, the real heroes in these disaster narratives are the ones who choose love despite the prospect of losing everyone and everything that matters to them. Writing this unexpectedly hopeful and malleable ending for the "horror" stories of human existence was Shelley's intellectual gift to the traditions of postapocalyptic political thought, existential philosophy, dystopian fiction, and plague literature.[136]

What is Plague Literature?

Before we go any further, I ought to define what I mean by "plague literature." I have taken for granted that the term needs no formal definition in the era of the novel coronavirus. On an intuitive level, we all know what plague literature is, because our lives during the Covid-19 pandemic have become its narrative material.

So far, I have followed Shelley in conceptualizing plague literature on two parallel planes: (1) metaphorically, across religious, mythological, and literary texts that treat plague as a symbol to "stand for" something else, such as hardship or misfortune (i.e., the Biblical plagues of Egypt, or the plague of Thebes in *Oedipus Rex*), and (2) sociopolitically, across literary and other historical documents that capture diverse elements of the human experience of plague as contagious or infectious disease, across time and place (i.e., the bubonic plague, malaria, or dysentery). A third and broader category that contains the other two can be described as *plague writing*. Plague writing is not necessarily for publication. It is any written response to the experience or depiction (factual or metaphorical) of a contagious disease (such as the bubonic plague or Covid-19) or an infectious disease (such as malaria or dysentery). The scope of plague writing can cover anything from a localized or regional epidemic, which touches some or many people, to an international or global pandemic, which afflicts multitudes or perhaps even all of humanity. In the era of Covid-19, the *New York Times* coronavirus tracker—which tells me as I write that over 6.5 million people have died from the novel contagion worldwide—is a prime example of how plague writing itself can be global.[137]

In this book, I focus on recovering the philosophical significance of Shelley's private and public plague writing. I treat not only her novel *The Last Man*, but also her journals and letters that use metaphors of plague or explore real-life experiences of epidemics, against the background of a wider tradition of published plague writing. Some of these published works are understood as canonical, such as Boccaccio's *Decameron* (1353) and Defoe's *A Journal of the Plague Year* (1722), because they defined the emergence of a recognizable Western genre of plague literature in the late medieval and early modern periods. Other published works predate these classics of plague literature by centuries, yet gave rise to their themes due to their robust reception across multiple languages. These include Ancient Greek and Roman literary works such as Sophocles's *Oedipus Rex* and Ovid's *Metamorphoses* (A.D. 1), which drew on the history of the Plague of Athens of 430 B.C.E. to develop rich allegorical accounts of plague that continue to shape poetic, theatrical, fictional, and historical descriptions of epidemic and pandemic.[138]

In a lecture given in 1890, the prolific British historian of books Henry R. Plomer was the first scholar to venture a definition of "plague literature" in English.[139] He did so via a "bibliography of the plague" in England, based on his research in the British Museum and the Guildhall libraries in London.[140] He identified five types of plague writing in English: (1) "proclamations and orders," (2) "medical works," (3) "theological works," (4) "general literature," and (5) "advertisements and bills of mortality."[141] He cited Defoe's novel *A Journal of the Plague Year* as the most prominent work of fiction in "general literature" about the plague in England.[142] Plomer knew that Defoe based his novel on his uncle's journal of the 1665–66 visitation of the bubonic plague to London, as well as other political, medical, religious, literary, journalistic and legal documents from the other four categories of plague literature. He must have judged that it was general knowledge by 1890 that Defoe had written the most famous novel in English plague literature, for it was the only novel he cited, alongside many poems and plays from the early modern period.

From this vantage, Shelley's decision to ground the narrative and imagery of *The Last Man* in the classics of plague literature, including Defoe's renowned novel, looks bold. Nearly seventy years before Plomer defined "plague literature" for their nineteenth-century British culture, she aimed at nothing less than to reinvent the genre before it had even solidified in form. Defoe was her main rival, so she took him on. She incorporated references to his *Plague Year* and *Robinson Crusoe* (1719) into her journals and *The Last Man,* alongside classical and medieval sources of plague imagery from the Bible, Homer, Sophocles, Thucydides, Lucretius, Ovid, and Boccaccio.[143] She also studied and alluded to more recent landmarks of the genre of plague literature after Defoe, by the American novelist Charles Brockden Brown and the Scottish playwright John Wilson.[144] After she published *The Last Man*, she continued to build on her knowledge of the genre to compose two scholarly biographies of the great fourteenth-century chroniclers of the bubonic plague in Florence, Villani and Boccaccio.[145] There is perhaps only one other major modern author of fiction who researched epidemic literature and history as widely and deeply as Shelley. This was Camus, who began *La Peste* with an epigraph from Defoe's *Journal of the Plague Year,* and studied the history of outbreaks of the bubonic plague in Algeria as part of his research for his great existential novel.[146]

Shelley's amalgamation of the themes of plague literature turned contagion and infection into pointed metaphors for the global politics and conflicts that drive humans to destroy one another and the world around them. In 1974, the historian, literary critic, and philosopher René Girard argued that the canon of plague literature, extending back to *Oedipus Rex*, has always implicitly made this very point.[147] By contrast, I show that Shelley's profound literary innovation was to make this point *explicit*, by foregrounding the conflicts that drive plagues—not the plagues that drive conflicts—in both her private writings and in her published pandemic novel. *The Last Man*, in turn, begat a new and vital genre of fiction, which overlaps with the older tradition of plague literature. Postapocalyptic literature from Edgar Allan Poe to

Emily St. John Mandel follows Shelley in diagnosing plagues and pandemics as symptoms of deeper human conflicts, instead of blaming them as the root causes of our individual and collective misfortunes. The success of this modern postapocalyptic genre in music, art, novels, short stories, film, and television means that Shelley has now surpassed Defoe as the prime model for the tropes and themes of the world's plague and disaster literature. She is the Oedipus Regina for our time of corona.

What She Predicted: A Monster Pandemic

Shelley is most famous for conceiving the original monster story of the modern horror genre, *Frankenstein*, for a ghost story competition held at Lord Byron's Genevan villa in 1816. She should be similarly celebrated for publishing the pandemic novel that unleashed the dominant tropes of postapocalyptic literature upon modern political science fiction. Published eight years after *Frankenstein*, her fourth novel *The Last Man* pictured the near annihilation of the human species by an unprecedented and highly pathogenic plague that surfaces during a war between Greece and Turkey in the year 2092.

The Last Man is the first major modern novel about a fully global and lethal pandemic, not merely a localized epidemic of a contagion that threatens a discrete population. Shelley was familiar with classic depictions of plague by Homer, Ovid, Boccaccio, Defoe, Charles Brockden Brown, and John Wilson, which were set within a single city or battlefield. By contrast, *The Last Man* chronicles a war-driven "epidemic" that spreads through travel, trade, and military routes across oceans and nations.[148] It is this global and artificial spread of Shelley's "epidemic" that makes her a visionary *political* theorist of how pandemics rise and overwhelm the world.

Although Shelley used the standard nineteenth-century English medical term "epidemic" to describe a twenty-first-century global plague, she knew the etymological origins of the term we now in fact use: "pandemic." While she lived in Italy with Percy in 1818, Shelley helped him translate Plato's *Symposium* (385–70 B.C.E.), which contains the Greek word πάνδημος.[149] In Plato's philosophical dialogue on the meaning of love, the goddess "Pandemos" is the "earthly Aphrodite" who oversees the bodily loves of "all" (*pan*) "people" (*demos*), men and women alike.[150] In the aftermath of the 1642–51 English Civil Wars and the 1665–66 Great Plague of London, the adjective "pandemic" gained salience in both political and medical contexts in seventeenth-century English. It could refer to either the disorders of democratic government by all people (as in monarchist John Rogers's 1659 condemnation of the "unjust *Equality of Pandemick Government*"), or the visitation of pestilence to undermine the stability of the entire body politic (as in the doctor Gideon Harvey's 1666 description of "Endemick or Pandemick" diseases that "haunt a Country").[151]

According to Justin Clemens, two important homophonic variants of "Pandemick" emerged in the English language in the aftermath of the English Civil Wars. The political philosopher Thomas Hobbes's *Leviathan* (1651) defined "Panique Terror" as a contagious "passion" of fear that happens to "none but in a throng, or a multitude of people."[152] The Reformed Christian poet John Milton invented the word "pandaemonium" for his epic poem *Paradise Lost* (1667) to depict Satan's hell as a kingdom where all the little devils lived in sin-infected chaos.[153] Indebted to her and Percy's study of Plato, Hobbes, and Milton, Shelley's *The Last Man* conceived the global plague as an "epidemic" that affects or touches upon (*epi*) all (*pan*) people (*demos*) precisely because it stems from the disruptions of collective human corruption, panic, and politics.[154]

In her first novel, Shelley had metaphorically rendered the revenge of Frankenstein's "monster" upon his uncaring scientist-maker as an unstoppable "curse," "scourge," and "pest" upon their family and potentially "the whole human race."[155] This unnamed "creature" was nothing less than a "catastrophe," brought to life by the chemist Victor Frankenstein from an artificial assemblage of the dead parts of human and nonhuman animals.[156] In her second great work of political science fiction, she found new horror in reversing the direction of the metaphor. No longer was the monster a plague: the plague itself was the monster.

With her great pandemic novel, Shelley panned out to see all plagues as human-made monstrosities that leave "a scene of havoc and death" behind them.[157] What made plagues so ghastly was their exponential power to multiply, causing a concatenation of disasters for their human authors and other afflicted people on "a scale of fearful magnitude."[158] Her distinctive philosophical contribution to plague literature was to conceive all plagues—real and metaphorical—as human contaminations of their wider social environments. Bad human behaviors corroded the people closest to them, then spread like toxins through the cultural atmosphere to destroy the health and happiness of others. The ancient plagues of erotic and familial conflict, war, poverty, and pestilence had reproduced together and persisted into modernity through centuries of modeling, imitation, and replication of humanity's worst behaviors in culture, society, and politics.

It is its explicitly political plotline that distinguishes *The Last Man* from its closest literary precedent, the long prose poem by Jean-Baptiste Cousin de Granville, *Le Dernier Homme* (1805).[159] Loosely translated from French into English in 1806 as *Omegarus and Syderia*, this theological fantasy reversed the story of Milton's *Paradise Lost* to end with a descendent of Adam as the last (not first) man. Granville's work did not feature a literal plague or epidemic, but rather a divinely predestined scourge of infertility visited upon humankind as a punishment for their collective sin against God. *Le Dernier Homme* soon inspired other English poems based on the apocalyptic idea of a dying Earth or the end of humanity, such as Lord Byron's "Darkness" (1816) and Thomas Campbell's "The Last Man" (1823). Mary Shelley knew of the former and most likely the latter of these two, much shorter, yet vastly influential, poems, and may have been familiar with Granville's longer, but more obscure, epic.[160] She certainly shared her major poetic muse with Granville, given that she drew the epigraphs for both *Frankenstein* and *The Last Man* from Milton's *Paradise Lost*.

On 19 February 1825, Shelley wrote to her literary agent Charles Ollier that her publisher Henry Colburn "mentioned to my father that there was a romance entitled The Last Man, in three thin volumes published some time ago. Now that I have finished mine I should like to see this."[161] This "thin" set may have been *Le Dernier Homme*, in French or translation. It is intriguing to consider that Shelley told her agent she had already "finished" a full manuscript draft of *The Last Man* before she expressed interest in seeing this literary predecessor. However, there is no record of her reading Granville as she brought her fourth novel to press that year. Godwin did note in his diary that he read *Omegarus and Syderia* in early January 1826, perhaps in anticipation of the publication of his daughter's contrastingly *thick* three-volume novel later that month.[162]

Reading *The Last Man* that winter, Godwin would have recognized his daughter's homage to his own anarchistic political theory. In his treatise *Political Justice* (1793), which Shelley kept in her traveling library, he had argued that corruption spreads in society due to the failure of people and their prevailing political institutions, laws, and leaders to stop or contain conflict and other injustice.[163] *The Last Man* follows this political logic but makes it personal. The first volume establishes how the interpersonal conflicts that arise from a cluster of five overlapping love triangles in the court circle of

Windsor Castle drive political fissures that eventually incapacitate England's leadership in the face of the plague. Adrian, the former prince turned republican, stands for Percy Shelley. Verney, his friend turned diplomatic aide, stands for Mary. In the first love triangle, Verney the shepherd boy and Adrian the prince share an unrivaled friendship until Verney falls in love with Adrian's sister Idris.

The next two love triangles involve Lord Raymond, who represents Lord Byron. Raymond is a philanderer like his aristocratic and licentious analogue. He dismisses the queen's machinations for him to marry her daughter Idris so that the royal family might regain political power in the new democratic government. Instead Raymond impulsively marries the commoner he loves, Verney's sister Perdita (who sometimes stands for Mary's stepsister Claire Clairmont), while carrying on a flirtatious romance with Evadne, the daughter of a Greek diplomat stationed at Windsor Castle. In the fourth and fifth love triangles, the aloof Adrian hints at a romantic interest in Evadne, but her undying obsession is Raymond, despite knowing that he and his wife Perdita are truly in love.

Suspecting an affair, Perdita separates from Raymond, driving him to abandon his democratically elected position as Lord Protector of England. Separately, Raymond and Evadne go to fight for the independence of Greece against the Turks in Constantinople. In the second volume, she dies cursing both him and the whole world to suffer a "plague" that appears to have infected her with a deadly "fever" on the battlefield.[164] He is crushed in the rubble of the Hagia Sofia before the war-driven "epidemic" crosses borders through diplomatic, trade, and travel routes to escalate into an international pandemic.[165]

The first volume of *The Last Man* also charts how decades of political corruption precede the visitation of the most devastating wave of plague to England. A monarchy until recently, England is a new and fragile democratic regime or representative republic in the late twenty-first century. Despite the appearance of the free and fair election of Lord Raymond to the executive position of Lord Protector, democratic institutions begin to erode from the moral corrosion of the elite white men in power who drive and manipulate the mechanisms of government behind the scenes.

It is in the second volume that the professed man of the people, Ryland, ascends to the highest executive office in the land. When Lord Raymond selfishly abdicates his position to escape his ill-fated love affair with Evade by going to war in Constantinople, Ryland takes advantage of the resultant chaos to ascend through electioneering to the position of Lord Protector. Although he claims to have the interests of the "popular" party at heart, Ryland dismantles the egalitarian system of social welfare put in place by his predecessor Lord Raymond.[166] Although the state has the technology and infrastructure to distribute food and other necessities to all of its citizens, it conspicuously fails to do so as the plague seeps into its most dense and populous city.

Ryland shows his true selfish character by renouncing responsibility for the people who elected him. The populist leader eventually abdicates his position, as did Lord Raymond. This leaves the former-prince-turned-republican, Adrian, to step in as the interim deputy Lord Protector just as the plague arrives in London—but it is too late for even a true defender of liberty to save democracy from falling apart.

In an ironic turn of events, Ryland flees London only to get infected by the airborne pathogen. But when he is found dead, "half-devoured by insects," alone in a quarantine bunker far from the capitol, it is not the final political tragedy to befall the republic.[167] The collapse of the democratic political system, and the decimation of its population by the plague, has yet to come.

In the third volume, a new and dangerous populist leader arises from the rubble of English democracy. This time he is a charismatic and authoritarian Christian preacher and "patriarch." The itinerant "methodist" evangelizes and manipulates the vulnerable remnant of plague survivors—targeting women, the poor, and children—by inveighing them to seek health and protection in his apocalyptic cult. His medical disinformation and religious propaganda make his followers naively believe that they are immune from the stealthy and invisible transmission of the deadly disease. As the "plague, slow-footed, but sure in her noiseless advance" besets even the "elect" of the cult, the patriarch lies about the numbers of the infected and even hides the bodies of his own followers in a desperate attempt to cement his prophetic authority among his chosen people.[168] Verney escapes the cult to lead a small remnant of survivors across France and into Switzerland, but by the time they reach the coast of Italy, there are only three people left. In a strange twist of fate, he ends up the last man to withstand the plague and other human-made disasters after his niece and Adrian drown in a sailing accident in the Mediterranean Sea, in a kind of recreation of the death of Percy.

Midway through *The Last Man*, Shelley has the Greek princess Evadne issue an apocalyptic prophecy: humanity would soon be incinerated in a vortex of war, passion, and betrayal. As she dies of "crimson fever" on a pestilential battlefield, she curses her beloved and the leader of the Greek forces

Lord Raymond for abandoning her for his wife Perdita. "Fire, war, and plague," she cries, "unite for thy destruction!"[169] As if on cue, the seasonal "visitation" of "PLAGUE" in Constantinople escalates into a deadly epidemic on an unprecedented scale.[170]

With her uncanny insight into the social genesis of epidemics and other plagues upon humanity, Shelley—through the voice of Evadne—anticipated the economic and political theory of pandemics that has gained currency in the twenty-first century. Back in 2005, the Marxist historian Mike Davis warned the world that zoonotic viral pandemics like the avian flu and SARS-CoV—whose genetically mutated strains enabled them to leap from nonhuman animals to a mass of human victims—were *The Monster at Our Door*.[171] While Davis did not cite Shelley in his book, he didn't need to: the allusion to *Frankenstein* was perfectly clear in the title.

Davis was writing in a long tradition of reading the monster imagery of *Frankenstein* through the technological lenses of Marxism. Based in London for much of his career, the German economic and political theorist Karl Marx was likely influenced by the massive cultural impact of Shelley's *Frankenstein* and her husband Percy's radical political poetry, as they filtered through the nineteenth-century British socialist tradition.[172] Despite his stubborn dislike of Marxist hermeneutics and other social-scientific readings of literature, the late Yale professor and literary critic Harold Bloom was always the first to admit that "it is hardly possible to stand left of (Percy) Shelley."[173]

Given his revolutionary-era philosophical debts to Rousseau, Wollstonecraft, and Godwin, it is not surprising that Percy Shelley felt outraged by the news of the August 1819 "massacre at Manchester."[174] The British calvary charged an assembly of sixty thousand workers, killing some and injuring hundreds more. While living in exile in Italy with his pregnant wife, in deep mourning over the recent death of their son William, the poet composed a timeless lyric to summon the poor to nonviolent protest. Not published until 1832 due to its controversial argument, "The Mask of Anarchy" became an anthem for the peaceful liberation of people from the slavery of poverty and political oppression:

Rise like Lions after slumber
In unvanquishable number—
Shake your chains to earth like dew
Which in sleep had fallen on you—
Ye are many—they are few.[175]

Completed two years before Percy's rousing defense of popular uprising against the power of the imperial state, *Frankenstein* made a parallel political point. Literary scholar Elsie B. Michie underscored that the tragic predicament of Frankenstein's abandoned Creature fits what Marx would call, in his *Economic and Philosophical Manuscripts* of 1844, the plight of "alienated labor."[176] Modern capitalistic society cruelly severed the poor from the material sources and products of their own making. Frankenstein likewise left his Creature bereft of any benefits of the "bodies," "work," and "labours" by which "the being" had been shaped into "a thing" such as "even Dante could not have conceived."[177]

When read against the background of Shelley's novel, Marx's theory of alienated labor recalls the dynamic of confrontation and separation that drives the conflicted yet magnetic relationship of the Creature with his technological maker. Taken out of the context of the *Economic and Philosophical Manuscripts*, some of Marx's words could easily be mistaken for a commentary on *Frankenstein*, as in: "The object that labour produces, its product, confronts it as an alien being, as a power independent of the producer."[178] While capitalism produced the workers from its elite economic control of the tools of science, technology, and economics, the workers received no benefit from those same tools that a truly benevolent maker might have otherwise bestowed upon them. What could such a creature do but confront their maker with a demand for the goods necessary for the development of their humanity?

In his 1857–58 "Fragment on Machines" from the *Grundrisse*, Marx rather poetically captured the process of human alienation from the products of their own technological labors: "Nature builds no machines, no locomotives, railways, electric telegraphs, self-acting mules etc. These are products of human industry; natural material transformed into organs of the human will over nature, or of human participation in nature. They are *organs of the human brain, created by the human hand*; the power of knowledge, objectified."[179] Reworking the twin Greek myths of Prometheus, in which the titan molds humanity from clay and then forges the mortals' rebellion from the gods through the gift of fire, Marx follows Shelley in depicting human beings as self-replicating machines, for they are artificial products of their own willful mind to dominate and transform nature through technology. As the political philosopher Marshall Berman argued in *All That Is Solid Melts into Air: The Experience of Modernity* (1983), Marx's bourgeoisie is a Promethean "sorcerer" akin to "Goethe's Faust" and "Shelley's Frankenstein," for it created new and unruly forms of artificial life that in turn raised "the spectre of communism" for modern Europe.[180]

What the late Mike Davis did so brilliantly, in the spirit of both Marx and the Shelleys, is to use this nineteenth-century techno-political imaginary to conceptualize humanity's responsibility for the self-destructive course of pandemics in our time. Generations of readers of *Frankenstein* have felt compelled to pity the Creature, despite his train of crimes, and come to view him as a product of the fevered madness of his father-scientist. In this rhetorically persuasive Shelleyan tradition, Davis pushed his readers to see Covid-19 and other pandemics as products of the myopic mindsets of the human beings who selfishly let them loose upon the world.

With the rise of the novel coronavirus, or SARS-CoV-2, Davis stoically set up his home office in his garage. As most countries around the globe went under lockdown during the endless winter of 2020, he sat down to update his book *The Monster at Our Door* for the second time.[181] Like Shelley and many writers of political science fiction after her, from Octavia Butler to Margaret Atwood to Emily St. John Mandel, the historian had predicted that a new, deadly, and devastatingly severe acute respiratory syndrome (SARS) or highly pathogenic avian influenza (HPAI) would visit the planet in the twenty-first century.

Reports from the World Health Organization had sparked Davis's concerns about the latest iteration of the avian flu, or H5N1 influenza.[182] H5N1 had fast and lethal outbreaks in 1997 and 2003—while exhibiting a terrifying 60 percent mortality rate.[183] It passed from chickens to humans in Hong Kong in 1997, and, on a much more alarming scale, through "commercial poultry farms" in South Korea, China, Thailand, Vietnam, and other regions of Southeast Asia in 2003, via a "highly pathogenic" and "novel strain," H5N2.[184] Like the epidemiologists, ecologists, and anthropologists whose work he studied, the historian feared that the "bird flu" could erupt into a pandemic that might kill more than the deadliest virus of the twentieth century.[185]

Davis recounted that an estimated "40 to 100 million people"—including his "mother's little brother"—had been taken by the H1N1 avian influenza of 1918.[186] The newspapers at the time described the pandemic as the "Spanish Flu," even though it started in the United States and elsewhere.[187] Because Spain remained neutral during the First World War, its press went uncensored. Spanish newspapers took the lead in reporting cases of the rising international wave of influenza. Far from war-torn continental Europe, the first recorded human outbreak of this flu mutation—which swiftly flew from birds to people—in fact began in a rural farming community and military base in Kansas.[188]

A dreadful rerun of 1918 loomed in our near future, Davis insisted, if nations did not prep for the worst. Governments needed to reduce "the virulence of poverty," improve health care, and stockpile medical and protective equipment.[189] They had to regulate international trade, factory farming, and flight travel with an eye toward protecting public health from a resurgence of uncontrolled zoonotic viral respiratory infections. And they must support the best virology and vaccine research before the next epidemic snowballed into a global economic and political disaster.

Under lockdown in April 2020, Davis changed the title of his updated book to *The Monster Enters*, to mark a shift in his historical perspective. Just a few weeks earlier, disease ecologist Peter Daszak announced in a *New York Times* op-ed that we had officially entered the "age of pandemics."[190] The monster pandemic of our political nightmares was no longer the threat of the avian flu at our door. It had already entered our world as SARS-CoV-2—a novel coronavirus initially transmitted from bats to humans near Wuhan, China—and it was leaving a mounting set of economic, social, and political disasters in its wake. More of these novel and volatile contagions stood on the horizon like the shadow of Frankenstein's Creature cast over the Earth. "As the hour of the pandemic clock ominously approaches midnight," Davis had reflected on the last page of *The Monster at Our Door*, "I recall those 1950s sci-fi thrillers of my childhood in which an alien menace or atomic monster threatened humanity."[191]

Without vaccines to stop their circulation across nations, these viral mutations threatened to destroy their human creators like Frankenstein's Creature had done. Ironically, they could upend the globalized economic and political systems that had proliferated their diseases through international trade, travel, and economic inequality. Never purely natural phenomena, SARS-CoV-2, SARS-CoV, and the latest strain of the avian flu were in fact the products and "plagues of capitalism."[192]

In the chapter titled "Plague and Profit," Davis made explicit his debt to both Marx and Shelley. He gave the name "Frankenstein GenZ" to the virulent "H5N1 superstrain—genotype Z."[193] At the turn of the twenty-first century, poultry factories in China unwittingly bioengineered this deadlier strain of H5N1, in the aftermath of the 1997 outbreak in Hong Kong. By inoculating ducks with an "inactivated virus" and breeding them for slaughter in their processing plants, they created a new and potentially leveling form of the avian flu, H5N2.[194]

Almost two centuries before our era's historical seer, the late Mike Davis, Mary Shelley saw the monster pandemic coming for us in the future. This book is about why she and some of her followers in the tradition of modern political science fiction have been able to predict with uncanny accuracy the political and economic problems that beset humanity in the "Plague Year" of 2020–2021.[195] For Shelley, the reasons were deeply personal. She experienced an epidemic of tragedies on a depth and scale that most people could not bear.

Truth Stranger than Fiction

Because she was the daughter of political philosophers, it is not surprising that Shelley used politics as a frame for interpreting the origins, forms, and scales of plagues, as well as human responsibility for them. Born of the leading women's rights advocate of the eighteenth century, Shelley received from her mother the weighty gift of the famous writer's maiden and married names: Mary Wollstonecraft Godwin. The dirty hands of the medical doctor, summoned by Godwin to remove the lingering placenta from his wife's uterus with sharp and bloodletting surgical implements, caused both the deadly infection of septicemia and a lifetime of pain for the surviving family. Since the fateful summer of 1797, Mary Wollstonecraft Godwin Shelley has had many lives, rebirths, and deaths. The international artistic successes of *Frankenstein* and *The Last Man*—especially in artistic, musical, theatrical, literary, and film adaptations since the nineteenth and early twentieth centuries—meant that Shelley never absolutely died. Her two best novels are responsible for generating a modern subgenre of science fiction, or what I have called "political science fiction," following the pioneering work of political scientist Clyde Wilcox and literary scholar Donald Hassler.[196]

Political science fiction is not necessarily about science. It is more broadly about human use of technology, science, art, and other culture to make choices and take actions with potentially disastrous consequences for the agents of change and the changing world around them. The postapocalyptic forms of political science fiction often draw on the themes and imagery of plague history and literature to examine the roots of human-made disasters in the artificial interventions of people in their wider environments. Following Shelley, works of fiction in this tradition trace the origins of plague to the deeper conflicts of romantic, social, and political relationships, beginning in the family.

Inspired by her deep reading of apocalyptic and plague literature from the ancient and modern worlds, *The Last Man* unveiled a mythic allegory for understanding the contagions of man-made misfortune that threaten the endurance of humanity.[197] "Humanity," in Shelley's usage, did not simply mean the human species.[198] It was rather the all-too-often untapped ethical capacity for resisting "coldness or inhumanity" through *humaneness*, or love and care for the whole of life beyond the selfish concerns and petty conflicts of human beings.[199] Displaying a kind of negative capability reminiscent of Keats's poetry, she had Verney denote the true meaning of humanity through a cascade of metonymic phrases: "frail humanity," "false humanity," "cloud of humanity," and "degradation of humanity."[200]

Given the global orientation of her ethics, there is a cosmic irony to the fact that Shelley finally fell to the internal malignancy of brain cancer. As the debilitating and slow-growing tumor filled her head, this once strawberry blonde beauty and still darkly imaginative genius was left with "her hair . . . silvery and her fine figure bowed," before entering an early grave.[201] She was buried according to her own gothic instructions, in a churchyard near her son's estate in the English seaside town of Bournemouth. There she lies with the calcified heart of her husband, saved from his funeral pyre on the beach at Viareggio, and the skeletons of her parents, removed from their resting place at St. Pancras churchyard in London, where she had begun her fateful affair with Percy in the summer of 1814.

After World War II, Mary Shelley and *The Last Man* resurfaced in literary criticism with the publication of a major biography of her life by the Scottish novelist Muriel Spark in 1951. Spark included an appendix with a long synopsis of Shelley's global plague novel.[202] Then in 1954, Spark produced an introduction for the first modern edition of the novel. Unfortunately, the press shut down after printing only six review copies. One of them, however, made it into the Bodleian Library, with a note from the publisher, suggesting he thought it was worthy of preservation. The next edition of *The Last Man* would have to wait until 1965 when the University of Nebraska press published an annotated version for scholarly use. The same year, Harold Bloom noted the importance of Spark's biography of Shelley and *The Last Man* for his scholarship on *Frankenstein*, apocalyptic literature, Romanticism, and the Shelleys.[203]

Before 1965, *The Last Man* had not been fully released in a new and widely available edition since 1833, when Edgar Allan Poe probably purchased it alongside *Frankenstein* from his publishers Carey, Lea & Blanchard in Philadelphia. Scholars have traced how the themes of Shelley's twin political science fictions as well as the poetry of her husband shaped some of his classic works of suspense and horror, including his 1833 short story "MS. Found in a Bottle," which paraphrases the ending of *Frankenstein*; his 1838 novel *The Narrative of Arthur Gordon Pym of Nantucket* about the last man to survive a shipwreck in the Antarctic; and his 1842 plague allegory "The Masque of the Red Death."[204] Shelley and Poe's combined impact on the modern horror and sf genres cannot be underestimated, as their American heir apparent Stephen King has often observed.[205] The 1964 film *Mask of the Red Death*—starring Vincent Price—helped to usher in the twentieth-century cinematic fascination with plagues of death: from the 1964 film *The Last Man on Earth*—also starring Price—to the 1994 and 2020 television miniseries adaptation of King's own epic postapocalyptic plague novel *The Stand* (1979), to the much-anticipated HBO miniseries based on the popular action-adventure game *The Last of Us*.

The multitudinous adaptations of the *Frankenstein* story for the cinema since the 1910s led to the rediscovery of her mother Wollstonecraft's life and works by feminist scholars in the 1960s and 1970s.[206] Shelley in turn became a leading twentieth-century icon of the modern gothic woman writer, rivaled only by the Brontë sisters. The early twenty-first century has seen a new—scientific and political—turn in her global reception. Haunting images from Shelley's political science fictions keep reappearing—like ghosts that refuse to rest in peace—in journalism and popular art on the life-and-death issues of the day: whether they be the specters of racism, endless war, imperialism, rising authoritarianism, mob violence, and democratic backsliding, or cloning, assisted reproductive technology, gene editing, artificial general intelligence, and the new wave of lethal and unpredictable airborne pandemics such as SARS, MERS, and SARS-CoV-2.[207]

Mary Shelley has never mattered more. In the three core chapters of *The First Last Man*, I take a fresh look at the relevance of her life and writing on two interlocking levels. First, the study of *The Last Man* and its literary and historical sources and legacies teaches us why epidemics play such an outsized role in modern political science fiction. Secondly, by reading her personal journals of sorrow and other private writings as forms of existential philosophy, we learn to better navigate the real-world ethics and politics of contagions of misfortune such as Covid-19.

A Series Finale

The First Last Man ties together my trilogy of books on why Mary Shelley's writings, both private and public, are uncannily prescient for theorizing human responsibility for creatures, creations, and disasters of our own making. *Mary Shelley and the Rights of the Child* (2018) treated her novel *Frankenstein* as an extended thought experiment on the duties of parents toward children, no matter how, from what, or by whom they are made. The conclusion used the novel's cascade of thought experiments on the ethics of creating life to speculate the rights of genetically modified children—or, what Margaret Atwood, in her 2013 postapocalyptic pandemic novel *MaddAddam*, called "Frankenbabies."[208] In *Artificial Life After Frankenstein* (2021), I expounded the relevance of Shelley's twin masterpieces of political science fiction for the ethics of using technology to make genetically modified organisms (including human clones, three-person IVF babies, and gene-edited children), robots, and artificial intelligences, and to a lesser degree, pandemics and other environmental disasters. *The First Last Man* picks up this argument to explore the existential, life-and-death question of personal and political responsibility for the spread of plagues and other contagions of misfortune.

This volume unfolds a comparative analysis of Shelley's archetypal postapocalyptic pandemic novel, *The Last Man*, and the journals, letters, and memoirs on plagues and other personal tragedies that she kept from 1814 to 1851. Chapter 1, "Journals of Sorrow: Mary Shelley's Existential Philosophy of Love," shows how Shelley developed from her life writing a prescient social and political theory of the growth of epidemics (real and metaphorical) into pandemics and other epic disasters that touch everyone. Following the ancient wisdom of Greek literature and the Bible, she rooted all plagues—whether natural pathogens or personal hardships, environmental cataclysms or political crises—in the interpersonal conflicts of human relationships. Shelley's diaries record her exposure to the major Western works of plague literature from the ancient world (the Bible, Homer, Sophocles, Thucydides, Lucretius, Ovid) to the medieval, early modern, and modern eras (Villani, Boccaccio, Defoe, Brown, Wilson). But her genius was not to copy or replicate the motifs of this tradition of plague writing, but rather to recreate the genre altogether through her imaginative engagement of her life story alongside major narratives of pestilence and works of political thought. In so doing she created two overlapping literary works of existential philosophy, both grounded in her lived experiences of tragedy: "The Journal of Sorrow" (c. 1822–26) and *The Last Man* (1826). Writing these twin masterpieces of personal prose led Shelley to see that the choice to love life and creation in the face of death and disaster was the only lasting cure for the many plagues of humanity.

Chapter 2, "The Plague of War: Salvaging the Significance of Mary Shelley's Translation of *Oedipus Rex*," presents a new archivally based study of Shelley and her reception of Sophocles and Aeschylus. It reveals her classically informed interpretation of Oedipus as a social and political pollutant whose history of wrongdoing brings a plague of evil upon those surrounding him. By redating her use of her under-studied "Greek Studies" notebook from 1820 to 1839 through an analysis of its contents, paper, and watermark alongside other manuscripts in the Bodleian Library, and contextualizing the thematic, biographical, and psychological significance of its translations and transcriptions of *Oedipus Rex* and *Philoctetes* in her broader corpus and life story, I salvage the personal, social, and political significance of her reception of Sophocles and Aeschylus from 1814 to 1839. Shelley wove her adaptations and translations of *Oedipus* from the first volume of her journals (1814–15) into her incest novella *Mathilda* (c. 1819–20) and her pandemic novel *The Last Man* (1826), as well as into her editing of Percy Shelley's "Greek Studies" notebook (1822–39). The author of *Frankenstein* systematized her identification with the dark and conflicted fate of Oedipus over the course of her adult life by infusing her private and public writing with thematic imagery—blood and vampirism, plague and war, crossroads and incest—that ran parallel to her translation work on Sophocles and Aeschylus.

Chapter 3, "Mary Shelley's *The Last Man*: Existentialism and International Relations Meet the Postapocalyptic Pandemic Novel," uncovers how Shelley mined the ideas of international thought to help develop three new subgenres of modern political science fiction. These Shelleyan forms of "poliscifi" are postapocalyptic, existential, and dystopian literature. As I argued in *Artificial Life After Frankenstein*, her two great works of *poliscifi* confront the social problems that arise from humanity's technological and cultural interventions in the wider environment. This chapter recovers *The Last Man* not only as the first modern postapocalyptic pandemic novel, but also as an important source for the existentialist tradition, dystopian literature, and their intersections with what I call "Literary IR," or a literary approach to theorizing international relations. Comparing *The Last Man* with its probable sources and the works that it, in turn, influenced—from Thucydides, Voltaire, and Vattel to H.G. Wells, George Orwell, Albert Camus, Richard Wright, and Ralph Ellison—reveals Shelley's ethical concern with the overlapping problems of interpersonal and political conflict, on a local and a global scale. *The Last Man*, alongside its later iterations in "Invisible Man" stories and films, dramatizes how interpersonal conflict, if left unchecked, can spiral into the wider sociopolitical injustices of violence, war, and other human-made disasters such as racism, species extinction, pandemics, and more metaphorical "existential" plagues like loneliness and despair.

Despite these dark themes and legacies, Shelley's authorship of the great plague novel of the nineteenth century inspired a range of paradoxically hopeful responses to crisis and conflict in music, painting, theater, and horror films featuring a lone (wo)man who survives an invisible pestilence or other stalking menace. This Shelleyan trend of finding hope amid an explosion of man-made tragedies crystallized in mid-to-late twentieth-century feminist existentialism and dystopian literature. The most important literary figures in this rising school of postapocalyptic political thought have been women: the Shelley scholar and existential novelist Muriel Spark; the Black Marxist playwright and Wollstonecraft scholar Lorraine Hansberry; and the leading authors of postapocalyptic plague fiction of the past fifty years, Joanna Russ, Margaret Atwood, and Octavia Butler, and more recently in the twenty-first century age of pandemics, Emily St. John Mandel and Sandra Newman.

Like her successors in feminist political science fiction, Shelley offered an account of a true—or hopeful—postapocalyptic ethos that challenged the reigning false—or fatalistic—conceptions of "apocalyptic thinking."[209] During her late twenties, and her thirties and forties, Shelley's journaling, her translation work on Euripides's *Alcestis*, her authorship of "The Invisible Girl," and her editing and publication of her late husband's translation of Plato's *Symposium* led her to a lasting existential epiphany, which she transmits to her readers even now. By daring to look inward, and letting her thoughts go dark, Shelley discovered that she could illuminate the dynamics of tragedy in her own life story in a way that revealed an unexpected path toward a sublime and transcendent sense of love for the whole of creation—for its solace and beauties as much as for its grief and horrors. Her philosophical insight has helped to inspire the modern tradition of postapocalyptic political thought, which has manifested over time and across genres in part through the adaptation of her ideas of the "last (wo)man" and "the invisible girl" in music, painting, literature, theater, film, television, and other art. I draw out the existential and ethical implications of a selection of these Shelleyan artworks for the possibility of building a hopeful postapocalyptic outlook toward life, politics, and everything—including the crises and catastrophes—that will continue to test our humanity in the future.[210]

* * *

[NOTE FROM THE EDITOR: In the year 2119, this book manuscript surfaced in an estate sale in Maine where the author is known to have family roots going back to the eighteenth century. After a research trip to England, she had been vacationing at her family's home, in the village of Island Falls, in late July 2022. As part of my research into the history of the first great Covid pandemic of the twenty-first century, I preserved the whole, crudely laser-printed copy—which had been left, apparently, on the author's desk (secured only by a rubber band) when she entered the hospital for treatment of a rare mutated hybrid of Monkeypox and Omicron BA.5, probably contracted during international travel to Britain. In the same auction lot as the book manuscript was the author's leather-bound diary, in which I found the following handwritten and dated entry near the end of its white lined pages. My subsequent search of digitized historical records of the (former) United States of America showed that the author, Eileen M. Hunt—who once used the pen name Eileen Hunt Botting—died before she could return to Oxford to complete her fellowship at the Bodleian, where she had been reading Shelley's journals and other manuscripts before going home to spend time with her son and parents.

—*Margaret Winston Smith*]

* * *

28 July 2022

The cough is getting worse and won't go away. The red pock marks on my skin look abhorrent. Thankfully I'm in the middle of nowhere, with only family to see me—so absolutely *no one* cares what I look like! At the urging of my mother, I shall make my way to the Millinocket Regional Hospital, forty miles away, where she used to work, later today. My book is almost done, and so I will leave it here to finish when I return. The final question is how to end it. In the process of reading Mary Shelley as an existential and postapocalyptic political thinker, I have tried to pay homage to her practice of life writing as a philosophical enterprise by beginning each book with an autobiographical preface. But as I look at my latest essay (or should I say attempt?), I see something different: a postface. For it explains in hindsight the reasons for my conception of this book as the finale to my trilogy on Shelley. Only upon rereading this piece—which I originally typed in my first quarantine journal more than a year ago—did I see how my archival study of Shelley's journals and the context for her authorship of *The Last Man* gave me the solace to write my way through my own traumatic experiences of a series of heartbreaking plagues as well as a world-stopping pandemic. Whatever its literary merits or demerits, its historical value is clear. So, I shall append my attempt at self-understanding to the end of this manuscript, for editing upon my return.

* * *

CHAPTER 1

Journals of Sorrow

Mary Shelley's Existential Philosophy of Love

Find my baby dead

—Mary Shelley, 6 March 1815, first journal book[1]

This is the Journal book of misfortunes—Read Livy—A great many of the plays of Alfieri—S writes—he reads Oedipus Tyrannos to me - On Teusday Sept 22nd he goes up to Venise—On thursday I go to Padua with Clare - meet S there—we go to Venise with my poor Clara who dies the moment we get there

—Mary Shelley, 24 September 1818, second journal book[2]

I begin my journal on Shelley's birthday—We have ~~now~~ lived now five years together & if all the events of the five years were blotted out I might be happy—but to have won & then cruelly have lost the associations of four years is not an accident ~~that~~ to which the human mind can bend ~~to~~ without much suffering

—Mary Shelley, 4 August 1819, third journal book[3]

It is better to grieve than not to grieve. Grief at least tells me that I was not always what I am now.

—Mary Shelley, 17 November 1822, fourth journal book, "The Journal of Sorrow"[4]

Her Philosophy of the Dark Side of Human Things

After the devastating loss of her first three children with Percy to premature birth, dysentery, and malaria between March 1815 and June 1819, Mary Shelley turned to private writing to find what meaning there was left in their volatile life together. As her friend Leigh Hunt observed in a letter of consolation to her in July 1819, she had a "tendency"—even a "philosophy"—to "look over-intensely at the dark side of human things."[5] Indeed, the author of *Frankenstein* would never fully "turn" away from reading her own life as "a tale of horror & despair."[6] At age seventeen, she had looked into a cradle to find her firstborn daughter, Clara, no longer breathing. "Find my baby dead," she found the strength to write in her first journal book that she co-kept with her married lover. From that tragic juncture in her young life, Shelley conducted in her personal writing her "philosophy" of confronting "the dark side of human things."

By the time she began the third volume of her journals, in August 1819, Shelley was writing for her life. She had taken two months away from keeping her diary, while mourning the sudden death of her beloved toddler William from an infestation of worms and a malarial infection that he contracted in Rome in the spring. She opened the new volume of her journals on Percy's birthday in August, only to wish they had never met. "We have now lived ~~now~~ five years together," she wrote in her journal in August 1819, "& if all the events of the five years were blotted out I might be happy." In September, she finally replied to Hunt's July note of sympathy: "I am much changed—the world will never be to me again as it was—there was a life & freshness in it that is lost to me," she confided in her friend, ". . . in fact I ought to have died on the 7th of June last."[7]

Little did she realize then that her worst troubles had only begun. Two children whom she fostered or supported would die. The baby she had adopted with Percy, Elena Adelaide, died of unknown causes under the care of her foster parents in Naples in June 1820.[8] Her sister Claire's daughter Allegra Byron succumbed to typhus in a Venetian convent in April 1822.[9] Soon thereafter on 16 June, Shelley suffered a late-term miscarriage that nearly killed her, followed by the trauma of losing Percy to the sea around "the fatal 8th" of July.[10] Less than two years later, Shelley learned by mail of the untimely demise of their friend Lord Byron, from sepsis contracted in battle for Greek independence at Missolonghi.

Like a feminine Oedipus, Shelley came to see tragedies—like the serial loss of five children she bore or cared for—as contagions of misfortune. As plagues upon humanity, tragedies seeped through families and societies due to the collective failures of people to prevent them. Akin to the ancient Greeks, Shelley envisioned epidemics of all kinds—psychological, social, and medical—as blights "upon" (ἐπί) the "people" (δῆμος), unwittingly caused by people themselves. In her first entry in her fourth journal book "The Journal of Sorrow" in October 1822, she mourned her past and future prospects in love as "blighted."[11]

Shelley knew that blight was worse than mere disease. In Ancient Greek, it connoted a perishing decay that overwhelmed crops and other populations. In her word-by-word, literal translation of *Oedipus Rex*, likely begun in late 1820, she twice translated "φθίνουσα" at lines 25–26 as "perishing."[12] In the opening scene, a Theban priest accosts King Oedipus with the "perishing in the fruit-bearing flowers of the earth, in the herds of grazing cattle, and in the unborn children of women." The priest demands an inquiry into the crimes that must have caused the god-sent plague.[13] By reversing these fatalistic images of decay, corruption, and infertility, Shelley would go on to transform her own "blighted" and "perishing" existence—with and without Percy—into an epic allegory for human endurance of death, grief, and suffering. Her 1826 roman à clef chronicles an "epidemic" that begins on a battlefield, passes across "infected countries," touches all "perishing creatures" like a "field of corn blighted in the ear," yet spares one man to muster the strength to pursue a new future for humanity.[14]

Writing through what her friend Hunt called the "double-dreariness" of her tears and grief, Shelley reconceived the ancient wisdom of plague literature from Sophocles to Ovid from the perspective of modern "political science."[15] She imbibed the Enlightenment-era idea of the science of politics from the writings of her parents, Wollstonecraft and Godwin, and other prominent eighteenth-century theorists of the evolution of society through the dissemination of the arts, sciences, and education.[16] During the 1790s, her parents' radical political treatises compared the vicious "spread" of moral "corruption" in aristocratic society to a deadly infection in the human body.[17]

Critical for Shelley's thinking on social and political diseases were the works of Jean-Jacques Rousseau, especially his novels *Julie or the New Heloise* (1761) and *Emile, or On Education* (1762). During her teenage years with Percy, she kept returning to read her parents alongside their common inspiration, Rousseau.[18] From all three she gleaned that a long succession of bad human decisions drove the widescale corruption of cultures and governments, the conflicts of war and imperialism, and even the environmental cataclysms of so-called natural disasters.

After the 1755 Lisbon earthquake killed as many as fifty thousand people, Rousseau made a public provocation: the disaster was neither purely natural nor God-given.[19] It was rather a product of poor human planning. The collapse of the city could have been averted, if only the bulk of the population had been dispersed across the countryside instead of packed in precarious "six-or-seven-story" buildings at the urban center.[20] With his philosophical response to the earthquake, Rousseau authored a new form of secular theodicy. He vindicated the ways of God and nature to humanity, by way of blaming humanity for bringing catastrophes down upon themselves.[21]

A few years later, in his epistolary novel, *Julie or the New Heloise*, Rousseau made a similar point about the dynamics of disaster. The story, set in eighteenth-century Switzerland, compares an illicit sexual love to an invasive contagion. The tragic romance of the aristocrat Julie with her tutor St. Preux embroils not only the lovers but also their friends and families in decades of emotional and social turmoil. Possessed by his passion for Julie, despite her betrothal to another man, St. Preux kisses her hand to inoculate himself with her smallpox and prove his undying loyalty to her. She responds with playful affection in a letter to her true love, "My friend, you have conquered me. I am not tested by so much love; my resistance is exhausted."[22]

Rousseau's most popular fiction dramatized a physiological paradox: love can be a dangerous psychic and physical contagion, and, in the correct dosage, the most effective vaccine for its malaise. Shelley became an avid reader of *Julie* alongside Percy and Claire soon after their elopement journey in 1814 and extending through their visit to Switzerland to see the settings for the novel in 1816.[23] Percy was then a twenty-four-year-old man with three living children from two relationships and a wife whom he had abandoned for Mary and an affair with Claire.[24]

As a married woman and a grieving mother, Shelley built on Rousseau's philosophy of social contagion. Plagues, to her, were human-made disasters, transmitted through the artifice of our feelings, deeds, and failures, yet still potentially contained by the power of true love and concern for others. By engaging with the "dark side" of Enlightenment political thought, Shelley arrived at a modern and political conception of plague as a collective and artificial disaster. Even with these eighteenth-century origins, similar *political* theories of epidemic continue to dominate twenty-first-century social science, epidemiology, and public health policy.[25]

In her journals and other unpublished writing, however, Shelley did not dwell on the broader and more obvious empirical effects of plagues, but rather made visible their hidden emotional dimensions. After the death of her one-year-old daughter Clara from "dysentery" and "fever" in Venice in September 1818, she wrote in her diary, "This is the Journal book of misfortunes."[26] She and Percy sought renewal by moving to Naples and then Rome with their three-year-old son William during the following winter and spring. Two months before their toddler would fall to "malaria," "worms," and "fever" amid the ruins of the Eternal City, Shelley ominously communicated to Hunt in London, "I suffer from ill spirits—God knows why but I have suffered more from them ten times over than I ever did before I came to Italy."[27] Her letter to her friend predicted that "evil thoughts will hang about me," like the oppressive "Roman air."[28] In letters written to her friend Maria Gisborne later that April, she feared that the city's seasonal "Malaria" encroached the fragile health of her son and husband with "colds, depression & even fever."[29] "We are delighted with Rome," she confided to the woman who had nursed her as an infant after her mother's death, "nothing but the Malaria would drive us from it."[30]

Sadly, her prediction was correct. On 29 June 1819, she wrote to Hunt's wife Marianne in the tragic mode of Oedipus after he discovers, to his horror, that he authored his own nefarious fate: "You see by our hap how blind we mortals are when we go seeking after what we think our good—We came to Italy thinking to do Shelley's health good—but the Climate is not any means warm enough to be of benefit to him & yet it is that that has destroyed my two children—I never know one moments ease from the wretchedness & despair that possesses me—May you my dear Marianne never know what it is to loose two only & lovely children in one year."[31] She paused to indent the next paragraph, as if to catch her bitterness before it infested her friend, like the parasitic worms that had swarmed her dying son's intestines, writing, "all my thoughts are nothing but misery it is not kind to transmit them."[32] She would spend the rest of her life resisting, out of love, this urge to touch others with the "misery" of misfortune.

Recovering Shelley as a Plague Writer

Early in her complicated polyamorous relationship with Percy, Shelley came to associate literary depictions of plague with her own brushes with conflict, war, and mortality. She bore witness to the scourge of the Napoleonic Wars when she eloped to France with Percy and her stepsister Claire in July 1814. In her first complete solo journal entry, from 12 August, she described the north-central French village, Le Pavillon-Sainte-Julie, as "a beautiful place but also desolated by the Cossac . . . they took the cows, sheep & poultry & tore down the houses for wood for fires."[33] The village had been plundered and burned to the ground by what she and the French called "The Cossacs," or the Russian soldiers in the coalition of the German armies that had invaded France to fight Napoleon in the winter of 1814.[34] In the aftermath, she observed, French peasants were impoverished, serving inedible food in their filthy abodes, surrounded by rats and other signs of pestilence.

One refugee whom they met on the road said that his child had been "murdered by the Cossacks."[35] War did not stop on the battlefield, Shelley saw firsthand, but rather seeped into every level of society, even homes and families. She later reworked these journal entries for her first book, a travel memoir of their trips to Europe in the summers of 1814 and 1816. In *A History of a Six Weeks' Tour* (1817), she asserted her "detestation of war, which none can feel who have not traveled through a country pillaged and wasted by this plague."[36]

Soon after she, Percy, and Claire settled into their new life in London after their first trip to Europe, they began the study of Ancient Greek together. Mary's "first lesson in greek" from Percy took place on 18 September 1814.[37] Around the same time, he ensued tutoring her stepsister in the language. Claire noted in her journal "Write and learn the Philoctetes" and "Write Greek again" on 21 September 1814.[38] Mary listed Thucydides among Percy's readings in 1815.[39]

Homer, Sophocles, and Thucydides's chronicles of war, conflict, infection, and pestilence would inform Shelley's plague writing, fictional and nonfictional, for decades to come. She consumed Pope's eighteenth-century translation of the *Iliad* in 1815.[40] Percy returned to the Homeric epic so often in the original Greek that the couple would have known, perhaps by heart, the verses from Book I in which Apollo, the sun god, emerges in a very different guise as the god of both plague and war.[41] The Greek sun god vengefully shoots down men with burning arrows of pestilence, after the Achaean leaders Achilles and Agamemnon fight over the child war brides whom they stole from their enemies. Homer recounts that "the corpse fires burned everywhere and did not stop burning."[42]

Although Thucydides is an historian and not an epic poet, there is a Homeric image of the overlay of war and plague in his *History of the Peloponnesian War.* In his account of the Plague of Athens that hit the city during its war with Sparta around 430–429 B.C.E., Thucydides recalls the horror of seeing his fellow citizens throw corpses onto funeral pyres intended for others, in a mad rush to rid themselves of the infected bodies that even predatory birds and animals would not touch or eat.[43] From this ancient Greek association of plague and war, Shelley reinforced in her mind what she had learned firsthand in France: politics is the driving force behind epidemics. In *The Last Man*, Shelley had her diplomatic alter ego Verney suggest this Thucydidean lesson when he watches with growing anxiety the rise of "the plague at Athens" after it spreads from the battlefields of Constantinople.[44]

Shelley also read, edited, and commented on Percy's 1817 poem "Laon and Cyntha"—published as *The Revolt of Islam* in 1818—which alluded to the "Plague" of Athens in Canto X: "First Want, then Plague, came on the beasts; their food / Failed, and they drew the breath of its decay."[45] Percy's epic poem dramatized the aftermath of the French Revolution in nineteenth-century "Constantinople and modern Greece," as he put it in a letter to his father, "without much attempt at minute delineation of Mahometan manners."[46] The emergent struggle for Greek independence against the Ottoman Empire also inspired the setting for the rise of the plague in Shelley's pandemic novel. When she referred to "the innumerous arrows of the plague," "poisoned arrows," "arrows of death," and "the arrows of pestilence" in *The Last Man*, her wording echoed *The Revolt of Islam*'s "the arrows of the plague," and both of their phrases alluded to Apollo's arrows in the *Iliad.*[47]

There were more proximate sources for the Shelleys' literary representations of the Plague of Athens: above all, Charles Brockden Brown's 1799 gothic novel about Philadelphia's 1793 yellow fever epidemic, *Arthur Mervyn*, and Daniel Defoe's 1722 fictionalization of his uncle's diary of surviving the 1665 Great Plague of London, *A Journal of the Plague Year.* In *The Last Man*, Shelley had Verney directly allude to *Arthur Meryvn* as the plague seeped into twenty-first-century London. "While every mind was full of dismay at its effects," Verney recalls, "a craving for excitement had led us to peruse De Foe's account, and the masterly delineations of the author of Arthur Mervyn."[48] Verney uses Brown's novel as a literary guide for understanding the leveling spread of a contagion through a populous city. As the Shelley scholar Richard

Garnett put it in 1902, "The description of the pestilence in *Arthur Mervyn* deserves to stand beside the other world famous descriptions of plagues by Thucydides, Lucretius, Boccaccio, Defoe, and Shelley himself in *The Revolt of Islam*."[49]

Before she wrote *The Last Man*, Shelley had familiarized herself with all of these classics of plague literature. In 1815, she read in Latin the most important adaptation of Thucydides's Plague of Athens in Ovid's *Metamorphoses* (A.D. 8).[50] In 1817, she read Defoe's *Plague Year*, as well as Brown's *Mervyn*.[51] While in Italy between 1818 and 1823, she intensified her interest in the study of politically exacerbated plagues in ancient and medieval literature.

In a strange coincidence, Shelley had recorded in her second journal book how Percy read aloud to her Sophocles's tragic drama *Oedipus Rex*—which opens with "bloody waves" of "plague"—right before the sudden death of their second infant daughter from fever and dysentery.[52] Less than nine months later, she would return, again and again, to Boccaccio's darkly comic-romantic response to the Black Death, the *Decameron*, in the weeks before the death of their three-year-old son William from malarial fever in Rome. In a moment of tragic irony, recognized only in retrospect by Shelley in her journals, the couple had chosen to remain in the "Eternal City" to enjoy the gorgeous spring, despite the fact that they knew of the seasonal threat of lethal infection by the "bad air" (in Italian and Latin, *mala aria*).[53] She immortalized this irony in her 1822–23 poem "The Choice," by linking the death of Percy to the "sharp:toothed Misery" that "tore the husk" of their marriage "in twain" during their first year in Italy:

> Now thou art gone, one lovely victim more
> To the black death which rules this sunny shore[54]

Shelley's poetic use of "black death" in "The Choice" and her dramatic, capitalized use of "PLAGUE" in *The Last Man* have origins in her Latin, Greek, and Italian translations. In the summer of 1820, she and Percy translated from Latin the poetic versions of the 430 B.C.E. Plague of Athens in Lucretius's *De Rerum Natura* (c. 99–55 B.C.E.).[55] Soon thereafter likely began her transcription and translation of Sophocles's *Oedipus Rex*.[56] In the autumn of 1820, she read in Italian the major fourteenth-century accounts of the Black Death's culling in Tuscany: Giovanni Villani's *Nuova Chronica* and Boccaccio's *Decameron*.[57] She continued to peruse Villani's historical chronicles of Florence into the summer of 1821. In the fourth and final issue of the literary-political journal *The Liberal* (1823), edited by Leigh Hunt, she published a biographical essay on Villani. She credited the realism of the Florentine historian to "living at a period when civil discord awakened the most violent passions and disclosed the workings of the heart carefully veiled from our politer eyes." Against this political backdrop, Villani wrote in "the style of one well read in human nature."[58] In her 1835 biographical essay on Boccaccio, she applauded his "description of the plague in Florence" as "the finest piece of writing" that he "ever composed," for "it presents a pathetic, eloquent, and vivid picture of the sufferings induced by that remorseless malady."[59]

Shelley creatively incorporated ancient, medieval, and early modern perspectives on contagion into a new, or modern, form of existential philosophy.[60] From the time she moved to Italy in 1818 to the publication of *The Last Man* in 1826, she acquired stoic grace and philosophic wisdom from her devoted study and translation of Plato, Spinoza, Sophocles, and Cicero. She forged a future-oriented prose style of self-reflective writing that can be regarded as an early form of existentialism, much like Montaigne in his meditative first-person essays that she devoured in two volumes in 1819.[61] Her style of personal writing was existential in the sense that it dwelled on the question of how human life could derive meaning from choice and love in the face of the specter of death, whose time of arrival was inevitable yet unknown. In her journals, letters, poetry, memoirs, fiction, and especially her roman à clef and pandemic novel, she took stock of her profound choices and losses in love—but did not stop there.

Through her almost lifelong composition of a mass of autobiographically inspired writings, Shelley challenged the fatalistic assumption that nothing can be done to remedy disaster. With her practice of personal writing, she modeled how one could seize the time to assess the destructive impact of the past on the present state of one's mind. In revisiting the past, one could quite literally summon the psychological power to rewrite it by reworking one's attitudes toward it. She undertook this difficult mental task by reconceiving the (auto)biographical narratives that would shape her future relationships with others: most importantly, her sole surviving child, Percy Florence Shelley, and his wife Lady Jane Shelley, who would become the heirs and literary executors of the vast and priceless Wollstonecraft-Godwin-Shelley family archive of writing.

Shelley's Existential Philosophy of Love

By crafting new life narratives to frame and understand her past, Shelley moved away from bitter hatred of her existence toward a paradoxical love of life, not despite but ultimately *because of* its plagues. In the earliest entries of her "Journal of Sorrow," composed on 2–7 October 1822, she envisioned the journey ahead in Old Testament terms. "I am in the valley of the shadow of death & soon shall be a clod," she wrote, evoking the wisdom literature of the Psalms and Ecclesiastes.[62] She compared herself to the cursed woman in the Book of Numbers who drinks of the water of bitterness: "I bear at the bottom of my heart a fathomless well of bitter waters, the workings of which my philosophy is ever at work to repress."[63] Paradoxically, this "philosophy" would lead her to "preserve" some "peace and tranquility of mind" by looking deep into the well of her heart to find the sources of her "sense of eternal & infinite misery."[64]

In the months after Percy's death, Shelley faced an immobilizing crisis, even worse than the "dreadfully depressed" spirits that she suffered in the summer of 1819, after the twin losses of her toddlers Clara and William to infectious diseases.[65] On 17 February 1823, she used the medium of her journal to communicate her desolation to the imagined spirit of Percy. In a sort of spiritual letter to him, she addressed the dead poet in her "Journal of Sorrow" as "my divine love." After this sublime invocation, she revealed the extent of her mental distress. Perhaps echoing the list of the "Principal causes of Misery" that she kept in her Italian papers, she confessed that "I desire death" as "the sole relief to my misery."[66] Percy's death felt like the final blow in the miserable chain of "loss of persons" she had loved.[67] Though she had not suffered the "misery" of literal "imprisonment," a claustrophobic "darkness" had closed around her like "prison walls."[68] Suffocating in her grief, she felt as if she was standing alone on a precipice:

> I go on from day to day & know that I am unhappy—know that I desire death only as the sole relief to my misery—but suddenly I awake—it is as a change from narrative to a drama—I feel the prison walls close about me—I feel in every trembling nerve that life has ~~none~~ nought but bitterness for me—that young—I can hope no more, enjoy no more—a palpable darkness ~~seems~~ surround[s] me, & I on [a] narrow pinacle of isolated rock, stand shuddering[69]

She used no final punctuation to demarcate the space between her precarious position on this "narrow pinacle" and her wish for death: for these were, sadly, one and the same.

Instead, she pulled back from the edge of suicidal despair with a simple indent. Beginning a new paragraph, she summoned hope for a new day, in which her work and the consolations of motherhood would fill her time: "But morning will come again—my studies—my occupations—my child."[70] By thinking of the light to come she could, paradoxically, relate the dark state of her soul more clearly. "I am very wretched tonight," she noted, before asking her "divine love," Percy, for inspiration to stay up writing toward dawn.[71]

Late that night, she ended her journal entry: "I go on scribbling till exhausted I throw away my pen—but I am so very wretched."[72] With a keen sense of irony, she wrote these words to her dead husband, while alone, yet probably with the very same pen that she said she threw away. Shelley would never truly relinquish her pen. On 17 February 1823, she preserved a private record of her existential choice to pick it up again: not simply to write, but to continue her life and reforge her identity through *being* a writer.

Her private prose in her "Journal of Sorrow" and other diary volumes left impressions on her lyrical essay, "On Ghosts," which she published anonymously in the *London Magazine* in March 1824.[73] In October 1823, she told Leigh Hunt that she had commenced an essay for a different journal than the short-lived one that he had founded in Pisa with Percy and Byron, *The Liberal* (1822–23).[74] Her new essay addressed the question of belief in the supernatural by relating a series of ghost stories, each drawn from her journals.[75]

At the heart of the personal narrative of "On Ghosts," Shelley recalled how she had once felt the real presence of the spirit of an unnamed loved—one whom she had recently lost. When she visited an apartment where they had resided in Italy, she "walked through the rooms filled with the most poignant grief."[76] After the "chimes of the Ave Maria had ceased," she was left in quiet solitude.[77] She pondered why the past existence of her lover in his "living frame" still seemed to be present in the empty space of their old abode: "He had been there," she thought in the past tense, "his living frame had been caged by those walls, his breath had mingled with that atmosphere, he step had been on those stones."[78] Alluding in sequence to Shakespeare, Lucan, and Isaiah, she reflected that "the earth is a tomb, the gaudy sky a vault, we but walking corpses."[79] And then she trembled as the "wind rising in the east rushed through the open casements."[80] For a moment, it felt as though he—the unnamed beloved—had manifested near her. As his almost palpable presence slipped from her consciousness, she reached a humble philosophical yet spiritual answer to the question of the existence of ghosts: "There is something beyond us of which we are ignorant."[81]

It was during this "wretched" year of 1823–24 that the lonely widow followed in the steps of Plato and became a philosopher of love.[82] During their first summer together in Italy in 1818, Shelley transcribed Percy's translation of the founding text on the philosophy of love in the Western canon: Plato's *Symposium*.[83] Soon after her arrival in London in August 1823, she bought a new leather-bound notebook into which she copied the manuscript.[84] While her friend Trelawny had salvaged this literary treasure from the wreck of the *Don Juan*, it was Shelley who saved its true value for posterity.[85] As she preserved and edited Plato's "Banquet" for eventual publication in Percy's *Essays* (1840), she wove its ideas into her own emergent theory of love's "mighty," godlike power to imbue the plagues of mortal life with eternal meaning.[86]

No matter how she looked at contagions of misfortune, Shelley concluded that they could be comprehended, borne, and ultimately transformed through the prospect of the realization of a higher or cosmopolitan love. This higher love, she theorized on the same sublime axis as the *Symposium*, could be reached only through a multitiered ascent to transcendence. Through his imagined dialogue of the mythic woman philosopher Diotima with his historic teacher Socrates, Plato had represented the ascent to a higher love of beauty as a tripartite ladder climb from love of the body, to love of ideas, and finally, to beauty itself.[87]

In a darker mood than Plato's Diotima, Shelley rooted transcendence in suffering. Alluding to the apocalyptic Book of Revelation in her "Journal of Sorrow," the widow wrote on 3 February 1823: "suffering is my ~~Apll~~ Alpha & Omega. Patience must be included."[88] With suffering denoted as the beginning and end of her existence, transcendence could not merely be the cognitive ascent to a metaphysical appreciation of abstract beauty. It required a more onerous path of "Patience" in accepting one's personal experience of pain as part of the reality of human mortality. The sources of one's suffering could not be kicked back, or packed away, like a ladder no longer needed to reach a higher level. The philosophical examination of the sources of one's suffering was rather the path to a holistic love of the shadowy, gothic beauty of life's interwoven joys and sorrows.

Shelley attempted in her "Journal of Sorrow" to find her own embodied way to a higher love of the whole creation, by examining her "grief," "sufferings," and "miseries."[89] First, she proposed that in the face of plagues—real or metaphorical—one must discover love for one's own existence, no matter how hard it has proven *to be*. Secondly, those afflicted by plague had to learn to move beyond their isolation and despair to feel compassion for their "fellow creatures," who shared the same mortal fate of suffering and death.[90] In these plague-oriented stages of her philosophy of love, Shelley seemed to agree with the practical medical perspective offered by Eryximachus in Percy's translation of the *Symposium*. The doctor argued that "Pestilence" and "other blights and diseases" are "produced from that excessive and ~~dis~~ disorderly love" that arises during "each season" of reproduction for plants and animals.[91] The "disorderly" passion of sexual love, in other words, led the human animal to experience the "pestilence" and "blight" of social conflict.

In her psychological adaptation of Plato's metaphysical ladder-climb to beauty, Shelley argued that a higher love could not escape but could heal the conflicts and suffering that "disorderly" sexual love had spread. This third and most difficult stage of ascent was to behold a panoramic appreciation of the beauty of the world as it was, is, and must be created. Inspired by her mother Wollstonecraft's unorthodox mix of Anglican and Dissenting Christian religiosity, as well as her own translation work on Spinoza's *Theological-Political Treatise* (1670), Shelley discovered that a deterministic outlook on one's place in the cosmos could resolve the problem of evil, or the ancient biblical question of why suffering and evil plagued the world if God and creation were good.[92] She reasoned that if an ineluctable chain of causal events made the world as it is, then all that has happened and will happen—good *and* evil—is part of that same necessary concatenation of creation and destruction.

In *The Last Man*, she dramatized this deterministic theodicy with the interior dialogue of Verney, alone in Rome, with the "unchangeable laws of Necessity": "Sudden an internal voice, articulate and clear, seemed to say:—Thus from eternity, it was decreed: the steeds that bear Time onwards had this hour and this fulfilment enchained to them, since the void brought forth its burthen. Would you read backwards the unchangeable laws of Necessity?"[93] Verney responds affirmatively to the voice of "Necessity" by exclaiming a line from Percy Shelley's Spinozistic poem "Queen Mab" (1813) and elaborating its existential meaning: "Mother of the world! Servant of the Omnipotent! eternal, changeless Necessity! who with busy fingers sittest ever weaving the indissoluble chain of events!—I will not murmur at thy acts. If my human mind cannot acknowledge that all is, is right; yet since what is, must be, I will sit amidst the ruins and smile. Truly we were not born to enjoy, but to submit, and to hope."[94] Once he accepts that life is not simply about pleasure but rather the acceptance of pain as part of the order of the cosmos, the lone human survivor resolves to "look my disaster in the face" by writing down his personal history of the global plague.[95] He vows to be the "servant of necessity, the visible laws of the invisible God."[96] Like her avatar Verney, Shelley strove to use personal writing as a spiritual path toward reconciliation with the whole strange gamut of creation. By accepting her part in the human artifice that has shaped suffering on the planet, Shelley learned to love the cosmic order of things, for its beauties as much as its miseries.

Several months before her husband died, Shelley articulated the germ of this existential philosophy of love. On 25 February 1822, she expressed it in a sort of private prayer in her third journal book: "Let me love the trees—the skies & the ocean & ~~all~~ that all encompassing spirit of which I may soon become a part—let me in my fellow creatures love that which is & not ~~imagine~~ fix my ~~love~~ affections on a fair form endued with imaginary attributes."[97] By embracing the flawed mortal reality of one's "fellow creatures" and the "all encompassing spirit" of creation, one might then transcend the egoistic delusion that personal suffering could somehow be greater, in magnitude or significance, than all the suffering in the cosmos. Most crucially, one might then abandon the dangerous fiction that the experience of suffering excuses anyone from responsibility for bringing pain upon others.

By adopting a cosmic perspective of love toward one's own life and the lives of others, Shelley saw that people had the power to turn plagues—or the worst burdens of mortal existence—into the cure for the social and political malaises that ail the entire world.[98] People could learn to see that their personal suffering could finally be transcended by identifying with the suffering of others, not perpetuating it. The deepest and most personal problems of individuals were roughly the same as those burdens shouldered by other people. These were problems made by a chain of human choices and human errors. They were social and political problems for which each person could claim some responsibility, however terrible it was to face that moral fact.

With this stoic wisdom, the widowed Shelley strove to inoculate herself against despair. At the time when she was writing *The Last Man*, she reflected in her journals on how she would read Cicero's philosophical dialogue from 45 B.C.E., *De Finibus Bonorum et Malorum*, "for hours."[99] Shelley, who had visited Cicero's tomb with Percy in November 1818, identified strongly with the Roman philosopher who had disseminated both Platonic and Stoic ideas.[100] One thing that might have drawn her to *De Finibus* was the fact that he had written it in response to the sudden death of his beloved daughter Tullia in childbirth.[101]

In an entry in her "Journal of Sorrow," dated 3 December 1824, Shelley "pondered . . . Cicero's description of that power of virtue in the human mind w^{h} renders man's frail being superior to fortune."[102] She concluded that she had nothing left "to fear" beyond the death of her sole surviving child Percy Florence, whose life anchored her to this world. She likewise had nothing "to cede" because she was free of the "tyranny of others," even as she endured the "negligence" of those whom she once counted as her closest friends.[103]

With her meditation on Cicero in mind, Shelley proceeded to paint a different picture of her solitude than she had done in Italy two winters before: "At the age of seven & twenty in the busy metropolis of native England I find myself alone—~~dese~~ deserted by the few I knew—disdained—insulted—to bear this I must indeed string my mind—I must awaken ~~conscio~~ conscious worth—memory & the hope beyond the grave to enable me to endure with equanimity this unkind treatment from my species—."[104] Like the hero of her novel-in-progress, Lionel Verney, she too was a last person, if her lastness—or her being *last*—meant somehow *lasting*. Though living almost alone as a widow in her cold home city, she was free to "hope" for a spiritual reunion with her loved ones "beyond the grave," as she awakened from a numbing depression to feel her "conscious worth" again.

Loving the Wondrous and Monstrous Creation

Back in November of 1822—a little more than four months after Percy's death—Shelley had reflected in her "Journal of Sorrow": "It is better to grieve than not to grieve. Grief at least tells me that I was not always what I am now."[105] She used this insight not to dwell in anguish but rather to move toward the transcendence of its worst pain. While losing Percy taught her that she once was made happy by what she had irrevocably lost, it also led her to see that change was always possible. If one could shift from happiness to grief in a heartbeat, then the converse must be true: even the bereaved might move through mourning to find happiness again.

A few days before Christmas 1822, Shelley sketched in her fourth journal book the chapter headings for an (auto)biography of her life with Percy:

> France—Poverty—a few days of solitude & some uneasiness—
> A tranquil residence in a beautiful spot—Switzerland—Bath—
> Marlow—
> ~~Ita~~ Milan—The Baths of Lucca—Este—Venice—Rome—Naples—
> Rome & misery—Leghorn—Florence Pisa—~~H~~ Solitude The
> Williams—The Baths—Pisa—These are the heads of chapters
> —each containing a tale, romantic beyond romance.[106]

Her elopement with Percy to postwar France had exposed her to "Poverty," as well as "solitude & some uneasiness." The emotional tumult of their open marriage and the serial loss of three of their children, a foster baby, and a late-term pregnancy brought her "misery" and even more desolate "Solitude." This chain of events reads like the list of the "Principal causes of Misery" she kept in her Italian papers.[107]

Less than six months into her widowhood, Shelley reflected that if she were to write a history of their lives together it would have to be more like a fiction—with a series of "chapters" that were "romantic beyond romance." Yet the narrative formula for capturing the truth and beauty of her life with Percy did not fit the staid conventions of tragedy, comedy, or romance. The brief yet arresting story of her first and only significant romantic relationship was, she thought, "romantic *beyond* romance." The exalted quality of her romance with a Romantic poet arose from her equation of true love with the enjoyment of life despite the fragility of its beauties and pleasures.[108]

In the very next paragraph, Shelley celebrated both her life with Percy and what she had learned by the loss of it. She addressed Percy, again, with the sacred "Thou": for he was still—in spirit—her "Beloved" husband. She challenged the permanence of death by writing *as if* Percy were reading her words in real time as she wrote them:

> I have lived. Love~~d~~ & joy have been mine. Thou hast left me,
> Beloved, but I charge thee take me soon. Thou has rendered me
> unfit for this air & it belongs to thee to make me again happy.—
> I no longer enjoy—but I love! Death cannot deprive me of
> that living spark, which feeds on all given it—& which is now
> triumphant in sorrow. I love—& shall enjoy happiness again—
> I do not doubt that—but when?—[109]

Through this extended meditation on her life as a widow after the death of Percy, Shelley reached a powerful existential conclusion. Because she "Loved" Percy, she had truly "lived"—for genuine "joy" had once been hers in his company. She darkly invoked her (dead) lover's power to "make me again happy." Their reunion would not take place in the flesh, but in the afterlife. Perhaps with poetic nods to Plato, Donne, and Keats, she looked forward to a spiritual reunion of souls. She expressed this faith simply but forcefully in her journal: "Death cannot deprive me of that living spark."

Even as Shelley insisted that she would enjoy "happiness again," the diarist dared to ask herself the open-ended question: *but when?* While this *when* was perhaps unanswerable, the *why* of her existence could be deduced from her capacity for "love" itself. By grasping the psychological fact that she still loved Percy, and would always love him, despite all their shared suffering and sorrows, the widow moved past the suicidal desire to join her lover in death. Instead, she stoically consoled herself with the wisdom that she loved life and her "fellow creatures" *enough* to keep living for the sake of their sole surviving child.

While the twenty-five-year-old imagined her reunion with Percy in the afterlife as the final consummation of her hope and happiness, she had the grace to recognize that through feeling "sorrow," her capacity for sharing "love" in this life had been enhanced. Despite her uncertainty about *when* happiness would come, and whether it would be in this life or the next, at least she knew in her heart that joy would come back to her and her son. From this point onward, Shelley carried a persistent hope: love of this world would always redeem the worst that life could bring, even death itself.

Verney likewise walked "the long road" to wisdom. His path "threaded a vast labyrinth" and "terminated" in the "Valley of the Shadow of Death."[110] As war, plague, and their political effects decimated his species, he realized that "life—life—the continuation of our animal mechanism—was the Alpha and Omega of the desires, the prayers, the prostrate ambition of the human race."[111] Love of life itself seemed to be the practical answer to the problem of evil: for it was the reason for being, or enduring, as human.

"Sorrow—Sorrow—Why am I here?" Shelley had asked her journal in December 1822, and then answered herself, "but that I am destined to be wiser, better and happier than I am."[112] She humbly added that "if it be not so—oh my God! Quickly extinguish this spark of life!"[113] Yet there would be no need for God to strike down her or Verney for failing to achieve wisdom, virtue, and happiness. S/he would "have faith" that life was worth living because of the lessons its suffering taught, and the chance it afforded to reach a higher love of the whole, wondrous yet monstrous, creation.[114]

To underscore the sublimity of this vision, Shelley orchestrated Verney's surprise experience of it in "Music—the language of the immortals."[115] Leading a frail remnant of survivors—his best friend Adrian, his niece Clara and his son Evelyn—Verney stumbles into a church in Geneva to find an organist playing Haydn's "New-Created World" or "Creation."[116] In December of 1823, Shelley had written to Leigh Hunt that her friend Vincent Novello had "converted" her to Haydn.[117] Among other works, Novello composed an organ score for "Creation."[118] Haydn's oratorio sang of the "wondrous being" of humanity made in the image of God as a foil to the "hell spirits" who fled into the "abyss" after disobeying their divine maker.[119] God's creation had been full of angels and monsters from its very genesis. Listening to these sublime and beautiful sounds, Verney realized that "as old and drooping as humanity had become, the world yet fresh as at creation's day, might still be worthily celebrated by such a hymn of praise."[120]

This Christian theological insight into the ever-renewing freshness of God's creation allowed Shelley to move forward in life with her love for Percy intact, as part of who she was as a woman, a mother, and a writer. It also enabled her as a novelist to think through the question of what comes after a seeming apocalypse. She ultimately answered this question in spiritual though unorthodox religious terms, derived from her reading of her late mother and husband's views on God and the problem of evil.

Though she was raised and remained formally Anglican her whole life, Wollstonecraft rejected the idea of original sin in the opening chapter of *A Vindication of the Rights of Woman.*[121] People were not born sinful, but rather made choices that brought evil into the world. Unlike Rousseau in his 1756 letter to Voltaire on the problem of evil raised by the Lisbon earthquake, however, Wollstonecraft did not argue that evil was simply a product of human error and bad behavior, which left God out of the equation.[122] Such a view, she insisted, "is as unphilosophical as impious," because it failed to recognize the "perfection" of God and his oversight of the cosmos.[123]

According to Wollstonecraft's more complex and expressly Christian view of divine providence, God—in his omnipotent, omniscient, and omnibenevolent wisdom—allowed evil to come into the world as a *by-product* of human choices. The "wise Being" allowed "that the passions should unfold our reason," she argued, "because he could see that present evil would produce future good."[124] According to Wollstonecraft's theodicy, humans could only learn the difference between good and evil by learning from their mistakes, which God permitted in the first place. She resolved the problem of evil by suggesting that it was part of the ethical machinery of God's tutelary cosmos. Human encounters with the evil consequences of their choices—both what they had done and failed to do—enabled them to grasp both *what not to do wrong* in the future and *what to do right* the next time.

As with other Anglicans, Wollstonecraft had a faith in God's providence that was fundamentally deterministic. But like the Rational Christian Dissenters in the church of the Reverend Dr. Richard Price on Newington Green, where she attended services in the late 1780s, she took a nonconformist view of most matters of Christian doctrine.[125] Following Price, her rationalistic moral theology allowed her to hold a view of free will's compatibility with both divine providence and the scientifically and empirically testable laws of nature. Following the chemist Joseph Priestley, a friend of her radical publisher Joseph Johnson, she was a Socinian, or eighteenth-century Unitarian, in her view of Christ as a God-ordained prophet not divine himself.[126]

Though she was the daughter of the atheist Godwin and wife to the atheist Percy, Shelley used her mother's creative mix of Reformed Christian moral ideas to develop her critical vision of Frankenstein's Creature as a product of bad education. She expressed through the poetic voice of the abandoned Creature that the *lack* of love and care turns people into monsters. Evil is not inborn, but rather ingrained by the privations of society and education. Having taught himself to read with a stolen copy of Milton's *Paradise Lost,* the Creature comes to identify with Satan, bewailing that he was born good, but became "monstrous" due to the tyranny of his father.[127] With biblical imagery, the Creature voiced a Wollstonecraftian principle of education that Shelley emphatically shared with the radical republican and atheist Percy.

Like her mother, Shelley remained a member of the Church of England even as nonconformist Christian traditions inspired some of her solidaristic and cosmopolitan ideals. These dissenting churches included the Protestant restoration Glasites in Dundee and the Calvinistic, hyper-rationalistic Sandemanian tradition of her father's early seminary training.[128] The Glasite Church had recently broken from the established Church of Scotland when she attended it between 1812 to 1814. While living in Dundee with the Baxter family, she participated in the Glasite Church's "Love Feasts" on Sundays. These meals of soup and bread shared among the congregation enacted a remembrance and ritualistic restoration of the last supper of Jesus with his apostles.

Shelley kept the Anglican church as the focal point of her unorthodox religious experience of Christianity's teachings on love, life, and death, as it had been for her mother. In the summer of 1814, she courted Percy at the Old Saint Pancras churchyard where Wollstonecraft was buried. On 30 December 1816, soon after learning of his wife Harriet's suicide, she married Percy at St. Mildred's on Broad Street in London.[129] In March 1818, she arranged for the christening of her children Clara and William alongside her stepsister Claire's daughter Allegra Byron at St. Giles-in-the-Fields in the West End, before they departed for Italy.[130] By January of 1820, she had befriended an English clergyman in Florence, Mr. Harding, who baptized her baby Percy Florence before they departed for Pisa.[131] In the winter of 1821–22, she resumed attending services in the Church of England with her friend the Anglican prebend Dr. George Frederick Nott, with much grumbling from the atheists in her Pisan circle.[132]

Shelley's deterministic spirituality drove her to protect her infant son, once more, from the fate that befell his late siblings. Enacting a secular baptism to save his body from contagious disease, she had her "babe vaccined," probably through inoculation with smallpox.[133] With this sweet yet matter-of-fact statement of his vaccination on 23 April 1820, her third journal book became a medical record of her deterministic faith: if she could *regret* choices she had made that led to her children's deaths, then she could *yet* make choices to positively affect the life of her "last child."[134] Perched on the dome of St. Peter's, her analogue Verney would be possessed by a similar prophetic vision: looking toward the good of future generations would be the only way to avoid the replication of the tragedies that had plagued generations of the past.

Journals of Sorrow: 2100, 2020, 1822

The Last Man is ultimately set in the year 2100, when Lionel Verney gazes upon the ruins of human civilization. Pre-apocalypse, he was the diplomatic advisor to the former-prince-turned-republican leader of England. Postapocalypse, he wanders through the empty "habitations of Rome," where he stumbles upon "writing materials on a table in an author's study."[135] One page had "an unfinished dedication to posterity . . . to whose everlasting benefit he bequeathed his labours."[136] "I also will write a book," Verney cries in inspiration. He dedicates this "record" to "THE ILLUSTRIOUS DEAD."[137]

As if the act of writing down the story of the "ante-pestilential race" could raise the dead, the author scrawls the spectral command on the title page, "SHADOWS, ARISE, AND READ YOUR FALL!"[138] A year later, Verney leaves his "HISTORY OF THE LAST MAN" amid the "prodigious relics" of Rome in the hope that some survivor will find it and learn from it.[139] We, the readers of *The Last Man*, are those survivors.

Verney's introspective turn, to reflect and write on the fate of his species, mirrors how our twenty-first-century world turned inward as Covid-19 spread across continents. In March 2020, Broadway and other theaters went dark around the world. Schools and dormitories shut down. Bars and restaurants closed. Universities moved online. People worked remotely and practiced social distancing. Even Disneyland—the purported happiest place on Earth—shut its gates for months.

Although the public enjoyment of arts and culture took a hit, private reliance on them spiked. People stayed home to watch Netflix—if not to chill, then to stay still. Writing from the safety of his extended self-imposed quarantine, the Slovenian communist political theorist Slavoj Žižek generously advised: "On the subject of movies and TV, gladly succumb to all your guilty pleasures."[140] Given his scathing critique of capitalism, the situational irony of this advice was not lost on him or anyone else.

Still controversial for his critical, far left take on the global disaster of 9/11 as a product of the failures of Western liberalism, Žižek managed a more pragmatic (even middlebrow) consistency between the theory and practice of social justice during the earliest months of the coronavirus pandemic. With some admirable prescience, he serenely "confined" himself to his apartment in February 2020, "with all the time needed to read and work."[141] He recounted the insightful words of his friend, the Lacanian psychoanalyst Gabriel Tupinamba, on why he preferred writing under lockdown: "People who already worked from home are the ones who are the most anxious."[142] Žižek added a telling postscript, writing that "if there is no great change in our daily routines, then the threat is experienced as a spectral fantasy nowhere to be seen and all the more powerful for that reason."[143] By April, he had published the first philosophical book on Covid-19—aptly titled, with some self-skewering wit, *Pan(dem)ic!* Even as he counselled others not to assume "panic" was endemic to "pandemic," he too felt swept up by worry about the invisible and stealthy transmission of the coronavirus through human social contact.

At the same time that Žižek was composing this short but riveting series of first-person essays—meditating on the ethics, politics, and culture of living and working in the haunting hyperreality of Covid-19—there was a rising popular interest in keeping pandemic diaries.[144] This trend initially called to mind great works of fiction such as Boccaccio's *Decameron* and Defoe's *Journal of the Plague Year*, which are based on first-person witness of visitations of the bubonic plague to medieval Florence and early modern London. But all plague journals, fictional or not, are in fact a literary tradition grounded in history.

One of history's most important yet still unsung keepers of a plague journal was Shelley. Her personal response to the plagues upon her family became the basis for *The Last Man*'s tale of a novel "contagion" that sweeps the Earth like an apocalyptic flood, triggering waves of other disasters.[145] Perhaps the only human immune to it is Verney, who reflects in his personal history that this "plague" was not like previous "contagious" diseases, like "the scarlet fever, or extinct small-pox."[146] While inoculation and vaccines had rid the world of the latter by the late twenty-first century, this new "epidemic" was uncontained due to the "unsettled" scientific question of how it "was generated and increased."[147] Healthy people and thriving towns might resist it at first, but "receive the death blow at the hundredth" instance of exposure.[148] This "made our legislators pause," Verney recalls, "before they could decide on the laws to be put in force."[149] Although "no care, no prevention could be judged superfluous," the world's countries failed to plan ahead.[150] Instead they reacted to the international trade, migratory, and health crises that the plague triggered, in the wake of their collective failure to establish policies that might have controlled or even prevented them.

Writing this personal yet political history, Verney looks back upon the anxious time of the rise of the plague and remembers how "every heart" felt like mother nature had played a mean trick upon her children:

> Nature, our mother, and our friend, had turned on us a brow of menace . . . She could take our globe, fringed with mountains, girded by the atmosphere, containing the condition of our being, and all that man's mind could invent or his force achieve; she could take the ball in her hand, and cast it into space, where life would be drunk up, and man and all his efforts for ever annihilated.[151]

These lines of prose poetry echo the postapocalyptic imagery of Byron's "Darkness" (1816), in which the poet pictured the end of the world and humanity after "the bright sun was extinguished":

> The waves were dead; the tides were in their grave,
> The moon, their mistress, had expir'd before;
> The winds were wither'd in the stagnant air,
> And the clouds perish'd; Darkness had no need
> Of aid from them—She was the Universe.[152]

Coincidentally, Byron composed these lines around the same time that Shelley began to write *Frankenstein*, while she and Percy were visiting the exiled poet in Geneva in the summer of 1816.

After completing her first gothic novel, Shelley followed Byron even further in her aesthetics, by going even darker in her fiction and her journals. She plaintively titled the fourth book of her private remembrances, "The Journal of Sorrow."[153] This pivotal volume contains her meticulous record of how she had lost almost everyone she loved or admired to contagion, infection, fever, or fatal accident since publishing her first novel at age twenty. Feeling as though she was a woman Oedipus—who was at once the plague upon her family and its worst victim—Shelley gendered the ravaging "PLAGUE" as a "her" in *The Last Man*.[154] Like Byron's all-consuming black hole, "She was the Universe." Both Shelley and her fictional global plague were unwitting mothers of a world of desolation.

Writing in the "Journal of Sorrow" after the death of Byron in Greece, Shelley rued that nearby Italy had been the "murdress of those I love & of all my happiness."[155] The heavenly Mediterranean had become her personal hell. Returning to her homeland of England in the fall of 1823 had brought little relief. In a sort of self-quarantine, she avoided society because of malicious gossip about her marriage to Percy. "Confined in my prison-room—friendless," she echoed the melancholic Hamlet, "my mind is as gloomy as this odious sky."[156] Yet she persevered to craft a futuristic novel around a fantastic existential and political premise: what if a former diplomat could give himself immunity against the worst effects of a global pandemic by retreating into an abandoned library to read and write in solitude?

Two hundred years ago, the widowed Shelley had the courage to sit down at her writing desk as she would imagine her simulacrum Verney do in the year 2100. Crying, she began to fill the blank pages of her "Journal of Sorrow."

"Well then," she wrote, "I am now reduced to these white pages which I am to blot with dark imagery."[157] Recalling Hamlet's judgment of "how flat & unprofitable" life seems to be, she confided to her diary: "I weep to think how unstable all that is. Those whom I most loved are gone for ever."[158] Still, she wrote. She filled two more volumes of her journals before 1844, around the time she published her last volume of travel memoirs, and her health began to fail. Yet she kept writing—mainly letters to her friends and family—until her long and painful struggle with a brain tumor ended in 1851.

Although people often feel overwhelmed by the "horrors of solitude" during times of lockdown, social distancing, self-quarantine, separation, or grief, there is also the chance to discover—like Shelley, Verney, and Žižek—the therapeutic value of isolation.[159] When paired with the practice of writing and reflection on one's relationship to the past, solitude has the power to produce a medicinal form of literature.[160] First in her journals and then in *The Last Man*, Shelley located herself in this august tradition of plague writing that acts to preserve what makes us most humane and deserving of survival. By immersing ourselves in the dark and somewhat perverse wisdom of plague literature, we readers gather the courage to trek through the "Valley of the Shadow of Death"—alongside Shelley and her double Verney—toward the unseen yet hopefully bright horizon of the future. Read in the wake of the isolation of people during Covid-19, Shelley's "Journal of Sorrow" is an existential reflection on the value of what her friend Mrs. Mason called "good mental health."[161]

CHAPTER 2

The Plague of War

Salvaging the Significance of Mary Shelley's Translation of *Oedipus Rex*

πόλις γάρ, ὥσπερ εἰσορᾷς καὐτὸς,
ἄγαν ἤδη σαλεύει κἀνακου
φίσαι κάρα βυθῶν ἔτ᾽ οὐχ οἵα τε φοινίου σάλου[1]

For the town, as you see yourself,
shakes dreadfully now, nor is able to lift
its head from the depth of the bloody
waves.[2]

ἔχθιστος	evil
λοιμὸς	plague
σκήψας	hanging over
ἐλαύνει	afflicts
πόλιν	the city

—lines drawn from Mary Shelley's transcription,
translation, and word-by-word crib of
Sophocles's *Oedipus Rex*, c. 1820–39[3]

What is the use of republican principles & liberty, if Peace
is not the offspring? War not Kings is the fleau of the world
—letter from Mary Shelley to Maria
Gisborne, 16 January 1833[4]

> I came to explore the wreck.
> The words are purposes.
> The words are maps.
> I came to see the damage that was done
> and the treasures that prevail
> —Adrienne Rich, "Diving into the Wreck" (1971–72)[5]

Diving into Mary Shelley's Translation of *Oedipus Rex*

In September 1814, soon after her elopement with the married poet Percy Bysshe Shelley, the seventeen-year-old Mary Wollstonecraft Godwin became a devoted student of Ancient Greek under her older lover's tutelage.[6] During the second half of 1820, the young mother—whose only child to survive into adulthood was still an infant—intensified her independent study of the language while living in Pisa with Percy, who was by then her husband.[7] In her journal, her annual reading list for 1820 concluded with the "first book of Homer. Oedipus Tyrannos. A little Spanish and much Italian."[8] Among fellow philhellenes and supporters of Greek independence in Pisa, she read Sophocles's great adaptations of the Oedipus and Odysseus myths for the Athenian stage over the course of the second half of 1820 through the summer of 1821.[9]

Composed and performed during the second Peloponnesian War, Sophocles's *Oedipus Rex* (429 B.C.E.) and *Philoctetes* (409 B.C.E.) intrigued the author of *Frankenstein; or, The Modern Prometheus*. Shelley fully transcribed and translated every word of *Oedipus Rex*, and recorded a partial transcription and more limited translation of *Philoctetes*, in a brown, leather-bound notebook. Like her third journal book, kept from 1819–22, her "Greek Studies" notebook was most likely manufactured in Italy, circa 1819–20, with coarse English watermarked paper and thinner Italian endpapers.[10] There is strong textual and contextual evidence that her friends Maria and John Gisborne purchased the notebook for her, as they had done her third journal book in 1819, from their "stationer at Livorno" in early 1820.[11] In March 1821, it was to Maria Gisborne that Shelley reported her progress in Ancient Greek during her daily ninety-minute tutoring sessions that winter with Prince Alexander Mavrokordatos. "I have finished the two Oedipi with my Greek," she wrote, "and am now half way through the Antigone."[12]

I have redated—and widened—the parameters of Mary Shelley's most likely use and consultation of her "Greek Studies" notebook from the second half of 1820 to at least 1839. By *use and consultation*, I mean her handwritten filling of its pages with her transcriptions and translations of Sophocles's *Oedipus Rex* and *Philoctetes* to serve as a source, guide and model for her ongoing reading, translation, transcription, adaptation, and editing work in this challenging ancient language. I accomplished this redating through a comparative analysis of the notebook's contents, paper, and watermarks alongside other manuscripts in the Abinger collection and related collections of the Shelley family papers at the Bodleian Library.

There are three main collections of Shelley family papers at the Bodleian. They share the same original provenance: from Mary Shelley to her sole surviving child Percy Florence Shelley to her daughter-in-law Jane Shelley. The first collection is "MSS. Shelley," which contains the initial deposit of papers and artifacts by Jane in 1893–94.[13] It includes R. F. B. Brunck's 1809 Oxford edition of *Sophoclis Tragoediae Septem*, found in Percy's "dead hand" after he drowned in a sailing accident off the coast of Tuscany in July 1822.[14]

The second collection is "MS. Shelley adds." Jane gave this collection to the inheritor of Percy's aristocratic title, Sir John Shelley-Rolls, whose family in turn donated the papers to the Bodleian beginning in 1946, and then the remainder in 1961 upon his wife's death.[15] It contains Mary Shelley's 1823–24 copy of Percy's translation of Plato's *Symposium*, which he completed with her transcription help during their first summer in Italy in 1818.[16] Percy's manuscript had been salvaged from the shipwreck that drowned him but was lost sometime thereafter, making Mary's copy invaluable.

The third is "MS. Abinger." Jane, who was close to her mother-in-law Mary, held onto this material for its sentimental value and bequeathed it to her adopted daughter Bessie Florence Gibson Scarlett. Bessie's son Shelley Leopold Scarlett inherited the title of the 5th Baron Abinger, which gave the collection its name.[17] The Abinger collection holds not only Mary Shelley's largely forgotten "Greek Studies" notebook but also the manuscripts of two of her most famous works: the five extant volumes of her journals and the surviving *Frankenstein* draft and fair copy.[18] "MS. Abinger" also houses the papers of Shelley's philosopher-parents, Mary Wollstonecraft and William Godwin. Although Duke University microfilmed the Abinger collection in 1951, followed by the New York Public Library's Carl Pforzheimer Collection of Shelley and his Circle in 1954, batches of the papers only began to be deposited in the Bodleian between 1974 and 1993.[19] Shelley's "Greek Studies" notebook (Abinger e. 52) was not deposited until 2004, when the Bodleian purchased the remainder of the collection after the 8th Lord Abinger James Scarlett's death in 2002.[20]

The fifty-three-year lag between the Duke microfilming and the depositing of Abinger e. 52 in the Bodleian only partly explains its neglect in the scholarship on Shelley. There has been a persistent assumption that her abilities in Ancient Greek were weak relative to Percy's, since (1) he studied the classics at Eton and, before his expulsion in 1811, at Oxford; (2) he was the one to introduce Mary and her stepsister Claire Clairmont to the study of Ancient Greek in September 1814; and (3) he involved Mary as an amanuensis in several of his translation projects, including Plato's *Symposium* in the summer of 1818.[21]

While these three facts are indisputable, they do not commit one to the view that Shelley lacked the skill in Ancient Greek to read, translate, or adapt it in any depth or accuracy, even with the assistance of Percy and Mavrokordatos at Pisa in 1820–21.[22] In defense of the view that Shelley was a serious though admittedly imperfect student of Greek from 1814 through 1827, Maria Schoina (2019) pointed readers to a defiant letter that she wrote to Percy's close friend from Oxford, Thomas Hogg, on 3 October 1824.[23] Hogg had "insulted her Greek" by implying that she as a "lady" could not match the linguistic work of a gentleman. Shelley, who was largely educated at home for her whole life, confronted head-on his masculinist derision toward her decade-long experience with Greek translation.[24] "It is not for amusement," she wrote with a classical rhetorical flourish, "but for the final improvement of my mind that I grub at Greek roots."[25] She coyly undermined Hogg's gender biases by implying that she would not want to be a mere "mistress" of the language who used a "smattering" of it to impress men of his "species."[26] With scholarly humility, she averred that she would never be "proficient" in Greek, but she insisted she would remain a dedicated student of it for its intellectual value alone.[27]

In her first journal book (Abinger d. 27) and her "Greek Studies" notebook (Abinger e. 52), I have uncovered three new pieces of textual and material evidence that further indicate her serious commitment to advancing and using her Greek learning between 1814 and 1839. First, my comparative handwriting analysis—verified independently by another expert, Will Bowers, in the summer of 2021—suggests that it was most likely she, not Percy, who adapted and wrote the Greek quote on the "heavy fate" of Oedipus from

Aeschylus's *Seven Against Thebes* (467 B.C.E.) in the endpapers of their co-kept 1814–15 journal book.[28] Second, my comparative study of the watermarks in Abinger e. 52 and her journals indicates that the terminus a quo (earliest possible date) for her use of her "Greek Studies" notebook is the second half of 1820—not early 1821, as Neville Rogers argued, when Mavrokordatos served as her tutor, nor 1827, as Alan Weinberg argued, while she was on holiday reading Greek.[29] Third, I have determined that Shelley did not give up her use of her "Greek Studies" notebook until at least 1839, when she corrected her late husband's translation of a line of *Oedipus Rex* according to her own word-by-word translation of the play, for publication in her edition of his *Poetical Works* that year.[30]

Prior to my examination of Shelley's "Greek Studies" notebook in its wider literary and political context, there has been a single systematic study of Abinger e. 52 in its material (not microfilmed) form. In 2019, Schoina authored a landmark in Romanticism scholarship by situating the notebook's use and contents in the context of Shelley's wider Greek studies from 1814 to 1827. However, Schoina followed the lead of Rogers and Weinberg in dating Shelley's use of her "Greek Studies" notebook from 1821 to 1827.[31]

Bowers (2018) also consulted Abinger e. 52 as part of his study of Shelley's partial translation of Homer's *Odyssey* in the summer of 1820, but focused on her other Greek manuscripts housed at the University of Iowa and in the Bodleian's "MS. Shelley adds."[32] Independently of Schoina, Bowers likewise began with the 1821–27 dating of Abinger e. 52 by Alan Weinberg in the *Bodleian Shelley Manuscripts* (volume 22, part 2, 1997), who had no access to the original notebook at the time and thus relied on the microfilm.[33] Bowers refined Weinberg's timeframe by suggesting that the "Britannia" watermark in Shelley's "Greek Studies" notebook meant that she might have acquired and used it only after she returned to England in August 1823—making the assumption that it was akin to the notebook that she purchased in London that year for copying Percy's translation of the *Symposium*.[34]

The problem with these previous attempts at dating Shelley's "Greek Studies" notebook is that they misidentified the watermarking within it. It is an empirical rule in archival research that by looking at manuscript pages under light one can identify any visible watermark and/or countermark. By studying the material form of Abinger e. 52 in the wider context of the Shelley family papers over a series of visits to the Bodleian between the summer of 2021 to the summer of 2022, I was able to identify two watermarks in Abinger e. 52: a double-oval Britannia (not the triple-oval Britannia that prevails in the Bodleian sample of Shelleyan manuscripts) and a "J&" signature countermark.[35] The section "Reconceptualizing and Redating Mary Shelley's 'Greek Studies' Notebook and Translation of *Oedipus Rex*" sets forth a study of this pair of watermarks to establish the terminus a quo for the manufacture and purchase of the notebook in Italy in 1819–20 and Shelley's likely initial use of it for her *Oedipus Rex* translation in the second half of 1820.

My widening of the parameters for Shelley's use and consultation of her "Greek Studies" notebook, in that section, is only one step in salvaging the significance of her understudied *Oedipus Rex* translation. The ultimate point is to recover its thematic meanings in a range of historical, philosophical, and literary contexts. Tracing a quarter-century of her reception of Aeschylus and Sophocles reveals her classically informed interpretation of Oedipus as a social and political pollutant whose history of wrongdoing brings a plague of evil upon those surrounding him. I uncover the meanings of this motif through a biographical and psychological approach to reading her published and private writings.

Toward this higher end, I demonstrate in the following sections—"Mary Shelley's Thematic Reception of the Oedipus Myth, 1814–1839" and "Shelley's Literary Incorporation of Oedipus into her Journals, *Mathilda*, and *The Last Man*"—that Shelley identified with Oedipus across a series of her own tragic life stories, particularly in her autobiographical prose writing, fictional and nonfictional. When we read her journals, her "Greek Studies" notebook, her gothic romance and incest novella *Mathilda* (c. 1819–20), and other work unpublished in her lifetime alongside her roman à clef and pandemic novel *The Last Man* (1826), we see how Shelley thematically connected her life to Oedipus by infusing her private and public writing with distinctive imagery—blood and vampirism, plague and war, crossroads and incest—that runs parallel to her translation work on Sophocles and Aeschylus. After establishing these three Oedipal themes in her writing in the section "Mary Shelley's Thematic Reception of the Oedipus Myth," I show in "Shelley's Literary Incorporation of Oedipus" how this process began with a holograph adaptation of Aeschylus's poetry on the "heavy fate" of Oedipus in the endpapers of her 1814–15 journal book.[36] This process of identifying with Oedipus continued through her authorship of *Mathilda* and *The Last Man*, while in grief over the losses of three children she had birthed and their father. It persisted through nearly two decades of transcribing and editing Percy's own Greek studies that were rescued from the hull of the sunken *Don Juan*.

Through a contrast of her reception of the Oedipal story with the most famous reclamation of it in Sigmund Freud's later nineteenth-century theory of the family conflicts that drive the unconscious, I argue in "Shelley before Freud" that Shelley's translation of *Oedipus Rex* was a part of her intentional psychological and philosophical attempt to salvage the wisdom of how *not* to live: in war with self and others. By "diving into the wreck" of her past, the leading gothic woman writer of the nineteenth century reclaimed the tragedies that befell her family and friends for the allegorical storyline of her global plague novel, a milestone of "post-apocalyptic, dystopian and existential literature."[37] By existential, I mean human contemplation of the meaning and value of life in the face of the ever-present specter of death. As Margaret Atwood has argued, dystopian literature—often rooted in plague literature of the past—serves as a "warning" of social and political disasters, or seeming apocalypses, that we should avoid in order to discover and preserve what makes mortal life worth living.[38] In the conclusion of this chapter, I reason that the existential literary innovation of the widowed Shelley was to uphold the grave conflicts and losses of her life as a warning for humanity on the order and magnitude of an Oedipal tragedy.

Reframing the Origins of Mary Shelley's "Greek Studies" Notebook

From July of 1820 through August of 1821, Shelley recorded in her journal her almost daily study of Ancient Greek.[39] In the second half of 1820, she most likely began her partial narrative translation and complete word-by-word crib of Sophocles's parricide, incest, and plague tragedy *Oedipus Rex* in her "Greek Studies" notebook.[40] Shelley wrote in her journal the word "Oedipus" on Saturday, 2 December 1820 and on the same day noted "a Greek prince calls. Prince Maurocordato."[41] This was her first of many meetings with the future Greek independence leader Mavrokordatos, who would aid her ongoing study of Ancient Greek from 23 January 1821 at least through 8 May 1821, if not until his departure from Pisa on 26 June 1821 to fight in the erupting Greek revolution.[42]

Bookending her 2 December 1820 entry on "Oedipus" and Mavrokordatos are notations that she "Read Greek" on 1 December and devoted time to her "Greek" on 3 December.[43] She could have been reading either *Oedipus Rex* or *Oedipus at Colonus* (401 B.C.E.), since she had alluded to the latter tragedy on the first page of her unpublished incest novella *Mathilda* (c. 1819–20).[44] She would go on to record her reading of *Oedipus Rex* and *Antigone* (c. 441 B.C.E.) at the same time she was studying "Greek" on her own, as well as regularly with "αμ" (Alexander Mavrokordatos), from January to March 1821.[45] Since July 1820, she recorded in her journal and correspondence that she had been reading Greek independently and "very seriously," including translating and memorizing "sixty lines of Homer's Odyssey."[46] She had devoted the first half of 1820 mainly to her Latin, while she was primarily responsible for working on the now-lost translation of Spinoza's *Tractatus Theologico-Politicus* (1670) that she and Percy began in November of 1817.[47]

Shelley noted in her journal that she read and finished "Oedipus Tyrannos" from 19 to 25 January 1821, and that Mavrokordatos gave her a "greek lesson" on 23 January. In March, her lessons with him increased in frequency, and she began using "αμ" as a journal code for him on days that they met to study Greek.[48] She may have begun to study Greek more independently, after 8 May, when she ceased to connect "αμ" with her "Greek" studies.[49] At the same time, she continued to record her regular social life with "αμ" until his departure in late June, and her almost daily study of Greek during this period.[50] On 3–4 July, she noted in her journal that she read and finished Sophocles's "Philoctetes," a play that appears to have shaped her earlier lessons with Mavrokordatos.[51] Among her papers in "MS. Shelley adds." is a manuscript of the Ancient Greek alphabet, with an epigraph from *Philoctetes* in the original Greek, which Mavrokordatos likely made for her in early 1821.[52] Given this timeline of the intensification of her Greek learning from summer 1820 through the summer of 1821, it is reasonable to infer that Shelley studied and discussed both *Oedipus Rex* and *Philoctetes* with Mavrokordatos and then continued to work on her translations, transcriptions and cribs of them after he left to help lead the battle for Greek independence.

The Political and Personal Background for Shelley's "Greek Studies" Notebook

The immediate political backdrop of the Greek revolution against the Ottoman empire shaped Shelley's enduring interest in the Oedipus myth, including her allusions to Sophocles's adaptations of it in her war-and-plague novel, *The Last Man*, which she set amidst an entrenched conflict between Greece and Turkey in the late twenty-first century. For the greatest of all Attic tragedies had been shaped by Sophocles's survival of the Peloponnesian War and especially the war-driven Plague of Athens in 430 B.C.E., which erupted in the wake of the siege of the walled city-state by the Spartans.[53] Aspects of *Oedipus Rex*, and other "Theban" tragedies about the House of Cadmus authored by Sophocles and Aeschylus, also ran parallel to Shelley's own past. Themes of sexual transgression, familial conflict, war, and plague in the history of her illustrious Romantic literary circle help to explain her studied attraction to reading, transcribing, translating, and adapting the myths concerning the interconnected fates of Oedipus and other members of the ancient ruling family of Thebes.

Shelley's extant corpus begins with the sixteen-year-old's journal entries on her elopement in the summer of 1814 to war-ravaged France with a married man—the republican, poet, free-lover, and atheist Percy Shelley—with her sixteen-year-old stepsister Claire Clairmont in tow.[54] This implicitly incestuous and publicly scandalous act of rebellion against prevailing standards of courtship and sexual propriety led to the girls' estrangement from their father William Godwin as well as the public branding of the group—including their notoriously promiscuous companion Lord Byron—as "The League of Incest."[55] Godwin's only daughter by birth, Shelley later admitted an "excessive & romantic attachment" to him in a 1834 letter to Maria Gisborne, who had nursed her in her infancy after the death of her mother Mary Wollstonecraft from a childbirth infection in 1797.[56]

By the time she was twenty-one, during her first year in Italy in 1818–19, Shelley had all the more reason to identify with Sophocles's metaphorical and thematic rendering of plague as incest, familial conflict, and the struggle for political succession in *Oedipus Rex*. A survivor of the Plague of Athens, Sophocles knew plague as both a dangerous pathogen and as extreme and widespread social hardship, caused by conflicts, losses, and betrayals that spill out to corrode the whole community.[57] In her own concatenation of plagues, real and metaphorical, Shelley had lost two of her beloved children under the age of three to infectious diseases, caught while accommodating her husband's peripatetic lifestyle during their first year of self-imposed exile in Italy with her stepsister Claire, who was likely having an intermittent affair with Percy.[58]

Also during her early twenties, Shelley most likely began to transcribe and partially translate Sophocles's *Philoctetes* in the same notebook as her word-by-word translation of *Oedipus Rex*. *Philoctetes* chronicles the political consequences of Odysseus's abandonment of an archer under his command, who suffers a debilitating and rancid wound from a snake bite during the Trojan War. Shelley's own compounding experiences of trauma, especially after the death of Percy, led the young widow to find solace in both her ongoing Greek studies and the preservation and editing of her late husband's translations of classical Greek texts, including Plato's *Symposium*.[59]

Shelley would also preserve in her papers a manuscript of the Ancient Greek alphabet with a quote from *Philoctetes* as its epigraph: "πάντα δεινὰ κἀπικινδύνως βροτοῖς κεῖται παθεῖν μὲν εὖ, παθεῖν δὲ θάτερα" (all things are full of fear and danger for mortal beings that after feeling good fortune they may suffer evil).[60] Her Greek tutor and friend Mavrokordatos—who would become the first president of the executive of a newly independent Greece in 1822–23—likely made the alphabet for her while he was living as a Greek expatriate in Pisa in early 1821.[61] Written twice more at the bottom of the alphabet manuscript, in a hand less polished than the style identified as Mavrokordatos above them, the quote from *Philoctetes* about reversals of fortune may have served as a mantra to Shelley as she buried herself in her own Greek studies and the preservation of Percy's in the wake of the "misfortune," "suffering," and "sorrow" that befell her family in Italy between 1818 and 1822.[62]

Handwritten in her "Greek Studies" notebook, Sophocles's ancient allegories of contagion, infection, and conflict inflected the composition of *The Last Man*. Shelley wrote the bulk of her pandemic novel from 1824 to 1825.[63] She published it in January 1826, a year before Alessandro Mazzoni released his popular and influential romantic novel, *The Betrothed*, which was set in seventeenth-century Milan during an outbreak of the bubonic plague.[64] Shelley's unique (and perhaps more influential) contribution to the ancient genre of plague literature was to combine an epic plotline about the near-extinction of humanity by a war-driven global epidemic with a roman à clef that processed her grief over losing almost everyone she had loved or admired. As in *Oedipus Rex* and *Philoctetes*, contagion and infection had become metaphors for the seemingly unstoppable spread of untimely death in Shelley's close-knit yet conflict-ridden community of expatriate Romantic writers.

Looking back on her life as she wrote her most explicitly autobiographical work of fiction, Shelley had her literary analogue Lionel Verney—the ostensible "LAST MAN" left after a lethal pandemic—identify with "Oedipus" as the unwitting spreader of a "sorrow-tainted life" to everyone around him.[65] For she too had felt the impact of infection and contagion, physical and psychological, upon her own unfolding life story. Sepsis took her mother Wollstonecraft eleven days after her birth in 1797. Suicide claimed her half sister Fanny Godwin and her husband's first wife Harriet Westbrook within two months in late 1816, as she was writing *Frankenstein*. Shelley's father Godwin admitted in 1820 that Fanny's suicide manifested from a deep and untreated wound in the Godwin-Shelley families: the young woman's jealousy and depression over Percy's rejection of her in favor of traveling and living with her half sister Mary and stepsister Claire in an apparent ménage à trois.[66] In her 1839 journal, Shelley would use the tragic language of fate and atonement to admit that Harriet's suicide weighed heavily on her conscience: "Poor Harriet to whose sad fate I attribute so many of my own heavy sorrows as the atonement claimed by fate for her death."[67]

Shelley's unorthodox relationship with Percy and their wider circle of literary and political collaborators, before and after their marriage in December 1816, faced its own dramatic series of plagues. A string of literal diseases—genetic or infectious—struck down five children she bore or cared for, between 1815 and 1822.[68] Then she nearly died from a hemorrhaging miscarriage before Percy drowned in the Mediterranean Sea.[69] Their mutual friend Lord Byron followed his fellow poet to an early grave, two years later, after contracting sepsis while fighting for Greek independence in Missolonghi in 1824.[70] With this unthinkable train of death in her wake, Shelley began to wonder, like Oedipus the King, whether it was she who was the reigning plague upon her community? Writing in her journal while in London in January 1824, the young widow imagined herself as a pestilential reaper, walking through a field with a scythe, leaving only the "grey stubble" of the grass, and the "flowers . . . strewn withered on the ground," in a trail of blight behind her.[71]

Given this real-life gothic personal backdrop, it should not be a surprise to contextually minded historians of ideas that Shelley focused her narrative translation of *Oedipus Rex* on the first twenty-four lines of the opening scene.[72] In it, a Theban priest brings to King Oedipus the pointed question: whose taint of guilt brought a "plague" of "blight" and infertility upon their city?[73] What follows from the priest's inquiry is the defining irony of the Oedipal drama and all tragic spectacles modeled after it, including Shelley's father-daughter incest novella *Mathilda* (composed in 1819–20, suppressed by Godwin, and finally published in 1959) and her autobiographical pandemic novel *The Last Man*.[74] Known as tragic irony, this literary device—as perfected by Sophocles and adapted to modern postapocalyptic fiction by Shelley—captures the ethical predicament of an apparent hero who is the last to understand what the audience (or readership) grasps through the disaster unfolding on the stage (or on the page).[75] Shelley became a modern Sophocles through her self-conscious use of tragic irony to compare herself (and her literary analogues in *Mathlida* and *The Last Man*) to Oedipus.

Reconceptualizing and Redating Mary Shelley's "Greek Studies" Notebook and Translation of *Oedipus Rex*

In the following section, I use archivally based research methods to establish that the most likely parameters for Shelley's use and consultation of her "Greek Studies" notebook to complete her transcription and translation of *Oedipus Rex* and her partial transcription and translation of *Philoctetes* were late August to December 1820, on the one side, and at least to her 1839 publication of Percy's *Poetical Works*, on the other. Prior to this study, Schoina (2019) was the only scholar to have systematically studied the manuscript of Shelley's narrative translation of the first twenty-four lines and remaining word-by-word "crib" for reading Sophocles's *Oedipus Rex* as found in her "Greek Studies" notebook.[76] Schoina dated its composition between 1821 and 1827, due to Shelley's (and others') notation of her intensive study of Greek texts during this timeframe.[77] Schoina moved beyond the late twentieth-century judgment of Rogers, the editor of Percy Shelley's poetry for Oxford University Press, who argued in an undated note tucked into Abinger e. 52 that "Mary Shelley's Greek Studies in this notebook . . . were probably written between Jan. & March 1821 when Mary was studying Sophocles with [Alexander] Mavrokordatos."[78] I build on Rogers's and Schoina's arguments to show that the most probable time in which Shelley became *intensively* occupied with translations and transcriptions of Sophocles (especially his *Oedipus Rex* and *Philoctetes*) was in the first half of 1821, when the Greek prince and independence leader Mavrokordatos regularly visited with her and Percy in Pisa until late June.[79]

As Bowers (2018) noted, it was in early 1821 that Shelley recorded in her journals her reading of all of Sophocles's Theban tragedies and *Philoctetes* and likely worked from an Ancient Greek alphabet (probably in Mavrokordatos's hand) with an epigraph from *Philoctetes*.[80] I agree with Bowers that she may have further intensified her study of the Greek texts of Sophocles's *Oedipus Rex* and *Philoctetes*, as well as Homer's *Odyssey*, as part of her mourning for Percy, while she lived in England in 1823–24, as a tribute to her late husband's devotion to the study of these Greek poets.[81] Furthermore, I concur with both Schoina and Bowers on the likelihood that she continued to use and work on her Sophocles transcriptions and translations from the summer of 1821 through 1827, when she wrote to her friend Jane Williams Hogg that she was studying Greek while on vacation.[82] However, I disagree with Weinberg, the editor of volume 22, part 2 of the *Bodleian Shelley Manuscripts* (1997), that the voluminous (roughly two-hundred-page) contents of Shelley's "Greek Studies" notebook may have been produced around, during, or after her 1827 vacation. I concur with Schoina that it is far more likely, given the match between the watermarks on her stationery from this trip, her Greek exercises from this period, and her very short and partial transcription and translation of *Alcestis* (438 B.C.E.), that it was Euripides, not Sophocles, that she was reading on this 1827 holiday, given the "scrupulous" transcript of the first 106 lines that she began sometime after 1825.[83]

To the burgeoning literature on Shelley's Greek transcriptions and translations, I add that she likely used and consulted her "Greek Studies" notebook well into the 1830s, since she mentioned her ongoing study of Greek in a 24 August 1832 letter to Maria Gisborne.[84] As we shall see in the section on "Mary Shelley's Thematic Reception of the Oedipus Myth," she also corrected her late husband's translation of line 67 of *Oedipus Rex* in her 1839 edition of his *Poetical Works* in a way that runs parallel to her translation of the play in her "Greek Studies" notebook.[85] After examining the handwriting, paper, and watermarks in her "Greek Studies" notebook alongside some of her dated manuscripts at the Bodleian Library, and asking the leading experts Schoina and Bowers to independently examine the same materials to verify my empirical observations and analyses, I am also able to redate the manufacture of Shelley's "Greek Studies" notebook (after 1819, from thick and coarse watermarked English paper, but most likely bound in Italy with brown leather and thinner Italian endpapers), as well as its purchase (with contextual and textual evidence pointing to Livorno in February 1820), and Shelley's earliest plausible use of it (after 26 August 1820).

As a result of my archival research, I am not inclined to narrowly date her use and consultation of her "Greek Studies" of Sophocles to her time in England in 1823–24 via the notebook's "English" style of paper and "Britannia" watermark, as Bowers speculates on the basis of the editorial commentary of Weinberg and Bruce Barker-Benfield in *The Bodleian Shelley Manuscripts*.[86] Although this dating is possible prima facie, the physical inspection of the manuscript notebook suggests otherwise. The editors probably could not see the watermark for the "Greek Studies" notebook on microfilm. They could not physically inspect it or include it in their beta-radiograph studies because it was not given by the family of the recently deceased Lord Abinger to the Bodelian until 2004.[87]

Perhaps because he could not do a beta-radiograph analysis of the "Greek Studies" notebook, Weinberg suggested dating the this notebook to 1827 via a system of handwriting analysis and the comparison of the microfilmed notebook with the watermarks on her post-1825 "Alcestis" transcription and a series of dated letters written while she was studying Greek on holiday in 1827.[88] Upon physical inspection, however, the primary watermark in the "Greek Studies" notebook proves to be an undated "double oval" Britannia symbol (not a "triple oval" Britannia identified as a standard watermark in the beta-radiograph study of Shelleyan watermarks) (Figure 8). The expert on Shelleyan watermarks, Barker-Benfield, had identified the "double oval" Britannia only once in the Bodleian Shelley manuscripts: Mary Shelley's "Cyrus fragment," variously dated from 1815 to 1817.[89] Given this pre-1818 dating of the "Cyrus" fragment with the same "double oval" Britannia watermark as the "Greek Studies" notebook, it is *possible* that the originally blank "Greek Studies" notebook could have traveled to Italy from London via the Shelleys or one of their many expatriate connections (such as the Hunts or the Gisbornes) between the time she came to Italy in 1818 and her return to England in 1823. However, in the summer of 2022, I uncovered a second, previously undetected watermark in Abinger e. 52—an English-Italian papermaker's signature countermark of "J&"—that supports my theory that the Gisbornes bought the notebook for the Shelleys at their stationer in Livorno in 1819–20 (Figure 9).

According to the watermark studies in volumes 22–23 of the *Bodleian Shelley Manuscripts*, the double-oval Britannia and "J&" watermarks in Abinger e. 52 suggest that the paper in this leather-bound notebook was made by Joseph Ruse and one of his partners, Bondon and Turners.[90] Joseph Ruse was an English papermaker who, in collaboration with others, made English-style paper for Italian markets, with the manufacturing most likely in Livorno. Following the detailed scholarship of the *Bodleian Shelley Manuscripts* editors, I was able to establish that Abinger e. 52 was (like her third journal book) most likely purchased in Livorno in 1819–20 by the Gisbornes and given to Shelley.

As Barker-Benfield argued on the basis of Shelley's letters, Maria and John Gisborne "supplied at least one blank book (that used for 'Prometheus Unbound') or more likely a batch of blank books well before December 1819 . . . and . . . in February 1820 of a second batch of a dozen similar notebooks."[91]

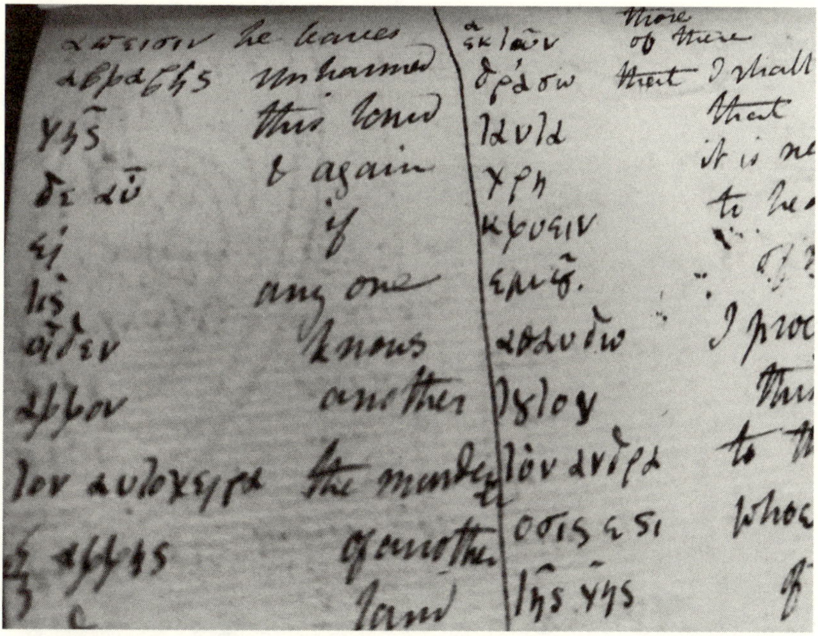

Figure 8. Mary Shelley's "Greek Studies" notebook. Abinger e. 52, Bodleian Library. On the left side of the page, the undated "double oval" Britannia watermark is visible. Reproduced courtesy of the Bodleian Library, Oxford University.

There is a Joseph Ruse watermark visible on a list of books that Shelley sent to Maria Gisborne in October 1819, after she had received her third journal book from the Gisbornes from their stationer at Livorno.[92] This supports my theory that Abinger e. 52 was purchased by the Gisbornes for Shelley at Livorno, most likely in the second batch of notebooks that they sent her in February 1820.

These Gisborne-purchased notebooks, including volume three of Shelley's journals that she kept from 1819 to 1822, had thick and coarse English paper (like the "Greek Studies" notebook) but were bound in brown leather in Italy, with thinner Italian endpapers.[93] Despite the fact that her third journal book is larger and horizontal in orientation and her "Greek Studies" notebook is smaller and designed to be used vertically (like a present-day artist's sketchbook that flips upward), they have several obvious similarities in material form: (1) coarse English paper in the interior, but endpapers of thinner style, which in the case of the third journal book have been identified as

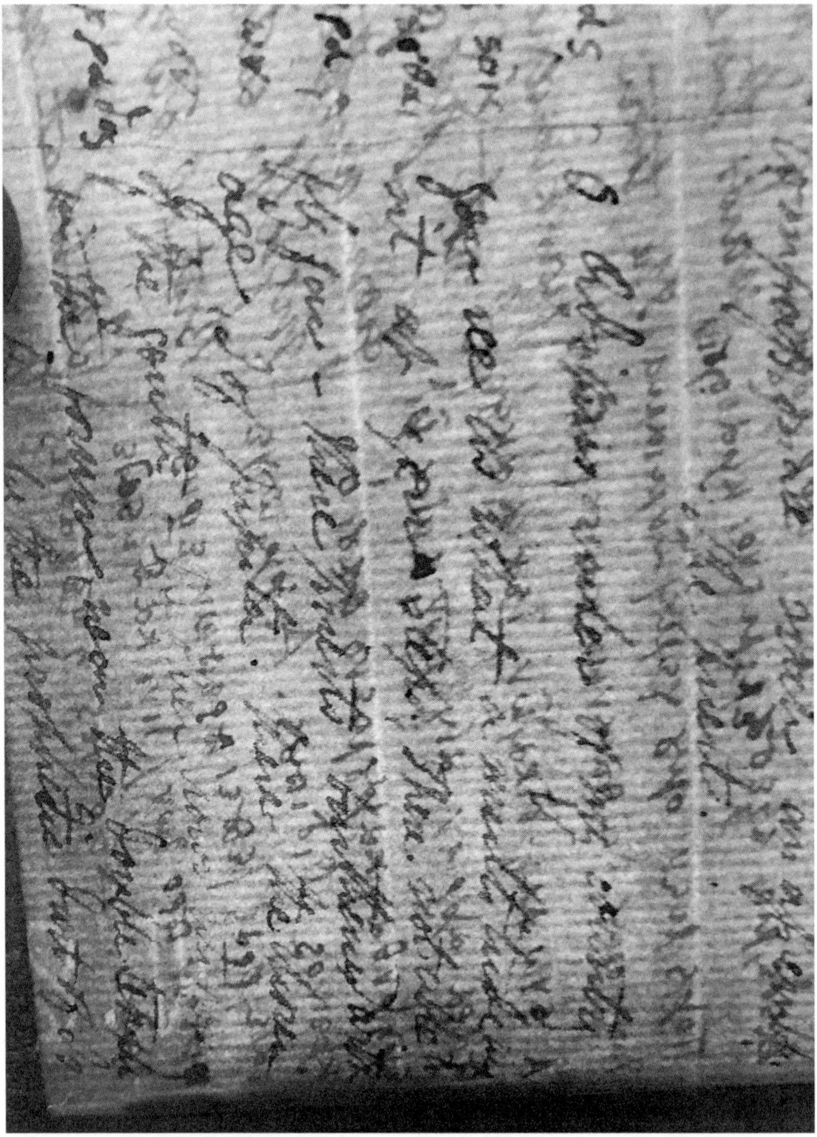

Figure 9. Mary Shelley's "Greek Studies" notebook. Abinger e. 52, Bodleian Library. On the bottom left of the page, the "J&" countermark is visible. It is the only signature countermark visible in the notebook's two hundred pages. Reproduced courtesy of the Bodleian Library, Oxford University.

Italian by the editors of the *Bodleian Shelley Manuscripts*, (2) brown leather rectangular bindings and covers, and (3) six vertical lines (though of different colors on each book) decorating the sides of the bindings (Figures 10–13). With these empirical archival observations and historical records in mind, I deduced that Shelley's initial use and consultation of her "Greek Studies" notebook most likely dates from the second half of 1820, when she recorded in her journal her almost daily study of Ancient Greek, her independent translation and memorization of sixty lines of Book I of Homer's *Odyssey*, her and Percy's extensive reading of Sophocles, and her perusal of "Oedipus" on the day she met her future Greek tutor Mavrokordatos on 2 December.[94]

After establishing the double-oval Britannia watermark and "J&" countermark for Abinger e. 52 and the terminus a quo (1819–20) for its manufacture and purchase, I reexamined some stubs of paper that had been ripped out of the notebook before her translation of *Oedipus Rex* began. In Shelley's hand, there is a date ("August 26") and a translation of the first line of *Oedipus Rex* visible on the stubs. Without a year, it is impossible to tell for certain if she began to translate *Oedipus Rex* on 26 August 1820. But, coincidentally, she recorded in her journal on 25 August 1820 that Percy began to write his satirical play based on *Oedipus Rex*, "Swellfoot the Tyrant."[95] The next day, she wrote the date "26 August," but left the entry blank after it.[96] From 27 August to 3 October 1820, virtually every entry notes "Greek" as one of her central activities.[97] Perhaps she started to translate *Oedipus Rex* in her notebook around 26 August 1820, but ripped the pages out when unhappy with it, and began again around the time she recorded reading "Oedipus" on 2 December 1820. Regardless, her earliest use and consultation of the notebook likely dates to the second half of 1820 and continued to at least her 1839 publication of Percy's *Poetical Works*.

"Metaphrase": Shelley's Literal and Literary Mode of Translation

Once she began her study of Ancient Greek in September 1814 alongside Claire and under the tutelage of Percy, Shelley followed the early nineteenth-century practice of using transcription and literal translation as a basis for lifelong language learning.[98] By the time she moved to Italy in 1818, she was a published novelist, but one who had chosen to publish *Frankenstein* anonymously due to the perceived impropriety of a woman writing on a topic so "hideous" as the making of life from the dead parts of humans and other animals.[99] As

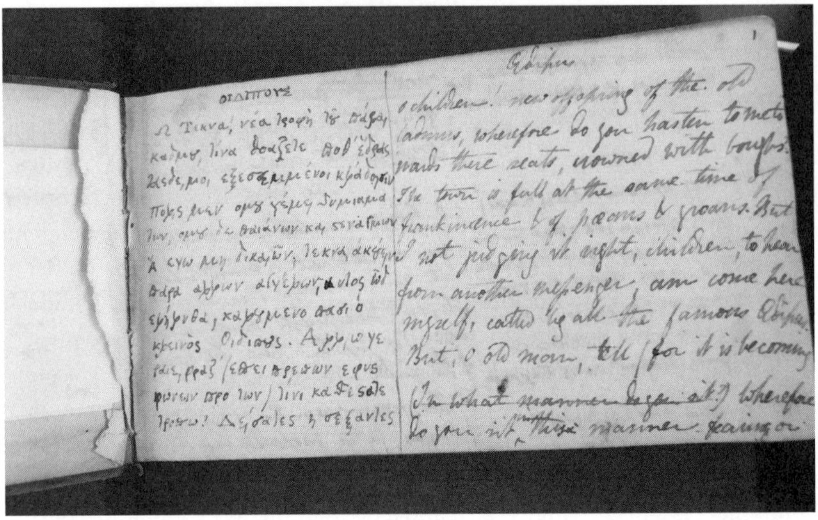
Oedipus
O children! new offspring of the old
Cadmus, wherefore do you hasten to me to-
wards these seats, crowned with boughs?
The town is full at the same time of
frankincense & of paeans & groans. But
not judging it right, children, to hear
from another messenger, am come here
myself, called by all the famous Oedipus.
But, O old man, tell (for it is becoming
(In what manner say it)) wherefore
do you sit in this manner fearing or

Figure 10. Mary Shelley's "Greek Studies" notebook, the first complete page (coarse English paper). Abinger e. 52, Bodleian Library. Reproduced courtesy of the Bodleian Library, Oxford University.

a woman hovering on the edges of men-dominant fields of study and creative work, Shelley understood that she had to package her contributions to both classics and literature in different forms than men. Rather than try to create publishable translations (as she did with Percy's Greek studies manuscripts after his death in 1822), she elected to take literary inspiration from the act of literal translation to weave imagery drawn from the Oedipus myth into her own tragic forms of plague writing.[100]

By literal translation, I do not mean a literal paraphrase. Shelley typically translated as accurately as possible into English each word in any given passage on Oedipus in Aeschylus or Sophocles. She did not merely give the "sense" of each line or simply imitate it. Even when she completed a narrative translation of the first twenty-four lines of *Oedipus Rex*, it was literal. Its exactness meant that her line-by-line translation of the opening scene sacrificed some fluidity in English translation for the sake of capturing the text's original meaning in Greek. Her method might be aptly described according to John Dryden's 1680 definition of "metaphrase," which he distinguished from both paraphrase and imitation as "turning an Authour word by word, and Line by Line, from one language into another."[101]

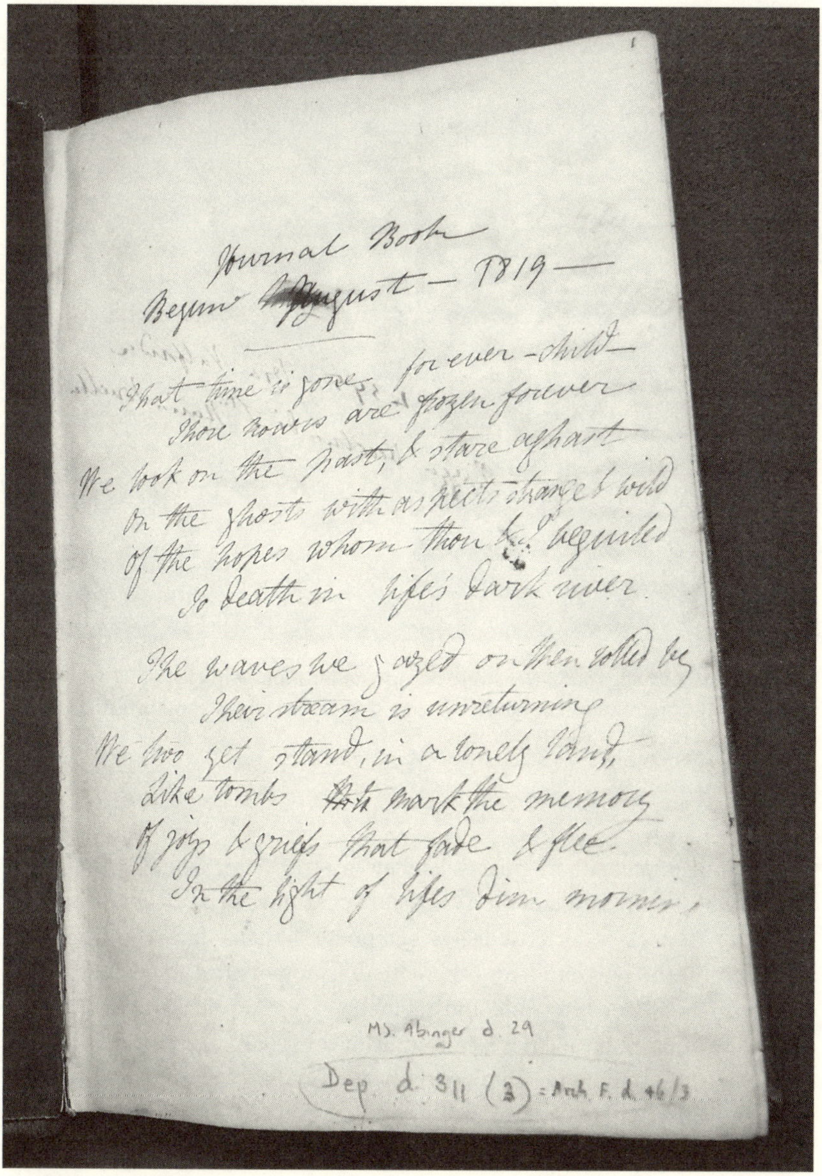

Journal Book
Begun August — 1819 —

That time is gone forever — child —
Those hours are frozen forever
We look on the past, & stare aghast
On the ghosts with aspects strange & wild
Of the hopes whom thou & I beguiled
To death in life's dark river.

The waves we gazed on then rolled by
Their stream is unreturning
We two yet stand, in a lonely land,
Like tombs that mark the memory
Of joys & griefs that fade & flee
In the light of life's dim morning.

MS. Abinger d. 29

Dep. d. 311 (3) = Arch. F. d. 46/3

Figure 11. Mary Shelley's third journal book, the first page (coarse English paper). Abinger d. 29, Bodleian Library. Reproduced courtesy of the Bodleian Library, Oxford University.

Figure 12. Abinger e. 52 (left, vertical orientation) and Abinger d. 29 (right, horizontal orientation), Bodleian Library. Reproduced courtesy of the Bodleian Library, Oxford University.

What ultimately distinguishes Shelley as a translator from her first tutor Percy—whose translation of the *Symposium* continues to be critiqued by classicists for its lack of exactitude—is her poetic balance between linguistic accuracy, on the one hand, and thematic harmony with the original work, on the other.[102] Her linguistic and thematic reception of Oedipus into her own body of writing provides a case study of this dual-level method of literal translation. By tracing her literary reception of Oedipus from 1814 to 1839, we see how her skills as a translator improved, evolved, and expanded to the point that she collaborated on the translation of a political call to arms for the Greek Revolution, "The Cry of War to the Greeks," probably from Modern Greek into English, in the spring of 1821; saved, transcribed, and edited several of Percy's Greek translations for publication between 1822 and 1839–40; and likely incorporated her own translation of a passage of Sophocles's *Oedipus at Colonus* into *The Last Man*.

Figure 13. Six vertical lines on the respective brown leather bindings of Abinger e. 52 (above) and Abinger d. 29 (below), Bodleian Library. Reproduced courtesy of the Bodleian Library, Oxford University.

Mary Shelley's Thematic Reception of the Oedipus Myth, 1814–1839: Plague, Blood, War

Shelley wove imagery from the Oedipus myths into her prose fiction and nonfiction via her literal translation of *Oedipus Rex* in addition to passages from Aeschylus's *Seven Against Thebes* and Sophocles's *Oedipus at Colonus* and *Antigone*. She drew out three main themes from the ancient myth of Oedipus and his cursed family, the house of Cadmus at Thebes, who together suffer the collective consequences of uncontrolled passion, anger, and lust for power. This trio of Oedipal themes in Shelley's journals and novels revolve around plague, blood, and war: (1) plagues, real and metaphorical, are borne by deeper conflicts in the family from whence they transmit through the wider society, (2) the incest taboo is a tragic crossroads from which the transgressor of the blood tie cannot turn back, and (3) love, like war, can be a fatal contagion when unchecked passion and the conflicts it causes are left to drain the life blood from those it was meant to sustain.

Plagues Borne by Conflict

As king of a city overwhelmed by "bloody waves" of "plague," Oedipus realizes all too late that his unwitting murder of his father and marriage to his mother are the crimes that sent pestilence—literal and figurative—to visit his people. "*He* is the plague," the late twentieth-century translator Robert Fagles had Oedipus proclaim when the king calls upon his people to join him in finding the wrongdoer who caused the wrath of the gods to be unleashed against Thebes.[103] Although Fagles's poetic translation of this passage depicted the peak of Sophoclean tragic irony, for Oedipus is unaware that he is the "*He*" who "is" the cause of "the plague," it missed some of the nuances of the Ancient Greek words for plague and pollution that Shelley pinpointed in her word-by-word crib for the play. In this handwritten vocabulary list for reading *Oedipus Rex* that she kept in her "Greek Studies" notebook, Shelley accurately translated "μιάσματος" (*miasmatos*, or, in Latin/Italian, *miasma*) as "pollution" and distinguished it from "λοιμός" (*loimos*) or "plague."[104] She caught what Fagles did not in his famous English translation of the drama. While the word *loimos* (plague) occurs in the opening scene, long before the appearance of the word *miasmatos* (pollution), Sophocles's command of tragic irony shows the audience or reader how a human pollutant (Oedipus) caused the city's plague (the diseased state of the reigning family and the Theban community).[105]

Similarly to the ancient cultures of the Hebrews, Egyptians, and Romans, the ancient Athenians used their religion and their medicine to conceptualize pollution in a dual sense: as a moral taint and as a physical toxin. Whether it was seen through the lens of medicine or religion, pollution was the root cause of plagues, blights, and other manifestations of moral or physical corruption, decay, destruction, and death in society.[106] An enthusiastic student of ancient Greek mythology and culture since childhood, under the tutelage of her father Godwin, Shelley was right to literally translate Oedipus's *miasmatos* as the "one" who is "being a pollution to us."[107] Her linguistic distinction between *miasma* and *loimos* made it clear that she shared Sophocles's dual medical-mythological view that the plague (or symptoms of decay) should not be mistaken for the pollutant (or cause of corruption).[108]

Looking backward, this causal account of the relationship between pollution and plague originates in ancient Greek religious taboos on "incest, parricide, and cannibalism."[109] The Theban political tragedies of Sophocles, Aeschylus, and Euripides were all in the Shelleys' traveling library at various points. Together they thematize the breaking of this trio of taboos as the self-destructive expression of deeper familial and social conflicts.[110] When Euripides had King Pentheus torn to pieces by the women of Thebes, with his head taken to his grandfather Cadmus as a tribute by his mother Agave, the playwright tied this trio of taboos into a single orgiastic spectacle, and produced the most anarchic tragedy for the ancient Athenian stage: the *Bacchae* (405 B.C.E.).

Looking forward, we find that the ancient Greek conception of how pollution precedes plague corresponds to basic theoretical concepts in modern epidemiology of the growth of an infectious pathogen into an "epidemic." Shelley used the latter scientific term—built from the Ancient Greek words for "to touch upon" (ἐπί, *epi*) and "the people" (δῆμος, *demos*)—to describe the rise of the global "PLAGUE" in *The Last Man*.[111] Public health teaches us today that the pathogen (whether a virus, bacterium, fungus, or parasite) is the *pollutant* that proliferates infection, disease, and death. If the pathogen spreads through the air, by physical contact, as a spore, or via a vector such as a blood-feeding insect, water, or a fomite surface, it can reproduce disease quickly via processes of infection (whether through human-to-human, or nonhuman-to-human relations) or contagion (human-to-human relations). The socially and physically exacerbated transmission of the pathogen creates an epidemic, or self-replicating system of corruption and destruction within a given network of lifeforms. If the epidemic grows beyond state borders and threatens to cover the globe, then the World Health Organization will declare an international pandemic as was the case with SARS-CoV-2 on 11 March 2020.

Sophocles shared our concerns with mapping the spread of disease. Immediately after King Oedipus calls for the people to identify the pollutant who caused the plague, he prays that "the doer of the deed"—whether it is a "single man" who has "gone undetected" or "one" who "has acted with others"—may "wear away a miserable life in misery, miserable as he is."[112] Whether the polluter is a lone and invisible man, or part of a secret cabal, Oedipus's curse upon him suggests the image of someone left to his own immeasurable misery. Oedipus himself, according to this self-curse, is the last infected man: the pollutant who outlasts everyone in bearing the brunt of the load of suffering generated by his own careless agency. The orphaned Oedipus became both the agent and the victim of disaster by failing to see the consequences of murdering a stranger, who turned out to be both the Theban king and his father, in an act of rage on the road to uncover his family history. This triggers a tragic epiphany in the parricidal and incestuous King, but it is not the narrow view that "*He* is the plague," as Fagles put it.

After he blinds himself with the dress-pins of his dead mother and wife, who has hung herself after realizing she bore the children of her own son, Oedipus is liberated from the oppressive weight of his tragic search for identity. With his eyes self-bloodied, he can finally see the bigger, darker picture of the human condition. When its passions are left unbound by reason, law, or a sense of duty to others, the individual ego (ἐγώ)—the myopic, self-absorbed "I"—is the source of pollution for the plagues that strain and test humanity, as a compassionate way of life and a lifeform.

In her autumn 1822 annotations to her transcript of Edward Williams's journal, Shelley appeared to allude to the egocentric blindness of Oedipus. Williams's journal had been recovered from the shipwreck that drowned him and Percy, who could not swim. Shelley reflected on their tumultuous and portentous time at Casa Magni on the coast of Tuscany in the spring of that year, with Jane and Edward Williams and her stepsister Claire. She critiqued her circle for failing to see how their myopic and reckless behavior would cause their own "miserable fate" to come that summer: "Were not almost insurmountable obstacles placed to our miserable fate—& we, mad blind fools, triumphed in conquering them all."[113] Through the trial of grief, Shelley herself moved from the egocentric "I" to the all-seeing "we": understanding herself, her husband, and their friends as sharing a tragic fate like Oedipus, by seeing all too late how it could have been averted.

As Shelley documents in her "Greek Studies" notebook, Oedipus typically speaks in the first-person singular. On the first page of her translation, this tendency reveals his egocentric and condescending manner toward his own people: "But I not judging it right, children, to hear from another messenger, am come here myself, called by all the famous Oedipus."[114] Before he punctures his eyes with pins, the king's insistent use of the "I" signifies his short-sighted selfishness in contrast to the communal concerns of the priest and chorus. After he turns his sockets into open wounds, Oedipus's use of the "I" changes in tone. Calling for his own exile or permanent self-isolation, he starts to see his personal history of selfish passion as a dangerous form of corruption that must be removed from the community in order to stop its reproduction by others.

Blood and Crossroads: Breaking the Incest Taboo

By the end of her crib, Shelley makes it explicit that Oedipus, still bleeding from his self-inflicted wounds, has recognized that he is a lethal carrier of *miasma*. The transmission of this term through Latin to modern Italian meant that *miasma* would have connoted a geographically specific airborne disease for Shelley, such as the seasonal malaria (or "bad air") that had infected and killed her son William in Rome in May of 1819. In her literal translation, Oedipus decries the crossroads (or the place of the "three ways" or "triple ways") where he turned into a cannibal who "drank my blood from my father."[115] With her evocative imagery of the "triple ways," Shelley alludes to both the trident-like path of the road to Thebes and the trio of taboos—parricide, cannibalism, incest—that Oedipus would break as a result of the choices he made at this pivotal juncture in his adulthood.

In her 1839 edition of the *Poetical Works of Percy Bysshe Shelley*, she corrected her late husband's translation of line 67 of *Oedipus Rex*, "πολλὰς δ' ὁδοὺς ἐλθόντα φροντίδος πλάνοις," which was originally rendered in his manuscript "Notes on Shakespeare and Sophocles" as "Coming to many paths[ways] in the in the wanderings of careful thought."[116] Selecting his superadded, figurative translation of "ὁδοὺς" as "ways" over his more literal, initial translation of it as "paths," she more precisely and poetically rendered the passage as "Coming to many ways in the wanderings of careful thought."[117] In her own translation of this line in her crib for *Oedipus Rex*, she omitted "careful," making the passage in English even more economical and allusive.[118] As part of preparing Percy's fragment on Sophocles as the "Greek Shakespeare" for publication in 1839, I argue, she likely consulted her crib for *Oedipus Rex* not only for her translation of "ὁδοὺς" as "ways" at line 67 but also for "τριπλαῖς ὁδοῖς" as "triple ways" at line 1399, where she evoked the literal and figurative crossroads where Oedipus "drank my blood from my father."[119]

By "my blood," Shelley seems to mean the tainted bloodline of the house of Cadmus, Oedipus's great-great-grandfather. The founder of Thebes, Cadmus accepted his grandson Pentheus's decapitated head as a regicidal and incestuous totem from his daughter Agave (the butchered king's mother). In her literal translation of this scene, Shelley's strikingly vampiric word choices—"drank my blood"—suggest that Oedipus not only killed his father with his own "hands," but also feasted from the family bloodline.[120] Whether this was a literal or a figurative act of cannibalism is irrelevant. What matters is that Oedipus finally understands himself as a blood-drinking cannibal who catches and spreads the taint of guilt upon his royal household by replicating its history of rage, violence, and heartlessness toward its own kindred.

On this Shelleyan reading of Sophocles, Oedipus is a kind of vampire who transmits the pollution, or *miasma*, that causes "bloody waves" of "plague" to drown the whole city of Thebes. Shelley knew of ancient Greek legends of blood-drinking gods, monsters, and revenants. Revenants were the ancient analogues to the modern vampire: corpses who rose at night to prey upon their loved ones.[121] Homer's *Odyssey*—a text that Shelley began to translate in 1820, right before she attempted *Oedipus Rex*—features many vampiric creatures, both on the island of the giant Laestrygonians and amid the shades of Hades.[122]

Beyond her study of the bloodlust of ancient Greek mythology, Shelley had witnessed the creation of the modern legend of the vampire. During the summer of 1816, while she, Percy, and her sister Claire lived in Geneva, Shelley became friends with John Polidori and Lord Byron. Polidori was a classically trained medical doctor, with a thesis on somnambulism written in Latin, who went on to publish a novel with the subtitle *The Modern Oedipus* (1819).[123] Byron hired him to be his personal physician while traveling on the Continent. The libertine poet had recently fled his homeland of Britain due to the scandal that erupted around rumors of his incestuous relationship with his half sister Augusta and the resultant breakup of his marriage.[124] The Shelleys, too, had been hounded by rumors of their illicit sex lives since Percy, a married father and advocate of free love, eloped to France with the teenage Godwin sisters in 1814. Thus, the members of the Godwin-Shelley-Byron circle were known as "The League of Incest."[125]

At the Villa Diodati, overlooking a dark and stormy Lake Geneva, this motley crew of British artist-expatriates held a ghost story competition, to pass the rainy days away, in mid-June of the nearly sunless "year without a summer."[126] While Shelley composed the incipit to *Frankenstein*, and Polidori began his incest tragedy, *Ernestus Berchtold; or, The Modern Oedipus* (1819), Byron produced a tale that defined the revenant—or what Bram Stoker would later call "The Un-Dead"—as a staple monster of the modern horror genre.[127] Perhaps because he never finished the ghost story, Byron's "A Fragment" (1819) inspired Polidori to write his own novella, *The Vampyre* (1819).[128] Both are set against the cultural backdrop of the Eastern Mediterranean, especially Greece and Turkey, where Byron had traveled in his youth. Six years before his "Fragment" appeared in the same volume as his poem *Mazeppa*,

Byron disclosed to the public his interest in the vampire legends of the Aegean. In *Giaour: A Fragment of a Turkish Tale* (1813), Byron observed that "The Vampire superstition is still general in the Levant . . . The Greeks never mention the word without horror."[129]

Sir Christopher Frayling argued in his classic of modern monster history, *Vampyres*, that Polidori's blood-draining villain "Lord Ruthven" was somewhat spitefully modeled after the ruthless sexual appetites of Lord Byron.[130] The poet had dismissed the doctor from his service after a fight over the care of his horses in August 1816.[131] The fictional Ruthven, and his historical analogue Byron, became the prototypes for the modern idea of the seductive, fanged, bloodthirsty aristocrat, to be popularized by the image of the Transylvanian count in Stoker's *Dracula* (1897).[132] Much to Polidori's chagrin, his most influential work would be mistakenly attributed to his former employer (and subject of his vampire-satire). This irony may have contributed to Polidori's presumed suicide by cyanide poisoning at the age of twenty-five in August of 1821.[133]

The vampires of the Levant, ancient and modern, may have been on Shelley's mind as she likely worked on her translation of *Oedipus Rex* under the tutelage of Mavrokordatos in the winter and spring of 1821.[134] Born to a Phanariot family with long-standing political ties to Constantinople, the young prince had lived in the Ottoman court of his uncle, the ruler of Wallachia, from 1812 to 1818.[135] One wonders if Shelley heard from her tutor some of the rich vampire folklore from that region of Romania or his native Greece. If not, there is another obvious source. By then associated with his epic poem *Don Juan* (1819) and Polidori's figure of the "vampyre," Byron was also a contributor to the intellectual life of the Shelleys' philhellenic circle of friends and compatriots at Pisa.

The Plagues of Love and War

Shelley shared with her literary collaborators Percy, Byron, and Mavrokordatos a fervent devotion to the liberation of the people of Greece from Ottoman domination. In her editor's note to Percy's "Hellas" in his *Poetical Works* (1839), she recalled that "The South of Europe was in a state of great political excitement at the beginning of the year 1821."[136] In April 1821, she worked with Percy and Mavrokordatos on an English translation of a Greek independence manifesto by Alexander Ypsilantis, probably from Modern Greek. She may have learned some Modern Greek from Mavrokordatos, but also their shared use of French together no doubt played a role in their collaborative translation work on the project.[137] Written in English in her hand, "The Cry of War to the Greeks" represented the political views of her Pisan circle of Greek revolutionaries including her tutor the prince.[138] Intended to publicize their cause of independence in a British newspaper, the manifesto portrayed the imperial tyrants as slaves to the worst passions of human nature, and the revolutionaries as the true heroes who sought "happiness" for their people. "Who are the mercenary & vile slaves," the manifesto demanded, "who will dare oppose a nation fighting for its independence?"[139] Another translator beat them to the English press, however, so the one written in her hand remained unpublished.[140]

This act of protest with her pen may have inspired the passion of a Greek count, George Metaxas, who belonged to the circle of exiled Hellenic rebels at Pisa.[141] He idolized Shelley in an undated pen-portrait, handwritten in his clumsy but charming French. His letter upheld her as "the goddess of the Athenes," then effusively praised the beauty of her "petite" frame and features, even her "jolis petits pieds" (pretty little feet).[142] The count's ostensible love letter must have been of sentimental value to her, perhaps as much for, as despite, its overenthusiastic praise of her petiteness; she kept it among her papers unto her death. Shelley may have also harbored romantic feelings for the "glamorous . . . black-haired, dark-eyed" soldier Mavrokordatos, according to the biographer Charlotte Gordon.[143]

Surrounded by seductive aristocrats—including her husband Percy—who were all well-versed in Greek mythology, Shelley was in a good position, among the philhellenic rebels of Pisa in 1821, to appreciate the vampire imagery in *Oedipus Rex*. Oedipus himself might be considered such a seductive aristocrat with a tendency toward war and rebellion. He was born to the line of the rulers of Thebes, who were known for violating taboos in the extreme, as seen in their animalistic dismemberment of their kin and king in *The Bacchae*. Cadmus had been cursed by the god of war for slaying the deity's dragon near the site of his future kingdom. Oedipus's father, Laius, was infamous for kidnapping and raping a boy before his own son killed him at the crossroads of the "triple ways." Years after his royal parents exposed him as an infant in order to avert the prophecy that he would murder his father and marry his mother, the adult Oedipus returned to Thebes, only to seduce queen Jocasta and seize the crown. In a horrific act of self-vampirism, Oedipus drew his own blood when he learnt of his crimes, by penetrating his eyes with the sharp points of his dead mother's dress pins.

As the major tragedies of her life unfolded during their time in Italy, Shelley grew to see her husband Percy as a sort of Oedipus: a man unable to grasp in advance the consequences of his own passions, choices, and actions for the fate of his family.[144] Ironically, Percy's first teenage wife arrived at a similar conclusion soon after he abandoned her and their children for Mary and Claire. On 20 November 1814, Harriet Westbrook Shelley wrote to her friend Catherine Nugent that her estranged husband—"the man I once loved," Percy Shelley—"is dead." In his place, she wrote, "is a vampire."[145] With this morbid image, she implied that the poet drained the life from the women and children around him. Two years later, Harriet confirmed her own theory by drowning herself, while pregnant, in the Serpentine.

Marrying Percy within two weeks of learning of Harriet's suicide, because her father Godwin threatened to kill himself if they did not, Shelley would build the character of Victor Frankenstein upon the eerie life (and death) histories of her new husband and the Godwin family.[146] Both Victor and Percy aspire to be the modern Prometheus: rebels who openly reject the rules of religion in pursuit of their radical intellectual ideals and dangerous creative goals. Like the demigod Prometheus, who causes the wrath of Zeus by stealing fire from Mount Olympus to empower humanity, Percy and Victor author their own tragedies.

Near the end of *Frankenstein; or, The Modern Prometheus*, composed in 1816–17, Victor describes the "monster" he has made through his rule-breaking science as "my own vampire."[147] Frankenstein's Creature is a murderous "scourge" that leaves its victims limp, pale, "bloodless," and bruised on the neck.[148] This artificially made, bloodletting "pest" wipes out Victor's family and friends while it slowly drains the life from him.[149] With this pestilential imagery, *Frankenstein* paved the way for Shelley's contribution to plague literature, *The Last Man*. But another, less studied but more proximate, source for her pandemic tragedy is her translation work on Aeschylus's and Sophocles's versions of Oedipus.

Shelley's Literary Incorporation of Oedipus into her Journals, *Mathilda*, and *The Last Man*

Shelley's most dramatic allusions to Oedipus occur in her journals in relation to the escalating familial conflicts in her life with Percy. In the endpapers of her first journal book, concluding in May 1815, there is a lament adapted from the chorus in Aeschylus's surviving play on Oedipus, *Seven Against Thebes*. I have determined—with the corroboration of another expert, Will Bowers—that this lament is likely in her hand.[150] Aeschylus's tragedy concerns the sons of Oedipus, Eteocles, and Polynices, who go to war over the right to rule Thebes. Here is the passage in the original Greek alongside the Loeb translation:

ἰὼ	O
Μοῖρα βαρυδότειρα μογερὰ	Destiny, grievous dispenser of heavy fate,
πότνιά τ᾿ Οἰδίπου σκιά	and mighty shade of Oedipus!
μέλαιν᾿ Ἐρινύς, ἦ μεγασθενής τις εἶ.	O black Fury, truly you are powerful![151]

The version in the endpapers added and rearranged several of Aeschylus's words for tragic emphasis, especially in the rendition of the first line, which can be literally translated as "O O O fate fate":

> ἰὼ ἰὼ ἰὼ μοῖρα μοῖρα
> βαρυδότειρα μογερὰ πότνιάτ᾿
> Οἰδίπου σκιά
> Μέλαιν Ἐριννεος
> Η μεγα θενής τις εἶ.[152]

Below it, Shelley added Percy's nickname for her, "Pecksie," as her signature, with the repetition of her exaggerated choral lament, "O O O/ fate fate":

> Pecksie/f/5
> ἰὼ ἰὼ ἰὼ
> μοῖρα μοῖρ[153]

The meaning of the "/f/5" after her nickname is unknown, but Shelley often used "symbols" in her journals, presumably to keep some of the meaning secret from the other adults in her complicated household.[154] Especially during the first year of their elopement, Percy often wrote in Mary's journals, while Claire kept her own. Mary may have written in code to keep one or the other in the dark.

This esoteric pattern persisted into her fiction. When she composed *The Last Man*, she encoded it with a reference to Aeschylus's tragedy of fraternal war that she had studied in the first conflicted year of her elopement with Percy and her sister. In her novel, Lord Raymond is the English-aristocrat-turned-Greek-freedom-fighter who represents Lord Byron. He falls in love with a Greek princess, the daughter of a diplomat from the "free States of Greece," despite his happy marriage to Perdita.[155] Perdita primarily stands for Claire, who also had an affair with Byron. This fictional love triangle escalates the political conflicts that cause the spread of the plague from a battlefield near Constantinople to topple governments and threaten the extinction of humanity. Princess Evadne's name alludes to one of the wives of the Argive captains who fight for Polynices's claim to his brother's and father's throne in *Seven Against Thebes*.[156]

The original meaning of the journal's Greek quote adapted from Aeschylus, however, might be inferred from its probable writing in Mary Shelley's hand, and its placement at the very back of her first notebook, which ends in May 1815. Her copying and modification of this passage from *Seven Against Thebes* would suggest that she was a quick study. Perhaps it was Shelley's guilt over disobeying her father Godwin during her elopement that inspired her preoccupation with the choral lament of the "heavy fate" of Oedipus. In 1834, Shelley disclosed in passing to the woman who nursed her, Maria Gisborne, that her stepmother Mary Jane Clairmont noticed "long before" she was fourteen that she had an "excessive & romantic attachment to my Father."[157] Mary Jane may have attempted to purge the family of a younger female rival for Godwin's attention by helping to arrange for the adolescent's departure in 1812 to live with the Baxter family in Scotland.

Akin to the exposure of the infant Oedipus by his parents, Shelley's youthful exile would backfire upon her family. Upon her first return to London from Dundee, in November 1812, she met Percy at a dinner party at her father's table.[158] Upon her next return, in 1814, they fell in love, courted on her mother's grave, and ran away to France with Mary Jane's daughter Claire.

But Mary and Percy's scandalous three-way elopement with her stepsister did more than anger their joint father-figure Godwin and his second wife. It infused an incestuous and conflictive dynamic in their romantic relationship from the very start. As she filled the final pages of her first journal book in the spring of 1815, Shelley's cursive grew ever larger and more uncontrolled.[159] Percy's intensifying affair with Claire may have led to an unplanned pregnancy. Claire moved out of the household that summer. One theory is that she went into hiding to have the baby, which did not survive, or to have an abortion.[160]

The more certain explanation for Claire's departure, backed up by the journal, is that Mary and Percy wanted to start over. In the last entry in volume one, Shelley predicts their "regeneration" as a couple with the conclusion of the volume (covering the first year of their romance) and the opening of a new volume (now lost).[161] Her repeated, emotional appeal to Oedipus's "fate" in the endpapers and association of it with her pet name "Pecksie" may also be a cry to Percy, her poet-lover and the co-keeper of the journal, to be mindful of the tragedies that incestuous conflicts bring to the greatest figures of literature.

An even more powerful reference to Oedipus is woven into the second volume of her journals. It occurs in Shelley's account of the death of her one-year-old daughter, Clara Everina, in Venice in late September 1818. Just a few days after the infant died of a fever while in her arms, the young mother plaintively wrote a tragic literary history of what she and Percy were reading and doing when Clara fell ill: "This is the Journal book of misfortunes—Read Livy—A great many of the plays of Alfieri—S writes—he reads Oedipus Tyrannos to me. On Teusday Sept 22nd he goes up to Venise—On Thursday I go to Padua with Clare meet S there—we go to Venise with my poor Clara who dies the moment we get there."[162] Shelley retrospectively identifies her fate with Oedipus by noting the tragic irony of hearing Percy read Sophocles's greatest tragedy as their baby daughter was, unbeknownst to them, dying from a feverish illness that they would only later identify as dysentery. She would come to blame Percy for causing the death of Clara by expecting them to travel for hours across Italy in hot weather to seek medical care for the sick child, all too late, in Venice.[163] Reflecting on their ineluctable loss as parents—much like the chorus contemplates the "heavy fate" of Oedipus and his children in *Seven Against Thebes*—Shelley used the term "book of misfortunes" to describe her second journal, and implicitly, her whole life with Percy.[164] After Percy died in 1822, she would formally title the fourth volume of her diary "The Journal of Sorrow."[165]

When their toddler William died of malaria less than nine months later, Shelley darkly wished in her journal that her and Percy's past "five years together" could be "blotted out."[166] Her next novel went even darker. Written swiftly, as she attempted to lift herself from a catatonic depression that her husband feared would end in suicide, Shelley's novella *Mathilda* (c. 1819–20) took on a trio of taboo subjects.[167] A teen girl, Mathilda, reunites with her long-absent father, only to gradually realize he has turned his passion for her dead mother into an incestuous desire for his daughter. Tormented by guilt, the father commits suicide by jumping into the sea after she elicits his sexual jealousy when other men begin to court her. Mathilda exiles herself to the wilds of Scotland, in a widow's black dress, where she attempts to seduce a poet into a suicide pact. "I procured Laudanum," she confesses, "and placing it in two glasses on the table, filled my room with flowers and decorated the last scene of my tragedy with the nicest care."[168] The poet resists the temptation, while the girl lets herself get sick, staying out all night in the cold damp air, and dies young.

Due to its overt engagement with the taboos of father-daughter incest, suicide, and the eroticization of death, the manuscript of *Mathilda* would be suppressed by Godwin when the author sent it to him via their friend Maria Gisborne in 1820. It would not be published until 1959. The parallels between the father and Godwin, the girl and Mary, and the poet and Percy were duly noted in the groundbreaking scholarship of Elizabeth Nitchie, who recovered the lost manuscript from the microfilm made of Lord Abinger's collection of Shelleyan papers in the early 1950s.[169]

On the first page of her incest tragedy, Shelley had the cursed female protagonist, Mathilda, directly reference Sophocles's *Oedipus at Colonus* as she looks back on her tragic personal history. "While life was strong within me," she ominously relates, "I thought indeed that there was a sacred horror in my tale that rendered it unfit for utterance, and now about to die I pollute its mystic terrors. It is as the wood of the Eumenides none but the dying may enter; and Oedipus is about to die."[170] Through the "female gothic" voice of Mathilda, Shelley identifies as a feminine Oedipus.[171] She reflects back on her tragic family history of incest and self-destruction, like the exiled Theban king does at Colonus. In another robustly autobiographical novel, *The Last Man*, Shelley had her analogue Lionel Verney compare himself to "Oedipus." However, Verney did not think of himself as the self-assured solver of the riddle of the Sphinx, but rather as the tragic figure "whose agonizing pangs, and sorrow-tainted life were to be the engines, wherewith to lay bare the secrets of destiny."[172] To underscore the incestuous conflicts in her family that led to this "sorrow-tainted" sense of self, she made Verney the orphan brother of Perdita, who primarily stands for Claire.

In *Mathilda*'s first-page allusion to Sophocles, Shelley presented the imagery of pollution, expiation, isolation, and exile that would also characterize her translation of *Oedipus Rex* that she likely began in 1820–21. But in *Mathilda*, the grieving author goes darker than even Sophocles's Theban trilogy—*Oedipus Rex*, *Oedipus at Colonus*, and *Antigone*—which she studied between 1818 and 1821.[173] When Oedipus at Colonus shares his story with his daughter Antigone and others, he models a way of reconciling oneself to even the gravest evils of the past by taking responsibility for one's role in making a collective tragedy. The telling of his story is cathartic, as Aristotle theorized, for it expels the emotional pollutants of rage, regret, and selfish despair from both Oedipus and his audience.[174] In *The Last Man*, Shelley had her simulacrum Verney compare his future wife Idris to "the beauty and matchless excellences" of the "heroine . . . Antigone, when she guided the blind Oedipus to the grove of the Eumenides, and discharged the funeral rites of Polynices."[175] Late in the novel, when the plague has taken his wife, Verney turns to the poetry of *Oedipus at Colonus* for consolation as he contemplates "the sea of calamity" before him:

> As an unsheltered northern shore
> Is shaken by the wintry wave—
> And frequent storms for evermore,
> (While from the west the loud winds rave,
> Or from the east, or mountains hoar)
> The struck and tott'ring sand-bank lave.

These lines, the editors Jane Blumberg and Nora Crook speculate, may have been translated by Mary Shelley herself, as no other source could be located for them.[176] Perhaps they were a product of the period of intense grief after Percy's death, from 1822 to 1825, when she devoted much of her intellectual energy to preserving his Greek translations and creating her own, and composed her "Journal of Sorrow" and her roman à clef.[177] If so, Shelley's translation work on Sophocles directly informed her writing of *The Last Man*.

By contrast to Verney's hopeful allusion to the seer-like wisdom of Oedipus at Colonus, *Mathilda* offers little in the way of consolation, redemption, or virtuous example, for it is a suicide note disguised as a gothic romance. Shelley's feminine Oedipus narrates her story to her would-be suitor, the poet she tried to seduce to drink laudanum with her, before she ends her own life. In the ambiguous final scene of the first draft of the novel, Mathlida seems to speak from the "grave," "where the turf is fresh," like a revenant who awakens at night to stalk her loved ones.[178] Whether she is a sickly writer of a suicidal love letter, or a vampiric seductress plying laudanum from her "grave" while "the violets are blooming on it," Mathilda's romantic horror story is meant to "pollute" the mind of the reader, not redeem it.[179]

The writing process proved to be cathartic for the author, however. As she pulled herself out of her own suicidal death-spiral, Shelley conceived a story that outdid even the dark mood of Sophocles's Theban trilogy. By infusing the tragic drama of Oedipus with the sinister and supernatural elements of the gothic romance, she made Mathilda into the prototype of the modern antiheroine: an innocent girl twisted by fate into a feminine version of the Byronic vampire.

Shelley before Freud: Her (Auto)Biographical Approach to Oedipus as a Plague Tragedy

Almost eighty years after Shelley had begun her translation of *Oedipus Rex* at Pisa in 1820–1821, Sigmund Freud published what has become the most famous interpretation of the play. Like Shelley, Freud translated Sophocles's greatest tragedy in his youth, as part of his gymnasium (secondary school) examinations in 1872–73.[180] Revivals of *Oedipus Rex* were popular in late nineteenth-century Vienna and Paris, where the neurologist saw it performed.[181] In his 1899 book *The Interpretation of Dreams*, he theorized that "it may be that we were all destined to direct our first sexual impulses toward our mothers, and our first impulses of hatred and violence toward our fathers; our dreams convince us that we were."[182] In the next line, Freud tied his theory of the meaning of dreams to the tragedy of Sophocles, which he had translated as a teenager: "King Oedipus, who slew his father Laius and wedded his mother Jocasta, is nothing more or less than a wish-fulfillment—the fulfillment of the wish of our childhood."[183] The iconic play, and the myth behind it, shaped the development of Freud's psychoanalytic concept of the "Oedipus complex": the conflict that emerges in the young child's mind as a result of feeling sexual desire for the mother and jealous anger toward the father.[184]

Perhaps because they translated the original Greek of Sophocles, Shelley and Freud did not forget the dramatic frame for *Oedipus Rex*. They both read it as a plague tragedy. In *The Interpretation of Dreams*, Freud pointed out that "Sophocles' tragedy begins" when "a plague breaks out."[185] The plague triggers the people "to consult the oracle" who had once predicted that the son of Laius would kill his father and marry his mother.[186] The messengers report that "the plague will stop as soon as the murderer of Laius is driven from the country."[187] On Freud's reading, the rise of the "plague" in Thebes is a mere symptom of a deeper "conflict" that Oedipus and his clan brought to the city.[188] The source of conflict, Freud reveals, is the intergenerational replication of a pair of dominant "psychic forces" of the unconscious: lust and rage.[189]

In 1899, Freud applied this psychological conception of "plague" (in German, *plagen*) to the conscious interpretation of his own dreams.[190] In one such self-analysis of a dream based on his university days, he distinguished between his happy state as a student and "the desires which plague me."[191] This plague of desires he associated with "the technique of sex."[192] The example he gave was from his dream of wearing a former professor's stolen "overcoat," which he took to be wishful thinking for a "condom" to satisfy his nocturnal passions.[193]

In *The Ego and the Id* (1923), Freud elaborated his theory of the conscious, preconscious, and unconscious facets of the human mind via a rereading of *Oedipus Rex*. He wrote it in the wake of the Spanish flu pandemic of 1918–19. It brought the devastating loss of Freud's then-pregnant daughter Sophie to influenza-driven pneumonia in January 1920. Then her youngest son Heinele, Freud's favorite grandchild, died from tuberculosis in June 1923.[194] During this time of intense grief, Freud theorized how the conscious reason and pragmatism of the "ego" (the "I") resolves the Oedipal conflicts of early childhood by letting the "superego" (the parent-like moral conscience) help control and direct the drives of the "id" (the unconscious and untamed sexual and violent passions).[195]

One hundred years before Freud, Shelley had a dark yet creative period of grief, colored by the experience of plague. As Will Bowers has argued, she turned to Greek translation of Homer and Sophocles as a mental salve to heal the psychic wounds left by the serial losses of her children and husband.[196] And as Maria Schoina has shown in the first published study of Shelley's *Oedipus Rex*, Shelley focused her narrative translation on the first twenty-four lines, ending with her gothic depiction of the Theban plague's "bloody waves" that threaten to drown the whole city.[197] She had translated enough in narrative form to find the poetic imagery she needed.

By grappling with the Greek of *Oedipus Rex*, half a century before Freud did his translation of the play, Shelley saw that the human passions—if unchecked—acted as pollutants that caused a plague of tragic conflicts to suffocate the surrounding community like a wave of blood. As she worked with her "Greek Studies" notebook (c. 1820–39), kept her private "Journal of Sorrow" (1822–26) and finished her own contribution to plague literature (1824–26), Shelley learned not to myopically fix on blaming her dead husband for their family's many woes. She would learn to see that tragedies were made by each of our egos, in the collectivity of a "we." And this would become the resounding Sophoclean theme of her postapocalyptic pandemic novel, *The Last Man*. For she was a last woman, of sorts, who had witnessed and survived the tragedies of the second generation of British Romantic poets, who all died young. Left alone, she strove to represent and record this revolutionary literary and political movement.

In May of 1824, the night before she learned of the death of her friend Byron from sepsis near the battlefield at Missolonghi, Shelley confided to her journal that she knew what it meant to be "the last man," with everyone she loved "extinct before me."[198] In the next entry, she mournfully noted how prescient she was. Like Sophocles's Philoctetes, Shelley knew she was a soldier left behind on an island to suffer alone a festering wound: the compounding loss of nearly everyone for whom she cared.[199] It was a psychic wound made worse by her abandonment and betrayal by her friends still living, especially Jane Williams, whose husband had died alongside Percy.

In the first entry of her "Journal of Sorrow," begun the same time as she started to copy and preserve her late husband's Greek studies manuscripts in October of 1822, Shelley seemed to compare her own fate to that of Oedipus at the crossroads: "Methinks I was born to that end alone, since all events seem to ~~drag~~[lead] me to that one point . . . Father, Mother, friend, husband children—all made—as it were—the team that ~~dragged me~~ conducted me here."[200] The twenty-five-year-old widow was already beginning to see that a tragedy could not be made by a single person, but rather could only be a product of an intergenerational cascade of human mistakes. Her family, and her relationships with them, had *led* her to the place of the triple ways, to contemplate her destiny and its roots in interpersonal conflict. In her identification with Oedipus and Philoctetes, Shelley might be seen as a philosophical antecedent to Martha Nussbaum's conception of tragedy as a combination of avoidable and unavoidable disasters, made by oneself and others. In the 2001 preface to the revised edition of *The Fragility of Goodness*, Nussbaum pointed out, "Even Sophocles, whose dramas more frequently focus on disasters that even wisdom and goodness could not avoid (Philoctetes' wound, Oedipus' parricide), still draws attention, as well, to much avoidable wickedness."[201]

Brian Doerries—the award-winning director who produced a new translation of Sophocles's Theban plays in 2021—has made a similar observation, based upon audience responses to his Zoom productions of *Oedipus Rex* during Covid-19. "Mistakes are what make us human, as the Greek tragedies we perform always bear out," Doerries observes, "and acknowledging and moving on from our mistakes is the only way out of the messes we make."[202] On this theatrical reading of the enduring relevance of Sophocles, Shelley might be seen as an actor in her own Greek tragedy, who recognizes the error of her ways through the recitation of the story of Oedipus.

In *The Last Man*, she treated pandemic as a metaphor for this tragic fact: the destructive course of human life was self-perpetuated around the globe. The airborne pathogen spreads from a battlefield near Constantinople to escalate into an "epidemic" that suffocates human culture and political systems via trade, travel, and personal and political conflicts.[203] Even the world's leading republic, England, crumbles in its many attempts to withstand this plague made by an international war, as its democratically elected leaders are selfish, corrupt, and torn apart by a "civil war."[204]

As she wrote this explicitly political plotline, Shelley may have been thinking of the divisiveness and corruption of British politics in the early 1820s—publicly dramatized in the Queen Caroline affair, which Percy had satirized in his burlesque parody of *Oedipus Rex*.[205] In the autumn of 1820, he had published his political drama in two acts, *Oedipus Tyrannus; or, Swellfoot the Tyrant: A Tragedy*, which mocked how George IV put his estranged wife Caroline on trial for adultery in order to prevent her from taking her share of power when he ascended to the British throne in January of that year.[206] The play concluded with a "carnivalesque scene of civil war."[207]

Although Shelley shared republican political commitments with Percy, after his death she publicly identified more with the "Liberal" cause and privately more with "liberalism."[208] She would later write in a letter to Maria Gisborne in 1833, "What is the use of republican principles & liberty, if Peace is not the offspring? War not Kings is the fleau of the world."[209] Like her mother Wollstonecraft, who defended the French Revolution but criticized its violence and sympathized with Louis XVI on the eve of his execution, Shelley saw that the real problem was not monarchy alone but the way that it was weaponized to hurt people, including the occupants of the institution itself.[210] In a list that she possibly composed and certainly saved in the year after Percy's death, Shelley faced these deeper causes of social and political conflict. The undated and unsigned manuscript contended that the "Principal causes of Misery" arose from interpersonal and familial relations, especially civil wars writ small: "Living with persons we hate . . . Dependence_Disgrace_Solitude . . . Ambition–Envy–Jealousy–Hate–Strife — Revenge."[211]

This was a tough political lesson that she had learned all too well in her personal life. If war was the true "fleau of the world," and this scourge threatened to destroy humanity and other life forms by replicating within the most basic and immediate of social relations, then she knew that the cure for this global plague would be found neither in "solitude" nor in "strife," but rather in the humane restoration of love and care for life as a whole, despite all the death and tragedy that thwarted it. As a young widow writing in her "Journal of Sorrow" and copying out her dead husband's translations and commentaries on the Greek poets, philosophers, and tragedians, she dove into the wreck of her life with Percy, a life she had once wished could be "blotted out."[212] Among the treasures she salvaged was the text of his translation of Plato's *Symposium*, the famous dialogue on the meaning of love. In September of 1822, their friend Edward Trelawny gave her Percy's Greek studies manuscripts, recovered from the hull of the *Don Juan*.[213] In the process of transcribing Percy's translation of the *Symposium* in 1823–24, Shelley found the Greek roots for the modern word "pandemic" in "Pandemos," the goddess of love who touches upon all (or *pan*) the people (or *demos*).[214] Perhaps it was this etymology that inspired her to develop her own "cosmopolitan" philosophy of love as the global—psychological and social—cure for conflict and war, both in her journals and in her pandemic novel *The Last Man*.[215]

Conclusion: Diving into the Wreck of Her Past

By looking back into her difficult past and confronting her role in the escalation of the conflicts that contributed to the deaths of her children, a sister, a stepsister's child, her husband, and his first wife, Shelley learned to see her whole life—with all of its tragedies—as a dark yet illuminating well for existential wisdom. This wisdom she poured into the aporetic ending of *The Last Man*, wherein Verney sets out to sea, with just his adopted dog and the works of Homer and Shakespeare for company, in search of other survivors of the plague. He speculates that a "saved pair of lovers," already with child, are ready to "re-people" the Earth. He even dares to imagine that there might be a "survivor" like him, "in search of a partner for their solitude."[216]

If he finds them, waiting on some "sea-side" to wave his ship to their shore, they could together rebuild humanity in a new, as yet uncharted, peaceful way of life.[217]

Like her avatar Verney, and the sage Oedipus at Colonus before him, Shelley never gave up hope that life was worth living if only to seek, against all odds, the restoration of love and peace. The paradoxical guiding wisdom of her tragedies, real and literary, lived and translated, would teach people how *not* to get there: in war with self and others. As if to reinforce this point, Trelawny passed down to her son Percy Florence Shelley and his wife Jane a water-damaged volume of Sophocles's tragedies, said to be salvaged from the wreck of the *Don Juan* along with Percy's translation of the *Symposium* (Figure 14 and Figure 15).[218]

While Freud read *Oedipus Rex* as a plague tragedy in order to conceptualize the subterranean familial conflicts of the unconscious, Shelley turned to reading, transcribing, translating, and adapting Sophocles's greatest play to self-consciously dive into the wreck of her past. She salvaged meaning from

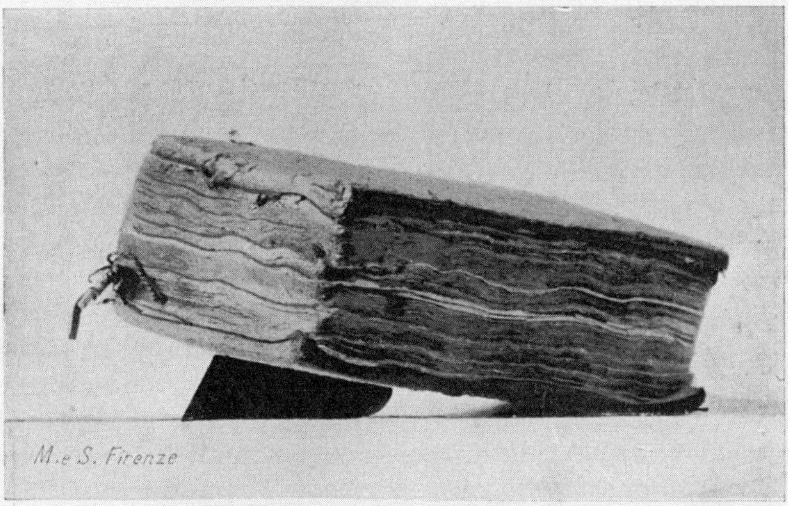

THE "SOPHOCLES" TAKEN FROM SHELLEY'S DEAD HAND

(Bodleian Library).

Figure 14. "The 'Sophocles' Taken from Shelley's Dead Hand." Illustration for Guido Biagi, *The Last Days of Percy Bysshe Shelley* (London: T. Fisher Unwin, 1898). Reproduced courtesy of Look and Learn.

Figure 15. *Sophoclis Tragoediae Septem* (1809). Shelley g. 1, Bodleian Library. Reproduced courtesy of the Bodleian Library, Oxford University.

the chain of tragedies that befell her, her family, and her circle of friends by infusing her philosophical contribution to plague literature and roman à clef, *The Last Man*, with allusions to Oedipus. The concrete act of translating *Oedipus Rex*, both literally and thematically, grounded the young widow and grieving mother in the present even as it allowed her to derive hard lessons from the past to guide her as the seeming "last woman" writer in the second generation of British Romanticism.

Shelley's "Greek Studies" notebook is a treasure of British literature as much as her journals also preserved in the Abinger collection, for both forms of her private writing served as a balm for her creative mind as she resisted the urge to wish her life "could not / End too soon" after the death of Percy in 1822. Through these mediums of personal writing, translation, and literary adaptation, Shelley transformed herself into a feminine Oedipus at Colonus. She modeled how to look at the past as a well of wisdom for what she and other humans might not do—or wish for—as they saved themselves from the appearance of meaninglessness in the face of the worst things life can deliver to mortal beings.

CHAPTER 3

Mary Shelley's *The Last Man*

Existentialism and International Relations Meet the Postapocalyptic Pandemic Novel

A Literary Style of IR

All too forgotten in the history of international relations (IR) and political theory, Mary Shelley ought to be foregrounded in the future, especially as these fields of political science grow to recognize their intersections with literature, existential philosophy, and women's intellectual work.[1] In her recent scholarship on existentialism and IR, Liane Hartnett has modeled how to engage literature, both "liminal" and canonical, as a source or "site" of political thought.[2] This extends a trend in mainstream IR scholarship, which has widened to consider literature and its relation to political thought.[3] This literary trend in mainstream IR arguably began in the aftermath of the First World War, when the Belgian playwright Émile Cammaerts argued in a 1922 article titled "Literature and International Relations" that "the artists and the writers who have been able, through their genius, to make their national temperament better known and better appreciated all over the world, are perhaps the first pioneers of a League of Nations."[4]

By folding Mary Shelley's futuristic war and pandemic novel *The Last Man* into the history of IR, this chapter contributes to a renewed literary movement at the forefront of contemporary IR. While this school of thought—which I label "Literary IR"—is just coming to be recognized as a distinct hermeneutical approach in political science and political theory, it has deep yet unsung historical roots, as this study of Shelley's novel *The Last Man* and its IR sources and existential legacies demonstrates. This insight into the long-range evolution of Literary IR—from Thucydides to Covid-19—is one of the realizations that follows from examining the philosophical relationship between IR and existentialism in the political thought and plague literature of Mary Shelley.

Mary Shelley, Literary IR, and Political Science Fiction

For her part in this process of developing Literary IR, Shelley creatively mined the ideas of international political thought as well as the themes of plague literature, the epic, the romance, and the gothic novel to help develop three new subgenres of modern science fiction (sf): postapocalyptic, existential, and dystopian literature. From this mélange of literary forms arose her two sf masterpieces: *Frankenstein* (1818) and *The Last Man* (1826). These works prove to be more "political science fictions" than "hard science fictions," for they are broadly concerned with tracing the often-harmful impact of human artifice on the whole world across families, societies, species, and nations.[5] Unlike later "hard science fiction" by Isaac Asimov and others that uses consistent scientific or mathematical reasoning to predict the consequences of making mechanized weapons, robots, spaceships, imperial galactic societies, and other forms of human artifice, Shelley's political sf is neither solely nor primarily concerned with rigorously extrapolating the future of technology and human society from present-day engineering inventions and scientific theories.[6]

Rather, *Frankenstein* and *The Last Man* are concerned with delineating the tragic emotions and unjust social consequences associated with the repeated human failure to make peace, share love, and care for others and the world at large. The gothic and domestic horror of *Frankenstein* arises from the destructive passion of a chemist who uses science and technology to create a "human being" without caring for it.[7] The existential and global terror of *The Last Man* derives from its slow and devastating exploration of the personal and political betrayals that exacerbate war, corruption, and a plague that appears to leave a lone human survivor, who lives to write the "history" of the near extinction of his species.[8]

Interpersonal and international conflicts, much more than science and technology, serve as plot devices for advancing the existential and postapocalyptic themes of Shelley's classics of *poliscifi*.[9] I use *existential* in two overlapping senses. First, I mean philosophical contemplation of the meaning of life and death and their relation to the psychological and social formation of personal and communal identities. Second, I mean the confrontation of death or a life-endangering threat. These two meanings of "existential" converge in my definition of "postapocalyptic" political thought. By *postapocalyptic*, I mean existential reflection or speculation on the aftermath of a devastating catastrophe that poses a life-endangering threat to a person, community, or species.

Both meanings of existential are integral to existentialist philosophy. While existentialism as a literary and philosophical movement is a twentieth-century phenomenon, largely canonized in France by the 1940s, existential philosophy predates it. Although most scholars ground the modern existentialist tradition in literary-philosophical writing of the late nineteenth century, especially Dostoevsky, Kierkegaard, and Nietzsche, I push the intellectual history of existentialism further back in time to Mary Shelley.

Shelley's *poliscifi* novels thematically represent the existential threat of death, abuse, war, and other catastrophes as surfacing in fraught familial and romantic relationships and spreading swiftly through and across cultures, states, and empires, like a "scourge," "pest," or "PLAGUE."[10] The escalating parent-child conflict between Victor Frankenstein and his abandoned Creature leads to the death of virtually everyone in his clan. The pestilential battlefields of a centuries-long war between Greece and Turkey spawn a lethal "epidemic" that leaves Lionel Verney, the titular "LAST MAN," alone to contemplate the future of humanity and the possibility of its extinction.[11] With her relentless focus on the deeper emotional conflicts that cause tragedy, injustice and the annihilation of life itself, Shelley foregrounded the social and political problems associated with humanity's selfish, careless, and violent interventions in their wider environment.

Both *Frankenstein* and *The Last Man* are modern postapocalyptic myths, in the sense that they use widely resonant allegories to envision the aftermath of human-made catastrophes.[12] Frankenstein's gigantic Creature is a hulking metaphor for humanity's monstrous potential for the destruction of the self and the other. The war-driven epidemic of *The Last Man* is likewise a metaphor, writ even larger, for humanity's failure to contain its self-destructive behavior even unto its own extinction. In Shelley's first novel, a man-made Creature turns murderous in his quest for vengeance against his neglectful father-scientist. In her fourth novel, a seasonal plague in Constantinople grows into a pandemic as domestic and international conflict circulates the airborne pathogen across borders and oceans through trade, travel, and war.[13]

Although *Frankenstein* is far better known and studied, it was *The Last Man* that contributed to the philosophical traditions we now associate with postapocalyptic, existentialist, and dystopian literature. By dystopian, I mean the opposite of utopian. Utopian literature depicts an ethical, social, or political ideal that is not yet realized. Utopia is Thomas More's neologism, combining the Greek words "οὐ" (not) and "τόπος" (place), meaning "nowhere."[14] Dystopian literature pictures the reverse image of utopia. As Margaret Atwood has argued from a liberal perspective, dystopias "warn" readers of what to avoid if they want to preserve freedom, peace, rights, happiness, and justice from attempts at tyranny, conquest, and oppression.[15] *The Last Man* hybridizes existential and postapocalyptic themes in its dystopian vision of a late twenty-first century Earth where even the world's leading republics of England and the "Northern States of America" crumble under the pressure of a war-spurred pandemic.[16]

Though most strongly associated with George Orwell's *Nineteen Eighty-Four* (1949) and Atwood's *The Handmaid's Tale* (1985), dystopian literature has roots in Shelley's *poliscifi*.[17] Orwell's original title for *Nineteen Eighty-Four* was "The Last Man in Europe," and he represented its hero, Winston Smith, as "the last man" in London to resist the contagion of totalitarian ideology disseminated by the all-seeing imperial regime of Big Brother.[18] A fan of gothic and sf literature since childhood, Orwell praised Mary Shelley in his 1944 review of *English Diaries of the Nineteenth Century*, and then, as we shall see, in the torture scene in *Nineteen Eighty-Four*, used language strikingly similar to this 1944 book's reprinting of a May 1824 entry on "the last man" from Shelley's journal.[19]

Atwood grew up reading Orwell and Shelley, and titled one of her first collections of poetry *Speeches for Doctor Frankenstein* (1966).[20] She set *The Handmaid's Tale* (and its 2019 sequel, *The Testaments*) in a postapocalyptic North America of the early twenty-first century. An epidemic of infertility—caused by sexually transmitted disease, the seeping of toxic waste into the environment, and the spread of political and sexual corruption in Western capitalist society—leads to a coup d'état of the United States by a fundamentalist Christian terrorist organization that seeks to restore female fertility by forcing a sector of women to serve as sexual slaves and surrogates for the military commanders and their wives.

Like any myth, ancient or modern, one recognizes the story of *The Last Man* before even reading it. This is due to the symbolic resonance and vast cultural influence of its central figure: the "last known survivor" of a massive existential threat like a postwar plague.[21] The cultural canonization of Shelley's story has been accomplished largely through its adaptation into two important postapocalyptic plague novels, M. P. Shiel's *The Purple Cloud* (1901) and Richard Matheson's *I Am Legend* (1954).[22] Shiel's novel is notable for introducing a recurring comic and romantic twist to the tragedy, wherein the seeming last man meets and falls in love with the apparent last woman.

Shelley's and Shiel's novels were also successfully translated for the screen and stage, beginning with a comic silent movie and Broadway musical *The Last Man on Earth* (1924) and extending to the Hollywood doomsday film *The World, the Flesh, and the Devil* (1959) starring Harry Belafonte.[23] But it was Matheson's novel about the "last man in the world" to survive a vampire plague that has secured the ongoing reception of the last man trope in contemporary sf and horror literature, cinema, and television.[24] After its initial filmic adaptation as *The Last Man on Earth* (1964), starring Vincent Price, Matheson's version of the last man narrative begot *The Night of the Living Dead* (1968), *The Omega Man* (1971), *28 Days Later* (2002), *I Am Legend* (2007), and countless postnuclear, pandemic, and zombie apocalypse movies and television series after them.[25] Another, less obvious but potent, line of influence from Shelley's *The Last Man* to modern monster cinema is through its overlapping thematic reception with her short story "The Invisible Girl" (1832–33) and her reader H. G. Wells's novel *The Invisible Man* (1897). Especially in the postapocalyptic and horror genres, the image of the "last woman" or "final girl" survivor of trauma and disaster has flourished alongside the "invisible" girl who endures abuse, isolation, and despair to find her way out of darkness to freedom, love, and community.

The Last Man Theme in Postapocalyptic, Dystopian, and Existential Political Thought

While the literary legacy of *The Last Man* has been woven into popular culture, the novel's significance for philosophy and political thought has only begun to be charted. In the era of Covid-19, *The Last Man* has been recovered as the first major modern postapocalyptic pandemic novel.[26] Here I foreground it as a vital literary and philosophical source for existentialism and its intersections with international political thought and dystopian literature. We can clearly perceive Shelley's ethical and political concern with the overlay of interpersonal and international conflict by situating *The Last Man* between its probable sources and influences. When placed between Thucydides, Hobbes, Vattel, and Voltaire, on the one hand, and Stoker, Wells, Orwell, Camus, and Atwood, on the other, *The Last Man* illustrates how conflict bleeds out of romantic and familial relationships to feed wider social and political injustices. These injustices include the material human-made disasters of racism, sexism, violence, war, pandemics, environmental crises, and species extinction. They also include metaphorical existential plagues upon humanity such as loneliness and despair.

Despite these dark themes, Mary Shelley's authorship of *The Last Man* led to the development of a hopeful, *post*apocalyptic existential response to the interlocking problems of interpersonal and international conflict. This future-oriented tradition of international political thought has aimed to rise above a pair of fatalistic fallacies: first, the metaphysical or existential belief that there is nothing after (or *post*) apocalypse, since extreme catastrophes may seem to bring to those who suffer them a final stop or absolute end to a state of human affairs; and secondly, following from this bleak premise, the nihilistic view that there is nothing to be done in the face of total war and other human-made apocalyptic disasters. Apocalypse, from this pessimistic perspective, is death without end.

By contrast, the postapocalyptic tradition after Shelley returns apocalypse to its original meaning in ancient Greek (ἀποκάλυψις): a "revelation" or "uncovering."[27] In this Shelleyan tradition of postapocalyptic political thought, it suggests the unveiling of a new way of life *after* personal or collective disaster. Shelley's dark yet ultimately hopeful vision of the future has informed the aesthetic behind modern existential, postapocalyptic, and dystopian fiction and philosophy, from Dostoevsky and Nietzsche, to Orwell and Camus, to Octavia Butler and Emily St. John Mandel. Shelley and her followers in feminist sf—especially Atwood, Butler, and Mandel—have created a vital imaginative space for thinking about how personal change in response to conflict and disaster can lead to global change toward diplomacy, justice, peace, and a new cosmopolitan world order.

Postapocalyptic political thought in this feminist vein offers a more hopeful and futuristic alternative to the pessimistic, absurdist, and nihilistic elements of canonical (and men-dominant) existentialisms, typically associated with Dostoevsky, Nietzsche, Sartre, and Camus. We need more feminist and literary approaches to addressing existential questions in *poliscifi* to save the concept of apocalypse from its reduction to mere annihilation and catastrophe. The Shelley scholar and sf writer Joanna Russ modelled such a feminist approach to existentialist political science fiction when she directly referenced Simone de Beauvoir in *The Female Man* (1975), a multiverse novel in which a future all-women society thrives after a plague wipes out all men from

Earth.[28] By adding the aporetic prefix "post-" to "apocalypse," we join Russ alongside Shelley, Atwood, Butler, and Mandel in making room in Literary IR for the theorization—or imaginative revelation—of new woman-friendly political futures *after* massive disasters. On this Shelleyan and feminist reading of the original Greek, apocalypse is never the end, but rather is always the beginning.

The Last Man: A Novel in Ideas of International Political Thought

As a roman à clef—or allegorical study of the author's life story—*The Last Man* is best understood as a novel "in ideas" instead of a novel "of ideas."[29] The plot of Shelley's global plague novel is driven by the political philosophies that she debated first with her father and later with her lover and husband the poet Percy Bysshe Shelley. But the novel, like *Frankenstein*, is not a mere ideological vehicle for the transmission of other writers' ideas.[30] It is rather that her dystopian novel questions and dissects these received ideas from the Western tradition to reveal a new, utopian, and cosmopolitan understanding of what world politics could and should be in the future.

Soon after the sixteen-year-old Mary Wollstonecraft Godwin eloped to Europe in the summer of 1814 with the unhappily married poet Percy Shelley, she noted in her journal that he read Thucydides.[31] Perhaps his interest in the *History of the Peloponnesian War* arose from the couple's recent trek through France, where whole towns had been razed by the invading forces of Russia during the last year of the Napoleonic Wars.[32] Since Mary kept an annual notation of her and Percy's reading in her journals, it is possible that they discussed Thucydides together or that she read the Greek historian but forgot to record it on the day or at year's end. What is certain is that *The Last Man* alludes to Thucydides's famous account of the Plague of Athens: Verney records with worry the arrival of the "plague at Athens" after it leaves the battlefields near Constantinople via trade, travel, and military routes.[33]

In 430 B.C.E., after the Athenian general Pericles ordered the masses to hide behind the city walls from the invading Spartans, he unwittingly sealed them up with the plague brought into the city-state through its busy trading and naval port. About one hundred thousand people—a quarter of the population—suffered reddening fever, stertorous breathing, and painful deaths because of this military strategy.[34] Shelley, it seems, derived a political lesson from Thucydides's account of the Plague of Athens, which she dramatized in *The Last Man*: bad political ideas and poor leadership decisions make for fatal public policies in times of war and other crisis. Like H. D. in Daniel Defoe's *A Journal of the Plague Year* (1722), Verney watches with anxiety as the plague sweeps into England from southern France, due to the failure of leaders in either country to prepare to stop it through suspension of trade, travel, military campaigns, and other politically institutionalized modes of disease transmission.[35] Set in the 2090s, her futuristic pandemic ultimately levels France, England, and all the world's other nations, enacting the war-driven political tragedy of the Plague of Athens on a global scale.

Following the insights of Jacques Derrida and his deconstructive philosophy, the feminist literary scholar Barbara Johnson argued that Shelley used the idea of "plague" more as a loose, figurative concept than as a fixed, literal disease.[36] Tellingly, the plague does not even appear until about halfway through the novel. When Verney recalls that it arose in the war between Greece and Turkey, he renders "PLAGUE" in all capital letters.[37] As Verney leads readers to comprehend his extraordinary existential predicament as the ostensible last man on Earth, "PLAGUE" functions more as a capacious symbol of varieties of human-made destruction than as an actual pathogen. By leaving mysterious whether its mode of infection was airborne, "contagious" by physical contact, or both, Shelley refrained from defining "PLAGUE" as a specific disease.[38] This omission is significant, given that she had a series of tragic experiences with infectious diseases, which took two of her children and a niece.

Perhaps because of the immensity of these losses, Shelley conceptualized "PLAGUE" as an existential abyss: a bottomless sign for catastrophes. The introduction of the word midway through the novel marks its transition from a romantic epic, set at the exotic locations of Windsor Castle and Constantinople, into a speculative dystopian fiction about the failure of the world's governments to contain a novel and lethal epidemic. This abrupt change in genre provokes in the mind of the reader a deconstructive philosophical process of unmaking, or breaking down, the prevailing meanings of a cascade of synonyms for disaster: war, conflict, contagion, corruption, hardship, disease, deprivation, and death. As the godlike author of the first novel to chronicle the global spread of a species-decimating pandemic, Shelley leads readers to see how the plague *unmakes* world leaders' bad political ideas and policies, revealing their tragic flaws as people and governments. This unmaking of a severely defective (or dystopian) world order uncovers the need to find new (or utopian) ways of making connections and communities on Earth. Shelley's political science fiction paradoxically reveals how critical analysis of the concept of disaster points the way toward overcoming it.

A studious reader of the Bible, Shelley revised the sacred story of Noah's Ark in the final scene of *The Last Man*, while giving the ancient Hebrew myth a distinctively modern existential and postapocalyptic twist.[39] In her fictional version of life after a flood of pestilence, the last man Verney packs his ship with his dog and the works of Homer and Shakespeare before sailing in search of other survivors.[40] He speculates that a new Adam and Eve must be awaiting the birth of a child in some remote location far from the threat of plague.[41] If he can find them, he thinks, there might be the start of a new Edenic society that preserves the best of human culture (compassion, companionship, literature) and discards the worst (the plagues of war and other man-made conflicts). The plague's unmaking of the global impact of war and imperialism leads, paradoxically, to Verney's remaking of the imaginative conditions for love, hope, renewal, and even the prospect of a cosmopolitan peace.

Beginning with their joint devotion to Wollstonecraft and Godwin's progressive political ideas, the Shelleys became experts on the history of Enlightenment political thought from Thomas Hobbes to Immanuel Kant.[42] They bought a copy of the 1816 French translation of Johann Gottlieb Buhle's *Histoire de la philosophie moderne* while they lived in Geneva that same year.[43] Buhle provided a lengthy summary of the international political thought of the Swiss political theorist and diplomat Emer de Vattel and its relationship to the earlier work on the law of nations by Wolff, Hobbes, Pufendorf, and Grotius. His 1758 treatise *Le Droit des gens* (The Law of Nations) was quickly translated into English.[44] It was well-known on both sides of the Atlantic for its contributions to just war theory and the idea of a diplomatic peace achieved through the cross-cultural and international leadership of "ambassadors."[45]

Vattel gained fame for defending the right of small nations to exist independently from more powerful states and empires. While he advanced a diplomatic and pacific view of the realization of international cooperation across sovereign nations, Vattel justified the intervention of more powerful states on behalf of less powerful ones vulnerable to conquest. When they read *Le Droit des gens* during the 1775 Continental Congress, American revolutionaries led by Benjamin Franklin found a two-fold model for a modern international practice of independent statehood: first, political leaders must show respect for the equal sovereignty of nations; and secondly, they must develop diplomatic alliances against imperial conquest and for international cooperation.[46]

Vattel's *Le Droit des gens*, with its final five chapters devoted to the theory and practice of ambassadorship, is the most proximate source in international political thought for Shelley's depiction of Verney as an "ambassador."[47] Born a shepherd boy in the north of the republic of England, Verney befriends the dethroned royal family near their country estate in the 2070s. Adrian, the former-prince-turned-republican-political-leader, sends him to Vienna to train as a diplomat, as "private secretary to the Ambassador."[48] After two years of diplomatic service abroad, Verney returns to the court circle at Windsor Castle, with "a reputation already founded," to serve his lifelong friend Adrian in his political career guiding the fledgling republic of England from a monarchical past into a democratic future.[49]

Also in Adrian's court is Evadne, a Greek princess and daughter of the Greek ambassador to England. In imagining an international diplomatic circle at Windsor Castle, Shelley likely took inspiration from her friendship with Alexandros Mavrokordatos, the Greek prince, diplomat, and leader of the 1821 Greek War of Independence from Ottoman rule. During the 1810s, Mavrokordatos lived in exile from his homeland in the court of his uncle, the prince of Wallachia, then was educated at Padua in the Austrian Empire before he befriended the Shelleys at Pisa in 1820–21, when he tutored Shelley in Ancient Greek.[50]

Beyond the example of Mavrokordatos's diplomatic career, Vattel's philosophy of ambassadorship as the art of forging "friendship" between nations likely shaped her characterization of Verney as a peacemaker.[51] Verney's life as a diplomat and citizen of the world begins with his friendship with Adrian and extends to shaping "friendship" in all domains of life: from the romantic relationships of their court circle, to the battlefields of Constantinople, to the English government's pandemic response in London, to aiding the remnant of plague survivors in France and Italy.[52]

The Shelleys likely encountered Vattel through Buhle, even though they probably bought his six-volume history of modern philosophy in Switzerland to learn more about his fellow German philosopher Kant. Buhle provided a lengthy summary of his late eighteenth-century contemporary Kant's three *Critiques*, which elaborate his epistemology, ethics, and aesthetics.[53] Buhle did not summarize Kant's political writings, however, including his utopian theory of a cosmopolitan peace achieved through a world federation of free republics. According to Kant's theory of "perpetual peace," these republics would be united not as a world state, but through mutual regard of their sovereign independence from one another.[54] In this and other political essays from the French revolutionary era, Kant argued that an essential feature of a free modern constitutional republic was to respect the "universal right of humanity" or "cosmopolitan right" of citizens, whether they were from one's own country or another nation.[55] In his 1795 essay on perpetual peace, Kant favorably placed Vattel among the "sorry comforters" of modern theories of international law: for he was a harbinger of an optimistic (though perhaps impractical) cosmopolitan philosophy of "universal hospitality" toward fellow citizens of sovereign republics and the world itself.[56]

Because Shelley did not record in her journals her or Percy's reading of Kant's political writings, it is more likely that the cosmopolitan and diplomatic themes of *The Last Man* are rooted in her exposure to Vattel and other French-Swiss cosmopolitan writers, rather than Kant. Another Francophone writer with ties to Geneva and Switzerland who may have inspired the character of Verney is Voltaire. Shelley noted in her journals that she read Voltaire's *Memoires*, his "romans," and his "Essay on Nations" between 1815 and 1816.[57] From the 1769 *Memoires* and her own extensive travels around Geneva, she would have known that Voltaire left the city-state for Ferney in 1759, just across the border in France, to protest the Swiss republic's ban on theater. Voltaire's fame in Ferney, and his liberal support of the theater, arts, and industry there, led the town to rename itself Ferney-Voltaire in 1791.[58]

The close match between the unusual surname Verney and Ferney-Voltaire suggests that Shelley may have wanted to associate the Voltairean town's avant-garde culture with the character of the "LAST MAN." Voltaire's riotously funny novel *Candide* (1759)—a satire of Rousseau's optimistic belief in providence even after the massive, human-exacerbated disaster of the 1755 Lisbon earthquake—may have inspired the dark humor of Verney, who says he will "sit amidst the ruins and smile" despite the very real possibility of human extinction.[59] Voltaire's anti-imperial, antislavery, and anti-church writings share *The Last Man*'s concern with the realization of true personal and political independence in opposition to past forms of religious and secular oppression. When he bravely strikes out to sea in search of other survivors, with Shakespeare, Homer, and his dog in tow, Verney evokes Voltaire's quixotic quest for a cosmopolitan conception of citizenship and independence, unlimited by national or religious roots, yet supported by love of the arts and compassion for others.[60]

In the biographical allegory of *The Last Man*, Adrian stands for Percy and Verney for Mary.[61] Following the political ideas of Percy's "Declaration of Rights" (1812), "The Mask of Anarchy" (1819), and "A Philosophical View of

Reform" (1819–20), Adrian is the radical visionary of peace made through nonviolent protest of oppression, modern representative republican government, and enfranchisement of the poor.[62] Mary/Verney take this radical vision of peace and justice and go global and existential with it. Despite being the last (wo)man left alone after losing everyone s/he loves, s/he finds a way to make peace with the world in all its darkness by summoning hope for the preservation of a new way of life on Earth, even if the human species faces almost certain extinction.

Like Vattel, Verney/Mary deduce that there are universal "offices of humanity" that extend beyond particular duties to care for and preserve one's own family, culture, and nation.[63] Vattel went so far as to argue that "every nation is obliged to cultivate the friendship of other nations."[64] He defined "real friendship"—whether between individuals or nations—as a "happy state" which "consists in mutual affection."[65] Verney/Mary take this argument about the duty to cultivate friendships one step further. Once they existentially identify as "THE LAST MAN" while writing down their strange life history, they extend Vattel's cosmopolitan ethic of friendship to other cultures and species. Back in panicked London, even the compassionate Verney succumbed to racism and xenophobia when he lurched from the outstretched arms of a dying "negro" who exposed him to the plague.[66] Overlooking a desolate Rome, the diplomat regains his cosmopolitan bearings. He keeps a mutt as his sole living animal companion after giving up hunting in favor of eating dried corn from granaries. To realize his "wild dreams" envisioned on "the height of St. Peter's," he takes a mere "week" to hatch a plan to travel to the "tawny coast of Africa" and perhaps the "spicy groves of the odorous islands of the far Indian Ocean" to find a "companion."[67]

After the apocalyptic flood of plague, Mary's avatar Verney is the modern existential Noah, setting sail toward an uncharted horizon of humanity with his dog and his books. What is left for him is the possibility of bridging a Voltairean cosmopolitan citizenship and a Vattelian friendship with the whole creation in an "international society" yet to be built.[68] This postapocalyptic hybridization of Voltaire and Vattel would entail a cosmic solidarity with and compassion for the world itself—what it was, what it is, and what it will be. In a reflection on the meaning of life and death near the end of his "HISTORY OF THE LAST MAN," Verney articulates this epiphany: human beings inevitably die, and may even become "extinct," but "humanity" understood as humaneness need not, and must not, be extinguished, if his life as a human is to ultimately have ethical meaning.[69] By reconceiving the meaning of humanity after apocalypse, Verney paves the way for understanding humaneness or genuine compassion as *post-human*: for it arrives after the Anthropocene, yet in time to save the world from human-made destruction.

Shelley, like her father Godwin, was a devoted reader of the Irish statesman Edmund Burke, who was influenced by Vattel's philosophy of international law. A Member of Parliament who prosecuted Warren Hastings for his crimes against the indigenous peoples of British India, Burke took seriously the Vattelian idea that the law of nations justified states' intervention on behalf of oppressed peoples against their tyrants.[70] In *The Last Man*, Shelley has the diplomat Verney quote or adapt the words of Burke on several occasions, reaffirming the wisdom of his pacific and optimistic views on being a good leader through following others, and on the persistence of the best of human culture even after war and other attempts to destroy it.[71]

Godwin's *Political Justice* (1793) alluded to Burke's traditionalist view of social life as people's membership in "little platoons," or small class-based communities, but took it in a radically anarchistic political direction.[72] In Godwin's theory of the ideal, or ultra-minimal, state, people would live most freely and ethically in families and other small social units. Citizens would come together only occasionally to work out essential matters of overarching government in localized representative bodies before returning to daily life in their little platoons.[73]

Godwin represented this anarchist vision of peaceful social life with minimal government as a critical retort to Hobbes's pessimistic vision of a violent state of nature without government. Building on his experience of the English Civil Wars, Hobbes famously theorized in *Leviathan* (1651) that the lack of a sovereign with sufficient power to enforce the law would inevitably entail the dissolution of society and government into a state of war of each against all.[74] A good pupil of Locke, Godwin thought (contra Hobbes) that people were social by nature and could live harmoniously in groups even without the oversight of government. Godwin took Locke's argument in the *Second Treatise of Government* (1690) about the state of nature in a more radical political direction.[75] True justice and happiness, Godwin argued, would be achieved by individuals in small communes without much government. *Political Justice* went so far as to theorize an inverse relationship between the amount of government and the capacity of people to deduce and perform the moral duties prescribed to them by the laws of reason. In other words, Godwin thought that the minimization of government intervention was the political key to making people realize their ethical potential as duty-bearers toward others.

In *The Last Man*, Shelley represented this philosophical debate between Godwin, Burke, and Hobbes as a political allegory. When the plague enters England, the government is unprepared, and society begins to crumble. In the initial fearful stages of self-quarantine, people retreat into their homes, living in relatively calm isolation. Meanwhile, the government—abandoned by its elected populist leader Ryland, then saved by Adrian and Verney—attempts to help the poor, provide medical care, and prevent the spread of the plague by imposing trade and travel restrictions. This amicable yet anarchistic stage of England's pandemic response reflects some of the communal ideals of Burke as refracted through Godwin's progressive theory of political justice.

But as the epidemic worsens in England, a more dangerous form of anarchy plagues the very basis of its society. Unburied bodies, panic, violence, invading forces, and apocalyptic cultists haunt the edges of Windsor Castle and weaken Adrian's republican government to the point that it finally collapses. This descent into leveling death and chaos is the final, Hobbesian, worst-case scenario of England's failure to adequately respond to the existential threat of the pandemic. Alluding to both the theory of the state of war in chapter thirteen of Hobbes's *Leviathan* (on "The Natural Condition of Mankind as Concerning their Felicity and Misery") and Ecclesiastes 9:10, Verney says "farewell" to culture itself when the plague unleashes anarchy and "sickening misery" upon Earth. "Farewell to the arts,—to eloquence," he proclaims, "farewell to poetry and deep philosophy . . . for 'there is no work, nor device, nor knowledge, nor wisdom in the grave, whither thou goest!'"[76] Shelley may too have been alluding to the list of the "Principal causes of Misery" that she kept in her Italian papers. It put "Strife" at the core of twenty-one psychological and social deprivations that stripped life of what made it humane and worth living.[77]

Immersed in misery, and without a government to lead, Adrian and Verney round up the last survivors—a frail thousand—and flee to France. There anarchy is no better. With the rise of this plague-driven state of war within and across states, Shelley signals her agreement with Hobbes's view that the state of nature is ultimately a state of war. When there is a vacuum of power on a national or international scale, the abyss of anarchy opens to swallow society whole.

Hobbes gleaned this dour lesson from the English Civil Wars, a political tragedy the Shelleys knew well from Percy reading aloud Hume's *History of England* in 1818.[78] Hume's *History* told the story of Sir Edmund Verney, an English aristocrat loyal to Charles I who died carrying the king's standard in the Battle of Edgehill in 1642.[79] His eldest son, Sir Ralph Verney, wrote an account of the Long Parliament and remained strategically neutral and diplomatic in his negotiations between the Royalists and the Cromwellians.[80] The Verney family held several estates, including one in Buckinghamshire, not far from where the Shelleys lived in Windsor in 1815–16 and in Marlow in 1817–18.[81] One wonders if Ralph Verney, a famous survivor of the English Civil Wars and the Great Plague of London of 1665–66, may have been an inspiration for Lionel Verney, the last survivor of a series of disasters caused by a cycle of war and plague.

Like Thomas Hobbes, Ralph Verney, and Emer de Vattel, Lionel Verney is wary of the danger of a state of war on the national or international scale. But Shelley uses the story of "THE LAST MAN" to make a Vattelian point about nonviolent closure of the vacuum of power. As a post-pandemic ambassador of "the offices of humanity," Verney models to himself and his readers how the international political void can and should be filled with a culture of friendly and hopeful diplomacy, which aspires to make peace over time with the whole world. This Vattelian diplomatic peace is governed by a "universalistic" law (or obligation) of a "moral person" (whether an individual or a state) to care for and protect the life and independence of oneself and others, especially the weak and vulnerable, across artificial borders of nation, culture, and species.[82] Verney acts on this diplomatic sense of obligation to care for the whole world when he refuses to succumb to despair and loneliness, and sets out with his dog and his books in search of a new community with whom to remake a planetary dystopia into a cosmopolitan utopia.

Shelley's Postapocalyptic Legacies for Existentialism, Dystopian Literature, and International Thought

There is a trail of intellectual influences from Shelley to Pushkin, Dostoevsky, Nietzsche, Stoker, Camus, Orwell, Butler, Atwood, Mandel, and the modern existential, postapocalyptic, and dystopian novel. *The Last Man* and the Russian poet Aleksandr Pushkin's influential play *A Feast in Time of Plague* (1830) borrowed decadent elements from the Scottish playwright John Wilson's *City of the Plague* (1818) by depicting people dancing or hosting dinner parties amid pestilence.[83] Fyodor Dostoevsky adored Pushkin. In *Notes from Underground* (1864), he alluded to the poet-playwright's famously paradoxical image of raising a toast to the plague.[84] Dostoevsky pictured a man living alone in a basement, reveling in the darkness of human existence instead of seeking an escape from it through the delusions of post-Enlightenment liberal-utopian politics. This "underground man," like Friedrich Nietzsche's "Last Man" after him, are riffs on the postapocalyptic literature of the era of the Napoleonic Wars, popularized by Shelley's sf novels and Lord Byron's poem "Darkness" (1816), which pictured the extinction of life after the death of the sun.[85]

A classicist by training, Nietzsche turned toward the writing of a new form of existential literature and philosophy in a similar vein as Dostoevsky, whom he first read in 1886.[86] Although we do not know for certain whether he read Shelley, Nietzsche suggested his cultural grasp of *Frankenstein*'s reworking of the ancient Greek myth of Prometheus. In *Beyond Good and Evil* (1886), he wrote, "He who fights monsters should see to it that in the process he does not become a monster."[87] This aphorism might be read as a philosophical abstract of the conflict at the heart of Shelley's first novel. Victor Frankenstein becomes a monster by fighting with his own monsters, internal and external—first, his perfectionistic psychological drive to create and dominate life, and then his material Creature made from this hubristic urge to become a tyrannical god.

In *Thus Spoke Zarathustra* (1883–85), Nietzsche used the figure of the "last man" as the allegorical antithesis of his "superman" or "overman."[88] Unlike the hopeful Verney who dares to believe that other people have survived the global plague, Nietzsche's despairing last man brings about the destruction of himself and humanity by sinking into the depths of a corrupt and pointless nihilism. Nietzsche bewails the descent of most of modern mankind into a "monstrous," beast-like state, and calls for the best of the rest of them to rise to the noble task of the "first man" or "overman": to take charge of reforming humanity as a whole by ascending to a higher level of individual virtue.[89] This superman/overman shares with Verney a future-oriented and poetic, empowered yet solitary posture, figured in Romantic painting of the nineteenth century as the lone woman or man looking over a sublime cliff or across a moonlit or sunlit horizon, made famous by the German artist Caspar David Friedrich.[90]

The Reception of Shelley and the Representation of "The Last Man" in Art

The most famous of the nineteenth-century artworks to directly represent the idea of the last man was a study and painting series (c. 1826, 1832, 1849) by the British Romantic artist John Martin.[91] Martin began the series during the year Shelley published *The Last Man*. He took inspiration from the public debates about the possibility of the end of humanity, reinvigorated by the publication of Thomas Campbell's short poem "The Last Man" (1823, 1825) and Shelley's novel (January 1826).[92] Martin became famous for painting scenes of apocalyptic disaster, which, according to art historian Barbara Morden, influenced the Brontës and the Pre-Raphaelites.[93] Well-connected in English society, Martin was friends with the gothic novelist, poet, and Member of Parliament Edward Bulwer-Lytton, who was in the social circles of Shelley and Godwin and corresponded with them extensively in the late 1820s and 1830s.[94] Shelley may have attended dinner parties with Godwin at Martin's salon in London in the 1830s.[95]

Martin wrote to Bulwer-Lytton in 1849 to thank him for sending his recently published poem, *King Arthur*. The poem drew explicitly from the language of both Campbell and Shelley's depictions of the last man as a seer overlooking a ruinous landscape, only to find hope on the horizon:

> . . . a dead great city's grave,
> Where, when the moon is at her full, behold
> Pillar and palace shine up from the wave!
> And o'er the lake, seen but by gifted seers,
> In phantom bark a silent phantom steers.[96]

Bulwer-Lytton's verse nicely captures the postapocalyptic ending of Shelley's *The Last Man*, with Verney steering his "phantom bark" into an unknown future like a new age version of Coleridge's ancient mariner. These lines inspired Martin as he completed his painting of "The Last Man" for exhibition at the Royal Academy and in Liverpool that year, in the midst of a cholera epidemic.[97] The canvas depicts a white-robed sage, raising an arm to greet a red sun, not a dead sun, over a stormy and desiccated landscape (Figure 16).

Bulwer-Lytton also corresponded with Thomas Campbell in the 1840s.[98] In London in 1823, Campbell had issued his hopeful Christian "evangelical" poetic response to the bleak vision of the death of the sun and the extinguish-

Figure 16. John Martin, "The Last Man" (1849), Walker Art Gallery. Reproduced courtesy of the Walker Art Gallery, Liverpool.

ing of life in Byron's "Darkness," but it met little attention.[99] Republished in London to great acclaim in 1825, Campbell's poem "The Last Man" sparked a public debate on apocalypse and human extinction that only gained steam with the publication of Shelley's novel in January 1826.

Returning to London from Italy in August of 1823, and supporting herself and her sole surviving child by writing for local publishers and periodicals, Shelley would have been aware of the controversy over Campbell and Byron's competing visions of the end times while she completed *The Last Man* in 1825. When the Shelleys were visiting the exiled poet in Geneva during the dark and stormy summer of 1816, Byron composed his great apocalyptic poem around the same time Mary noted in her journal that she had begun to write *Frankenstein*.[100] It was the "year without a summer" when the climatic impact of the eruption of Mount Tambora caused skies to darken around the world.[101]

In May of 1824, the night before she learned of the death of her friend Byron from sepsis near the field of the war of independence in Greece, Shelley confided to her journal that she knew what it meant to be "the last man," with everyone she loved "extinct before me."[102] Her distinctive use of the word "extinct" suggests a profoundly personal and psychological link between the shock of the loss of individual life and the mourner's ascent to existential contemplation of abstract and absolute nothingness. The next entry confirmed how prescient she was. She was now, in fact, the last (and leading) literary woman in the second generation of British Romanticism. Campbell's poem, reissued in 1825, would have resonated deeply with her in the wake of the death of her and Percy's close mutual friend Byron, author of "Darkness."

Indeed, the legacies of Campbell's poem for popular culture run deep throughout nineteenth-century Anglo-American art and music. In London, between 1826 and 1832, a comic play and a number of satirical cartoons and essays spoofed the concept of the "last man" (and, after the publication of Shelley's thinly-veiled roman à clef, the "last woman").[103] This international cultural hub also saw a serious tribute, the short opera scene "The Last Man" (1826)—with lyrics from Campbell's poem and set to music by William H. Callcott—performed four times in the same period.[104] In 1835, the best-known British Romantic painter J. M. W. Turner—whom Godwin took his daughter Shelley to visit in his studio[105]—illustrated an 1837 edition of Campbell's poems. It featured a watercolor of the last man as an angelic new Adam, guided by a golden cross in his leap of faith toward heaven over an orange-pink sun, which is setting, or perhaps rising, on the horizon (Figure 17).[106]

The religious resonances of Campbell's poem turned the last man into a mainstream nineteenth-century icon of hope. Music publishers in London, New York, and Boston reissued Callcott and Campbell's 1826 opera scene "The Last Man" from the 1840s through the 1870s.[107] In 1857, in Boston, Philadelphia, Cincinnati, and New York, it was printed as part of a series "Sweet Songs for Sabbath Evenings" for hymnals and churchgoers.[108] This popular sacred music, like Martin's painting, represented the last man in a prophetic manner, heralding not the nihilistic death of the sun but rather the sign of a brighter way of life to come. In the words of Campbell, as sung in the opera scene: "Yet prophet-like, that lone one stood, Saying, This spirit shall re-turn to Him That gave its heav'nly spark."[109]

In this Victorian evangelical context, the Irish artist Robert George Kelly exhibited his painting "The Last Man" to critical appreciation in Birkenhead, England in 1886 (Figure 18).[110] Its dark yet dramatic canvas offers a vista of hope through its vision of an orange sunset (or sunrise) that illuminates a bare man half-dressed in white like Christ after the resurrection. Facing away from the viewer, he raises his hand toward the horizon as though to welcome the light into the darkness engulfing the world. In nineteenth-century

Figure 17. J. M. W. Turner, "The Last Man" (1835), National Galleries Scotland. Reproduced courtesy of the National Galleries Scotland.

European art and literature, Campbell, Shelley, Martin, Turner, and Kelly's iconic images of last men, alongside Nietzsche's superman, gesture toward a new postapocalyptic future in which humanity resurrects itself in more positive and creative ways than ever seen before, despite the threat of

Figure 18. Robert George Kelly, "The Last Man" (1886), Williamson Art Gallery. Reproduced courtesy of the Williamson Art Gallery, Birkenhead.

extinction. These artworks depict a literal sunrise after humanity's sunset, as an affirmation that something does and will exist, even if we do not.[111]

The Reception of Shelley in Postapocalyptic and Dystopian Literature

Beyond her tantalizingly indirect connections to Dostoevsky, Nietzsche, Campbell, and other nineteenth-century creators of last men, Shelley directly and indirectly influenced countless works of postapocalyptic and dystopian literature. Among the most philosophically and politically significant are Bram Stoker's *Dracula* (1897), H. G. Wells's *The Invisible Man* (1897) and *The War of the Worlds* (1897), M. P. Shiel's *The Purple Cloud* (1901), Alfred Noyes's *The Last Man* (1940), Richard Wright's *Native Son* (1940) and "The Man Who Lived Underground" (1942), Albert Camus's *The Stranger* (1942) and *The Plague* (1947), George Orwell's *Animal Farm* (1945) and *Nineteen Eighty-Four* (1949), Ralph Ellison's *Invisible Man* (1952), Richard Matheson's *I Am Legend* (1954), Muriel Spark's *Robinson* (1958), Lorraine Hansberry's *A Raisin in the Sun* (1959), Joanna Russ's *The Female Man* (1975), Octavia Butler's *Clay's Ark* (1984) and *Parable* series (1993–98), Margaret Atwood's *The Handmaid's Tale* (1985) and *MaddAddam* trilogy (2003–13), Emily St. John Mandel's *Station Eleven* (2014) and *Sea of Tranquility* (2022), and Sandra Newman's *The Men* (2022). All of these novels use figures of stalwart last (wo)men and stealthy plagues to convey how the social pathologies and psychological contagions of political injustice are transmitted, often undetected, by man-made monsters across boundaries of family and nation. These monsters may be literal bloodsucking, man-eating cannibals, or figurative vampires or invisible pests, who seek to drain and dominate others through manipulative practices of mind control and physical torture. In twentieth-century dystopian literature, figurative vampires and invisible pests proved to be more effective than literal monsters in draining the life and humanity from society by taking the forms of racism, sexism, totalitarian states, and conquering empires.

At the time of his death, Stoker owned a Victorian pocket-sized edition of *Frankenstein*, printed in the 1860s. Its superadded subtitle—"the Modern Man-Demon"—eerily anticipated Stoker's depiction of Count Dracula as a monstrous hybrid of man and demon.[112] The shape-shifting vampire from Transylvania is less a person than an evasive spectral phenomenon or miasmatic disease that hovers around and possesses its hosts. Like an oppressive wave of plague spread by bats or rats, or even a violent poltergeist, Dracula takes on a variety of material forms and overtakes the most cutting-edge technology of the British empire—electric telegraphs and steam-driven international shipping—to target and prey upon his victims, raining death and chaos across the thresholds of homes and states. The international and technological bent of Stoker's novel, in turn, may have influenced the leading dystopian novel of totalitarian political surveillance: *Nineteen Eighty-Four.*

On Christmas of 1919, the teenage Eric Blair (later known as George Orwell) gave a copy of *Dracula*—arrayed with garlic and an ornate crucifix—as a love-gift to his sweetheart Jacintha Buddicom.[113] His monumental works of dystopian fiction, *Animal Farm* (1945) and *Nineteen Eighty-Four* (1949), are concerned with the two dominant themes of *Dracula* and Shelley's sf novels before it. First, there is the political problem of *cannibalism*, real or metaphorical, by which people in power cruelly use or prey upon their fellow creatures in order to advance their own craven and even bloodthirsty interests. Secondly, there is the political problem of *mind control*, literal or figurative, through which people's worldviews are manipulated and tainted by the insidious belief systems of those in power.

While he was at boarding school in the 1910s, Orwell loved to read plague literature and speculative tales of epidemics and disease, including Edgar Allan Poe's plague allegory, "The Masque of the Red Death" (1843) and H. G. Wells's novel *The War of the Worlds* (1897) and short story "The Country of the Blind" (1904).[114] Wells's novel chronicled a cataclysmic alien infestation of Earth, stopped only by a pathogen for which the invaders lacked immunity. In the final chapter, Orwell would have encountered the narrator deliriously singing lines from Thomas Hood's satirical poem, "The Last Man" (1826), when he discovers that the aliens have been defeated by the Earth's microbes. "The Last Man Left alive! Hurrah! The Last Man Left Alive!" he chants, forgetting in his delirium that other people around the world must have had the same ecstatic grasp of their survival.[115] Then he composes himself and continues in search of his wife.

Wells may have encountered Shelley's *Last Man*, too, as part of his research into Hood's ironic response to the "last man" trope of the 1820s. What we do know for certain is that Wells knew *Frankenstein*, for he directly referenced its title in the opening pages of the manuscript for his novel about making human-animal hybrids through science, *The Island of Doctor Moreau* (1896).[116] Published a year later, his novel *The Invisible Man* features another riff on the idea that Victor Frankenstein, not his Creature, was the real monster: the megalomaniac Griffin uses science to turn himself invisible so that he might enact crime, mind games, and other forms of tyranny upon others.

Unlike Wells, we do not have direct evidence that Poe read Shelley, but there is a consensus that he alluded to the final sentence of *Frankenstein* in the last lines of one of his earliest published stories, "MS. Found in a Bottle" (1833).[117] That same year, he might have acquired from his publishers their new dual-release of the first American edition of *The Last Man* with *Frankenstein*.[118] As with Poe, we also do not know for certain if Orwell read Shelley's novels. We do know that Orwell, a lifelong fan of sf, requested to review "anything by M. P. Shiel"—the author of *The Purple Cloud* (1901), the closest literary adaptation of Shelley's *The Last Man*—when working for the *Adelphi* magazine in the early 1930s.[119] We also know that Orwell praised the "lost art" of Shelley's journals—the basis of her roman à clef, *The Last Man*—in 1944, and that the original title for *Nineteen Eighty-Four* was "The Last Man in Europe."[120] He may have been directly referencing Shelley's novel when he had the hero Winston Smith described as "the last man" as he is tortured for his belief in love by O'Brien, the merciless agent of the totalitarian regime.[121]

While reviewing *English Diaries of the Nineteenth Century* in 1944, Orwell had encountered a three-page transcript of Shelley's journals, covering 14–15 May 1824. It was on 14 May that she invoked the concept of the last man: "The Last Man. Yes, I may well describe that solitary being's feelings: I feel myself as the last relic of a beloved race, my companions extinct before me."[122] James Aitken, the editor of *English Diaries of the Nineteenth Century*, underscored the term "The Last Man" with a footnote that identified it as the title "of a novel [Shelley] was writing."[123] As the research head of the Orwell Society, L. J. Hurst, has pointed out, "the key words "last man" and "extinct" also appear in O'Brien's one-paragraph address to Winston: "'If you are a man, Winston, you are the last man. Your kind is extinct; we are the inheritors. Do you understand that you are alone? You are outside history, you are non-existent.' His manner changed and he said more harshly: 'And you consider yourself morally superior to us, with our lies and our cruelty?'"[124] These neat parallels make one wonder if Orwell paid homage not only to Mary Wollstonecraft Shelley's existential meditation on the bleak sense of extinction that comes after the absolute loss of love, but also to the last two initials of her pen name, by calling the tragic diarist of *Nineteen Eighty-Four*—who is tortured by the state for having a love affair—"Winston Smith."

Malcolm Pittock made the case that Orwell may have changed the title from "The Last Man in Europe" to *Nineteen Eighty-Four*, just before it went to press in late 1948, due to the fact that Alfred Noyes, a well-known Catholic conservative writer, had recently published a popular novel titled *The Last Man*. Pittock did not explore whether Noyes appropriated the title from Shelley's novel or other representations of "the last man," but rather focused on unearthing parallels between the plot of this 1940 postapocalyptic novel and Orwell's *Nineteen Eighty-Four*.[125] Its parallels with Shelley's plague novel and its closest adaptation, Shiel's *The Purple Cloud*, are far more obvious.

Noyes's *The Last Man* is about a global war that seemingly leaves one man alive only to find a female survivor with whom he falls in love, much like Shiel's romantic twist on Shelley's existential thought experiment. Before the catastrophic war, Noyes depicts the world's nations split into two rival leagues or factions. They use bioweapons that spread lethal diseases across borders, harming both their enemies and themselves. Then the "two sides" mutually deploy a more effective and supposedly "secret" and "last resort" doomsday weapon that sends "all-pervasive" and "ethereal waves" to stop the "beating of the human heart."[126]

Noyes began his postapocalyptic novel in medias res. The narrator compares his incredible story of survival with nineteenth-century "Poems and works of fiction" about the "last man."[127] The narrator alludes to the plotlines of two of the best-known plague novels in this tradition, Wells's *The War of the Worlds* and Shiel's *The Purple Cloud*, as well as the "dying sun" imagery of Byron's "Darkness," before he recounts how he *in fact* endured a war-driven near-extinction event and found love despite it all.[128]

In 1944, Orwell described Noyes's poetry as "completely spurious bombast."[129] He reviewed Noyes's 1942 novel *The Edge of the Abyss* and judged the story so "silly" and "incoherent" as to not merit rehearsal, even as it raised a serious question: will rising amorality lead to the "destruction" of "western civilization"?[130] If Orwell also deigned to read Noyes's *The Last Man*, he was yet again exposed to the tradition of postapocalyptic literature rooted in the 1820s debates on "the last man" to which Shelley contributed the major plague novel.

Nineteen Eighty-Four, like Shelley's and Noyes's extended riffs on the "last man" theme, is as much a war novel as it is a novel of dystopian international politics. Writing in the wake of the bombings of London during World War II, Orwell knew firsthand the terror of living under the constant threat of destruction. Indeed, his wife Eileen O'Shaughnessy Blair died in 1945 during a hysterectomy intended to resolve her poor health, which had been exacerbated by the grief and tension of wartime. In 1950, Orwell also died young from the contagion of tuberculosis that he contracted as a child and that had crippled him for months on end as an adult.

Perhaps inspired by his wife's 1934 poem "End of the Century 1984," which imagined what her high school would be like fifty years in the future, Orwell's greatest novel is set in a dystopian Britain of the late twentieth century.[131] Alluding to Aldous Huxley and his *Brave New World* (1932), O'Shaughnessy's poem pictured girls' secondary education in the year 1984 without books and "colds" but with infantilizing technological and hedonistic means of mind control:

> For sun-bronzed scholars tune their thought
> To Telepathic Station 9
> From which they know just what they ought:
> The useful sciences; the arts
> Of telesalesmanship and Spanish
> Mental cremation should banish

Relics, philosophies and colds—
Mañana-minded ten-year-olds.[132]

In Orwell's starker version of a Huxleyan techno-dystopia, the "telescreen" is the visual equivalent of O'Shaughnessy's radio-like "Telepathic Station 9."[133] By spreading hateful xenophobic and sexist ideology through its telescreens, the "Big Brother" of the surveillance state produces the infantilizing "mental cremation" of the populace in order to exert totalizing control of its political behavior.[134] No longer a sovereign nation-state governed by an elected parliament through the consent of its citizenry, Britain in *Nineteen Eighty-Four* has been subsumed under the empire of Oceania. Constantly at war with other superstates, Oceania treats Britain—known as "Airstrip One"—as a mere landing strip for its airborne weapons.[135] By keeping a diary against the rules of the regime, (Mr.) Winston Smith leaves a private record of using writing to resist the oppressive force of Big Brother's fascist ideology. As with (Mary Wollstonecraft) Shelley's *The Last Man*, the narrator's journal is implicitly the futuristic dystopian novel itself.

The Reception of Shelley and the Rise of the Existential Novel

While in Paris in 1945, Orwell tried to meet Camus, a fellow journalist and critic of fascism. He later sent Camus a copy of the French edition of *Animal Farm*, a fable about how authoritarian and totalitarian regimes cannibalize their own by implementing a system of brainwashing and mind control.[136] Camus's two great existential novels from the 1940s, *The Stranger* and *The Plague*, share uncanny thematic resemblances to both *Frankenstein* and *The Last Man*.[137] The suicidal protagonist of *The Stranger*, Meursault, has often been compared to the Creature.[138] The characters share angst-ridden social isolation, the utter failure to thrive in emotional and familial relationships, and sudden descents into murderous crime because of the tragic sense of the absurdity of existence.

Although *The Plague* does not concern a pandemic but rather a localized epidemic of the bubonic plague, it follows both *Animal Farm* and *The Last Man* in treating contagion as a metaphor for how political ideologies (fascism, imperialistic war) manifest as social diseases that drain a society of its capacity for humaneness. And like Shelley's sf novels, Camus's existential narratives explore the psychological state of a lonely survivor of personal or political disaster. Dr. Rieux, the narrator of *The Plague*, is a survivor like Verney who lives to chronicle the implosion of a human community. Akin to Verney's "History of the Last Man," Rieux writes a synthetic account of the outbreak in his northern Algerian city by resourcing the memories, experiences, and journals of himself and his friends. Camus's and Shelley's dystopian plague survivors write diaristic histories that warn future readers of the danger of the resurgence of the social diseases of conflict, domination, and despair.

The fact that we avidly consume their plague narratives, in their original and artistically adapted forms, suggests that Shelley and Camus shared a paradoxically yet contagiously hopeful existential outlook. Despite the darkness of their epidemic literature, both existential writers leave open the possibility of delivery from the disasters of the past to a new and unknown, postapocalyptic blank slate. Humanity might then have a second chance to realize its potential for what had eluded it before: whether it be freedom or love, happiness or peace.[139] Before he died in a car accident in 1960, Camus titled his last unfinished novel—published by his daughter in 1994—*The First Man*.[140] One wonders if this conceptual reversal of the title of Shelley's pandemic novel signals his awareness of *The Last Man* and its many legacies in twentieth-century cinema and literature.

A reader of both Nietzsche and Dostoevsky, Camus was familiar with their existentialist ideas of "the last man" and "the underground man." In Dostoevsky's *Notes from Underground* (1864), the narrator's unforgiving sense of the meaninglessness of existence drives away the one woman in his life—a prostitute who cares for him—by coldly attempting to pay for her services. Flinging the money away, she flees his St. Petersburg apartment—or what he calls his "underground hole"—and disappears into the winter night, leaving him alone in the wet snow to trace back in time the reasons for her rejection of him.[141] This "underground man" prefigured both Nietzsche's "last man" and Camus's Meursault.[142] All three archetypes of the modern existential protagonist tie back to Shelley's sf novels and their sources in eighteenth-century English and German literature. Camus and Shelley explicitly based their plague novels on Daniel Defoe's tale of solitary woe under quarantine lockdown in *A Journal of the Plague Year*.[143] Frankenstein's Creature reads and identifies with Goethe's *The Sorrows of Young Werther* (1774). And in his 1942 essay on his philosophy of the absurd, *The Myth of Sisyphus*, Camus revealed his deep reading in the works of Goethe, Dostoevsky, and Nietzsche.[144] Through this intertextual overlay of influences, the idea of the last known survivor of a wider psychological or social catastrophe—living alone in a hovel, basement, or bunker—has become a predominant existential trope of modern literature.

In the early 1940s United States, Richard Wright developed an influential strand of Black existentialism from this image of the underground man. His novel *Native Son* (1940), like Camus's *The Stranger* two years after it, features a Creature-like outcast who becomes a murderer due to his sense of estrangement from society and humanity itself. In Wright's version of the *Frankenstein* story, it is racism and poverty that triggers the young Black American protagonist Bigger Thomas's desperate and tragic resort to a life of crime. Like Frankenstein's Creature and Camus's Mersault, Bigger Thomas is not an unsympathetic figure. In each of these criminal cases, the reader is left to critically judge the reasons why the central figure of the story became inhumane.[145]

Wright amplified the Dostoevskian and Shelleyan themes of his Black existentialism in his influential short story "The Man Who Lived Underground" (1942). After reading an August 1941 *True Detective* report of a Los Angeles man who staged "a series of burglaries from an underground bunker," Wright composed a novella about a Black man, Fred Daniels, who escapes into the sewers after being tortured by the police for a crime that he did not commit.[146] In his memoir of writing the 1941 manuscript for the novel *The Man Who Lived Underground* (2021), from which he excerpted the eponymous 1942 short story, Wright cited "Russian literature" and the "movies depicting the antics of invisible men" as his major literary inspirations beyond the true crime report.[147] In Spring 1942, Ralph Ellison read an excerpt of Wright's story in the *Accent*, and sent a note to congratulate the publisher.[148]

Ellison went on to publish in 1952 his own *Invisible Man* novel, another classic of Black existentialism and postapocalyptic literature. A short story based on the novel had appeared in a 1947 issue of *Horizon*, a progressive London literary magazine edited by Orwell's close friend Cyril Connolly.[149] Building on Wright and W. E. B. Du Bois before him, Ellison explores the ways that racism is an unseen yet oppressive force in American society that renders the true selves, or "souls," of Black folk invisible to others, including themselves, because of the socially prescribed "color-line" that separates and elevates whites above people of color in culture and law.[150] Ellison's *Invisible Man* famously began and ended with an unnamed Black narrator, living alone in a Harlem basement alit with thousands of stolen lightbulbs, powered by illegally diverted electricity. Doubly living off the grid, the narrator is finally able to see what it means to be Black in America. He is an "*invisible* man": unseen by the racist society that refused to see who he really was, because it systematically denied him the education, economic opportunities, and citizenship rights that he deserved in order to develop and share his talents with his nation and humanity itself.[151]

Making explicit what Wright left implicit in "The Man Who Lived Underground," Ellison opened *Invisible Man* with an allusion to the "Hollywood-movie ectoplasms" of the 1930s.[152] While neither American writer directly cited Wells as a source, the Universal Studios monster movies had turned his 1897 novel into a mainstay of mid-century global popular culture. As we have seen, Wells directly referenced *Frankenstein* in the draft manuscript of *Doctor Moreau* and alluded to the 1820s debates over the postapocalyptic idea of "the last man" in the conclusion to *The War of the Worlds*.[153] Given his fascination with Shelleyan literature, Wells could have also sought out her gothic romance "The Invisible Girl" in the 1891 edition of her *Tales and Stories* prior to writing *The Invisible Man*. Regardless, the overlapping themes of her three great dystopias—*Frankenstein*, *The Last Man*, and "The Invisible Girl"—were refracted through popular culture of the early twentieth century. Since James Whale directed *Frankenstein* (1931), *The Invisible Man* (1933), and *Bride of Frankenstein* (1935) for Universal Studios, the imagery of Shelley's and Wells's masterpieces of political science fiction commingled in the cinematic imagination. From Hollywood, images of invisible, last, and lonely men infused the classics of Black existentialism by Wright and Ellison.

Playing with the growing postwar and postnuclear fascination with the idea of the "last man" as an "underground man"—cut off from the toxic atmosphere of the outside world by hiding in a sewer, pit, or cellar—Matheson's horror-sf novel *I Am Legend* was pivotal for the development of the mid-century iteration of postapocalyptic literature.[154] It effectively combined the gothic plot lines of *Dracula*, *Frankenstein*, and *The Last Man* with the existentialist ideas of Camus, Nietzsche, and Dostoevsky. Matheson's proximate source for adapting the plot of *The Last Man* was M. P. Shiel's novel *The Purple Cloud* (1901) about a poisonous gas that instigates humanity's self-destruction through war and other conflict.[155] In a romantic version of the aporetic ending of *The Last Man*, Shiel had the last man abandon his misanthropy when he stumbles upon a female survivor and seer, buried in the ruins of Constantinople, with whom he falls in love. In a direct nod to Shelley, he framed the entire story as a "Sybilline prophecy," as she had presented *The Last Man* as her "latest discoveries in the slight Sybilline pages" that she supposedly discovered in a cave near Naples in December 1818.[156]

Blending elements of Stoker, Shiel, and Shelley as refracted through filmic versions of their novels, Matheson imagined a postapocalyptic America in which all but one human has been turned into a vampire by a bioengineered plague. This lone man, Robert Neville, quarantines himself in a bunker to fight off the invaders, until he encounters a woman with whom he falls in love. She turns out to be a vampire sent to stop his hunting of her fellow infected humans. As he awaits execution by the new people in power, Neville ultimately realizes that he is the aberration or monster, not the vampires, for he is the "last of the old race" of humans.[157]

Matheson's novel was adapted for the screen as *The Last Man on Earth* (1964), and later as *I Am Legend* (2007), starring Will Smith. The 1964 film almost single-handedly spurred the zombie apocalypse genre in film and television, led by the directorial work of George Romero.[158] However, Matheson's version of the last man narrative had disturbing racist undertones. If the Black British writer Shiel's *Purple Cloud* was the story of how a man and a woman from different cultures could remake society after the demise of a racist world built on conflicts between "'White' and 'Black' powers" then Matheson's *I Am Legend* was the story of the last white man's anxiety about the loss of his supposed "race" supremacy over people of color.[159] The casting of Will Smith as the hero in the 2007 movie turned *I Am Legend* into a post-civil rights allegory for the lasting, isolating and largely unseen struggle of Black folks' bare survival of the plague of racism. The 2007 film makes explicit what Wright and Ellison left implicit: the Black man is both the last man and the invisible man, while the White man is the vampire plague that seeks to make Black people and their culture not only unseen but extinct.

The gender biases implicit or explicit in "last man" narratives also came to be interrogated alongside racial prejudice in twentieth-century literature, theater, and film. In the interwar period, feminist sf gained traction, especially in the postapocalyptic mode. The art critic Helen Sunderland likely authored the anonymous short story, "The End of the World" (1930), which imagined a "plague" after the "third World War" that takes "the males of every nation," leaving women to mourn the death of "the Last Man" and the eventual demise of the human species.[160] In the 1940s, Richard Wright befriended Simone de Beauvoir. He gave her a tour of Harlem as she was writing *The Second Sex* (1949).[161] In her philosophical classic of feminist existentialism and phenomenology, Beauvoir credited Wright for showing her how racism worked in the same ways as sexism, such that the shared plight of women, Blacks, and Jews in the postwar period was to be culturally defined as the subordinate other to the dominant White man.[162]

During this postwar rise of second wave feminism and feminist sf, Muriel Spark, Lorraine Hansberry, and Joanna Russ recovered the work of Wollstonecraft and Shelley to revive the idea of the "last woman" and "invisible girl" in late twentieth-century literature, theater, and film. The novelist Spark not only produced one of the most important biographies of Mary Shelley in 1951, but also introduced the first modern scholarly edition of *The Last Man* for Falcon Press in 1954. Unfortunately, the press went out of business after only a half-dozen review copies had been printed.[163] Spark's scholarship on Shelley and *The Last Man* nevertheless left a deep impression on her first two novels.

Spark's *The Comforters* (1957) and *Robinson* (1958) are about young women survivors of trauma who use diaristic writing to save their own lives and their senses of themselves as autonomous subjects. In these allegorical, semi-autobiographical novels, the women narrators are avatars for Spark herself, who had endured domestic violence, divorce from her mentally ill husband, child custody issues, a life-threatening addiction to weight-loss pills, a difficult breakup with her lover during her conversion to Roman Catholicism, and a nervous breakdown in the run-up to producing her first major works of fiction.[164] In *The Comforters*, the female protagonist—an anxious writer and recent convert to Roman Catholicism who no longer sleeps with her boyfriend—hears a typewriter click in her own head as she becomes convinced she is a character in a convoluted novel of crime, mystery, and existential crisis. In *Robinson*, the "only woman" survivor of a plane wreck on a remote Atlantic island is a divorced convert to Roman Catholicism.[165] Stranded among a small group of strange men, she tries to use her diary to solve a suspected murder when the lone, Crusoe-like settler on the island goes missing soon after the crash. Modeled on Shelley's journals and roman à clef, Spark's early novels shaped two dominant tropes of modern feminist film and literature: (1) the existentialist and surrealist idea of being (or feeling like) a self-conscious character in your own novel or film and (2) the postapocalyptic concept of being (or feeling like) the last woman survivor of a mental or physical catastrophe that threatens to render one invisible to oneself or others.

A close reader of Du Bois, Wright, Beauvoir, and Wollstonecraft, the Black Marxist playwright Lorraine Hansberry combined the feminist tropes of the "last woman" and the self-conscious female character in her 1959 Broadway play *A Raisin in the Sun*. The young Black heroine, Beneatha, takes after Hansberry herself, who grew up near the University of Chicago in historically segregated neighborhoods. Beneatha seeks to escape the racism of her southside Chicago upbringing by going "to Africa . . . to be a doctor" with her fiancé. When her mother tries to persuade her to stay to marry another man with "some loot," she proclaims, "I wouldn't marry him if he was Adam and I was Eve!"[166]

Hansberry's Beneatha echoes a comic theme found in the first silent film and Broadway musical based on Shiel's romantic riff on Shelley's novel. In *The Last Man on Earth* (1924), Elmer proposes to his girlfriend Hattie only to have her turn him down, saying she wouldn't marry him if he was the last man left on the planet. Then a plague strikes, killing all men but Elmer, and leaving him the last available man for women (including Hattie) to fight over sexually.[167] Beneatha rewrites this absurdist (and sexist) Hollywood punchline, however, by asserting her Black womanly authority over her plan to blend love and vocation in her own unfolding life story. Refusing to become another victim of systematic American racism and sexism, she departs for Africa to become a doctor with her lover and thereby exits her mother's (and society's) limiting script for her and other Black women.

One of Hansberry's last major projects after the success of *Raisin in the Sun* was the drafting of an historical play on Shelley's mother Wollstonecraft. The typescript of the first scene depicts a teenage Wollstonecraft sticking her tongue out at her patronizing older brother. In her manuscripts held at the Schomburg Center for the Study of Black Culture at the New York Public Library, there are copious notes and annotated scholarly books on the Wollstonecraft-Godwin family. One of these notes dramatizes the playwright's passion for bringing Wollstonecraft to life on the stage.

One night in August 1960, Hansberry awoke at "3:38am" with a sense of urgency. She scribbled down a sliver of a dream in which "Vivien Leigh" had triumphantly played the role of Wollstonecraft on Broadway.[168] The poignancy of this note derives from the existential fact that Hansberry would die of pancreatic cancer less than five years later, at age thirty-four. She knew all too well that her historical feminist heroine had died young, at age thirty-eight, eleven days after delivering the future author of *Frankenstein*. Perhaps with Shelley's artistic tributes to her mother in mind, Hansberry conceived her play as another way to give birth to Wollstonecraftian ideas. The existential tragedy was that she would not complete this script before her time was up.

Left in her notes is evidence that Hansberry intended to make Wollstonecraft's youthful romantic friendship with Fanny Blood a central theme of the play. Identifying as bisexual since her college years at Madison, Hansberry seems to have sympathized with what Godwin called Wollstonecraft's enduring love for a person "of the same sex."[169] As it became clear that her undiagnosed sickness was severe, the young playwright took elements of Wollstonecraft's short life to heart. Hansberry quietly arranged with her husband to have an open marriage so that she could explore her sexuality. She had a series of lesbian relationships during the last few years of her life and contributed anonymously to a gay literary magazine. At the time of her death in January 1965, she left behind two unfinished historical plays that respectively centered on the leading figures of revolutionary-era women's and Black liberation: Wollstonecraft and Toussaint L'Ouverture.[170]

Alongside Muriel Spark, the lesbian feminist sf writer Joanna Russ was a pivotal author of literary criticism on Shelley's *The Last Man* in the late twentieth century. Like Spark, she sought to elevate *The Last Man* to the same level as *Frankenstein* in the English literary canon. Russ's tributes to Shelley include her futuristic plague novel, *The Female Man* (1975), in which a peaceful lesbian world arises after a plague kills all men on Earth. Russ took inspiration for this surrealist feminist utopia from pulp fiction and erotica of the postwar era. A standard plotline of the erotic paperback romance was women living out their sexuality "without men" in an anonymous city or island retreat. Another common storyline was a lone man stumbling into an exotic Amazonian community, only to encounter personal and sexual peril when he fell in love with one of the women already "taken" by a femme fatale.[171]

In Russ's feminist sf twist, this "last man" living among lesbians becomes a gender-hybrid last (wo)man, with a woman's body and a man's spirit, who time-travels across the ages of planet Earth in different incarnations of herself (and her avatar Russ). Each of these last (wo)men are from radically different cultures and epochs, yet all have first names that begin with "J" like their author. They reveal through their strange, funny, and sometimes traumatic lives the socially constructed differences in the actual and possible treatment of women relative to men across time. Together these gender-transfiguring last (wo)men expose and satirize the heterosexual and masculinist biases that lurk behind the apocalyptic premise, born of Wells, Shiel, Noyes, and Matheson, that the "last man on earth will spend the last hour before the holocaust searching for his wife and child."[172]

In direct homage to Russ and perhaps also mid-century pulp fiction, Sandra Newman has forged yet another novel combination of the Sparkian/Shelleyan "last woman" and "self-conscious character" tropes. In her feminist postapocalyptic novel *The Men* (2022), the woman narrator is a seemingly happy mother and wife, who is silently suffering due to being a survivor of child sex trafficking. Despite her love for her husband and son, with whom she is camping in the wilderness, she dares to imagine whether the world would be better off "without men"—only to find her dream come true as a waking nightmare. On this alternate Earth, transpiring on a different mental plane, she finds love in a lesbian commune but desperately seeks connection to "the men" who have been disappeared by some invisible power. The men and boys, including her own husband and son, can still be seen as captives in mysteriously made video clips circulating on the internet. When she repeatedly witnesses her son's cannibalistic murder by other men in the found footage of the captives, the compounding trauma triggers an awakening in her. She returns to her original—damaged but real—life story to embrace the fact that "the men" in her family are safe and fast asleep in their tent. Her fantasy of an all-woman world appears to have been a psychic dystopia that arose from ignoring, rather than addressing, the sexual violence in her past. Newman's novel received much criticism for its essentialist implications, since the invisible force that steals "the men" only takes people with Y chromosomes. Yet, this story of an alternate Earth ultimately vindicates the feminist idea that all forms of gender and sexual violence (including violence against trans people) must be rendered visible in society for the residual trauma to be addressed, rectified, and transcended.

With the feminist icon Elisabeth Moss in the starring role, the 2020 movie remake of *Invisible Man* dramatized on screen many of the same themes of domestic and sexual violence as Newman's *The Men*. The film opens with a woman escaping a glass house on the coast where her abusive boyfriend sleeps, surrounded by strange scientific equipment. Like Griffin in Wells's novel, the tyrant has learned to turn himself invisible. In a dystopian feminist twist, this invisible man does not seek power over the whole world, but only over his girlfriend. He uses a technological cloak of invisibility to both perpetuate and escape culpability for psychological and physical violence toward his sexual partner. In a second feminist twist, the female survivor uses her ex-boyfriend's stolen technology to make herself invisible. She manipulates her murderous ex into trusting her, then uses her cloak of invisibility to slit his throat—all while the police are waiting outside. With her cloak packed in her bag, Moss as the invisible woman finally leaves the glass house unscathed and undetected. By stopping the violence of the invisible man, the invisible woman becomes the last (wo)man standing.

This smart yet scary 2020 update of the 1930s *Invisible Man* films uncannily recalls the themes of Shelley's prototypical gothic romance. In "The

Invisible Girl" (1832), Rosina flees into the woods to barely subsist on her own. She lives like a ghost to escape the cruel tyranny of her adoptive father and aunt, who wanted to block her secret betrothal to the eldest male heir in the family. Rosina only becomes visible to society again after she reunites with her shipwrecked lover Henry in the tower. Henry creates a memorial in the tower to his wife's enduring identity as a once-lonely yet ever-valiant survivor of domestic tyranny. He restores a portrait from their happy courtship, names it "The Invisible Girl," and hangs it in the tower as a marker of her heroism. By allowing the invisible girl to triumph over the abuse that had threatened her very existence, both Shelley's 1832 short story and the 2020 film insist that the true horror would be to let domestic abuse remain invisible to a society that ought to prevent, prosecute, and overcome it.

Though made mainstream by generational iterations of the *Invisible Man*, *Halloween*, *Alien*, *Scream*, and other horror movie franchises, the last (wo) man and invisible person tropes have also cross-pollinated in some of the best feminist literary fiction, especially the plague novels of Atwood, Butler, and Mandel. While a young poet in the 1950s and 1960s, Margaret Atwood was a devoted reader of Orwell's *Nineteen Eighty-Four* and Shelley's *Frankenstein*.[173] Atwood's feminist dystopian fictions from the *Handmaid's Tale* and *MaddAddam* series are replete with monstrous imagery of blood, betrayal, cannibalism, and the ripple effects of toxic romantic and familial relationships.[174] Atwood's handmaid Offred is Creature-like in her diaristic recording of her social isolation and deprivation as a sexual slave forced to work for a Puritanical theocracy in the early twenty-first century. Made anonymous by her red handmaid's cloak, the nameless handmaid (only identified as "of" the military commander "Fred" whom she services) uses journaling to resist brainwashing and subordination. Since her diary becomes the novel itself, as in *Nineteen Eighty-Four* and *The Last Man*, Atwood's handmaid is a *once-invisible* girl survivor of sexual trauma and oppression, whose life story and suffering are made visible through a self-conscious decision to rebel through writing about oneself. Atwood's 2019 sequel, *The Testaments*, reinforces this theme by presenting the first-person diary entries of Aunt Lydia, who was thought to be one of the escaped handmaid Offred's oppressors. She turns out to be a double agent who is instrumental in arranging for the decades-later reunion of Offred and her daughters. Atwood represents a literary paradox with the journals of Offred and Lydia: private writing can make visible women's political struggles with man-made disaster.

A reader of *The Handmaid's Tale*, Octavia Butler shared with Atwood a fascination with the postapocalyptic image of the final girl survivor. The biracial sf writer and critic Samuel R. Delany called Butler the leading Black sf writer after Shiel.[175] A distinctive element of Butler's style was to draw upon the monster and vampire imagery of horror and disaster literature in the vein of Matheson, Stoker, and Shelley. Set in 2021, her novel *Clay's Ark* chronicles the dangerous outbreak of a highly infectious alien microorganism after a spaceship crashed in the desert with one contagious survivor.[176] This last man deliberately infects other humans who mutate into blood-drinking, cat-human hybrids, but a biracial girl endures the transformation with her humanity and her capability for building loving communities intact.

Also set in the twenty-first century, Atwood's prescient *MaddAddam* series envisions the invention of a CRISPR-like technology that would allow for the making of pig-human hybrids (such as scientists in fact began to make in petri dishes in 2017).[177] In this dystopian triptych, a nihilistic leader in the corporatized pharmaceutical industry cynically unleashes a bioengineered plague in the form of a sexual enhancement pill.[178] While his express purpose is to destroy humankind, two women survive him and a cannibalistic, patriarchal, apocalyptic cult that gained power in his wake. These last women bring humanity back from the brink of extinction by working in league with the genetically engineered animal hybrids as their pacific companions.[179]

Atwood's work inspired Butler's *Parable* series and Mandel's *Station Eleven*: especially their now-iconic stories of "last women" who, like Mary/Verney, find the strength to survive a devastating series of personal and political disasters to sustain hope of a better future. In *The Parable of the Sower*, Butler presents the diaristic story of a young African American woman, Lauren Oya Olamina.[180] In the year 2024, she escapes the breakdown of her impoverished and violent Los Angeles community by disguising herself as a man and hitting the road into the anarchistic world beyond the city walls. In the sequel, *The Parable of the Talents*, Olamina—a bit like Mina, the female lead of *Dracula*—uses her superhuman capacity for identifying with other people's thoughts and feelings to fight the social diseases of her time and work toward a new, postapocalyptic world of peace and justice to be realized on another planet.[181]

Mandel's *Station Eleven* has been poignant to read during the time of Covid-19, as it foresaw that a lethal flu-like pandemic could be unwittingly and swiftly transmitted via international air travel. Mandel directly referenced the existential philosophy of Jean-Paul Sartre throughout her postapocalyptic plague novel set in the near future of the twenty-first century. While Sartre pessimistically argued in his play *No Exit* (1944) that "hell is other people," Mandel has her young heroine Kirsten survive the state of war left in the wake of the Georgia Flu to realize that true hell is both "a world with almost no people in it" and "the absence of people you long for."[182]

Like a "final girl" survivor in a late twentieth-century slasher horror film, Kirsten narrowly escapes a brutal execution by a false prophet of doom when one of his abused followers turns on him to save her before committing suicide with the same gun.[183] Akin to Verney equipped on his ship with the works of Shakespeare and Homer, Kirsten's love of literature and its power to imagine a more hopeful future is what sparks this act of supererogation by a stranger. As she recites lines from her favorite comic book, *Station Eleven*, to the mad cult leader who also happens to own one of the few surviving copies, Kirsten distracts him long enough for his rebel sentry to finally revolt against the tyrannical ideologue. In the final scene of the novel, Kirsten gives her copy of the comic book to an airport museum established to preserve the vestiges of humanity's pre-pandemic past. Then she sets out to discover the mysterious source of the electric lights that have just been alit over the southern shore of Lake Michigan.

Mandel, like Atwood, writes dystopian fiction in the more hopeful and cosmopolitan mode of Shelley and Butler than in the dark and cynical mode of Orwell and Camus. This may be due to these women writers' concerted bridging of a variety of gendered and international perspectives in their novels. A lifelong environmentalist, the Canadian Atwood has used her fiction to explore social justice issues raised by the melting Arctic, the uncontained AIDS epidemic, legal attempts to strip women of reproductive rights, and the corporatization of bioengineering worldwide.[184] Now based in New York as well as Los Angeles, especially since she helped to produce HBO's critically acclaimed *Station Eleven* miniseries in 2021, Mandel came of age in Canada during the early twenty-first-century wave of SARS that hit Toronto due to traffic through its major international airport.[185]

Her most recent novel, *Sea of Tranquility* (2022), uses time travel, simulation theory, and parallel realities to explore her own experience of isolation and crisis during Covid-19. In this autobiographical metafiction, Mandel upstages Shelley in making a literary analogue to herself—a woman author of a pandemic novel—the pivotal character around whom the action unfolds. *Sea of Tranquility* becomes the author's pandemic memoir (or "pandemoir") about what it is like to be a plague writer in lockdown, like H. D. in Defoe's

Plague Year, Verney in Shelley's *The Last Man*, or Rieux in Camus's *La Peste*. Mandel's analogue Olive survives a SARS pandemic in the year 2203 through the selfless intervention of a time-traveler from the future, who was named for one of the characters in her novels. Mandel's sf allegory reminds us that, even as authors of our own life stories, we always have our fates intertwined with the lives of others, across vast overlapping scales of time and space, in ways that we can never fully comprehend as individuals. As in the aporetic ending to *Station Eleven*, Mandel's time-travel novel leaves her readers with hope that the imaginative medium of fiction can help us to map and make visible our ethical connections to others in the cosmos.

Conclusion: Literary IR from the Last Man to the Final Girl

Almost two centuries before Atwood, Butler, and Mandel shaped the contemporary field of feminist *poliscifi*, Shelley's seeming powers of augury likewise arose for deeply personal reasons with universal resonance. As a young English woman, traveling through Italy with her husband and children, she experienced an epidemic of tragedies on a depth and scale that most people could not bear. The original "last Woman," or final girl who outlasts them all, Shelley's emotional and intellectual resilience in the face of the many plagues upon her family is what made her a visionary and generative sf novelist, existential writer, and political philosopher of pandemic and other artificially made disasters.[186]

It is to Shelley that we owe the diverse evolution of the modern existential, dystopian, and postapocalyptic literary traditions—especially the hopeful feminist outlooks of Atwood, Butler, and Mandel—and their philosophical roots in Western international thought from Thucydides to Vattel. By reclaiming her within this feminist "counter-archive" of *poliscifi*, we reveal how postapocalyptic and dystopian literature can build pragmatic, creative, optimistic, and emotionally compelling bridges between existentialism and IR.[187] This interdisciplinary, bridge-building exercise in Literary IR is crucial for rectifying two long-standing biases of these critical areas of philosophy and political science: (1) gender prejudice against the value of women's contributions to and perspectives on existential questions and international politics, and (2) a pessimistic orientation toward politics and the human condition that obstructs the hope and love necessary to move forward through globally impactful disasters of our own making.

POSTFACE

The Last Woman in Self-Quarantine

[*Note from the Editor*:
During the year 2120, this text has been extracted from the word-processed and cloud-preserved travel journal of the twenty-first-century American writer Eileen M. Hunt for recording in ARCOVID, the United Nations of the Americas' digitized archival collection of papers marking the centenary of the novel coronavirus pandemic. All notes to the text are mine, using sources that the author likely accessed online or in print; the rest is rendered exactly in her own words.

Margaret Winston Smith
Editor-in-Chief
Global Pandemics Research Collective, U.N.A.
4 September 2120]

Sunday, 6 June 2021
London

Five days into a British-government mandated quarantine for international travelers to England, I feel like the last woman left in the existential limbo of the Covid-19 pandemic. Though fully vaccinated with two shots of Pfizer-BioNTech for almost two months now, I am required to take no less than five Covid tests in the space of three weeks to legally affirm what science has already proven: mRNA vaccines work to halt the spread of the novel coronavirus. Aside from the $600 total price tag for the tests (generously covered by Notre Dame), and my very first PCR throat swab that made me involuntarily dry-heave on a sidewalk last Thursday in Southwark, I'm psyched to be back in Britain on my *almost*-postapocalyptic and *nearly*-post-pandemic research trip to study Mary Shelley's correspondence, journals, and other manuscripts related to her authorship of the first modern global pandemic novel, *The Last Man*.

When I was awarded a grant to travel to London, Oxford, Hertford, and Bournemouth to study the lives, papers, and legacies of Shelley and her correspondents, such as her fellow gothic writer Edward Bulwer-Lytton, I was wary of the obstacles to realizing my somewhat fantastical research proposal written midway through the long dark winter of Covid-19. I had originally planned to visit Italy, where Shelley lost three children she bore or cared for to the infectious diseases of dysentery, malaria, and typhus.

But with the travel bans and lockdowns on the continent, I narrowed my trip to her homeland of England. Even then, the minimum five-day quarantine, the serial testing, the uncertainty of new travel bans and lockdowns, and the resurgence of new coronavirus variants all seemed to converge to make the trip seem impossible to plan. When one added in the labyrinthine online process to apply to read manuscripts and books at the British Library in London and the Bodleian Library at Oxford, then the very idea of the trip seemed preposterous.

My situation felt as absurd as the titular "LAST MAN"—or the sole known human survivor—of Shelley's fictional global "PLAGUE."[1] While I had the luck of winning the grant to support writing a book about Shelley, plague literature, and the development of a modern postapocalyptic aesthetic in literature and the arts, I could not control whether the U.S. or the U.K. would change their international travel rules before or during my trip. I could be prevented from flying there, or back again. With the rise of the new Delta variant in Britain, I could—in theory—become infected with the virus despite being fully vaccinated. I could not know if I would test out of quarantine in time to do the work in the archives that I was here to accomplish.

On the eve of my flight across the Atlantic, the infamously campy words of Bulwer-Lytton sprang to mind: *It was a dark and stormy night.*[2] And so, like Lionel Verney—the hero of *The Last Man*—I decided to go bravely into that good night. I was prepared for the worst but hoping for the best of comic adventure that only a postapocalyptic research trip can offer.

Quarantine upon arriving in Britain has been an exercise in government-mandated self-contradiction. Although I am required to self-isolate for five days, I have the option of going to a pharmacy or even an outdoor roadside lab to get my Covid testing done. If I elect the latter, how can I avoid *doing things* on the way? Especially tempting things, like buying croissants (and an almond flapjack, and scones, plus a loaf of raisin bread for good measure) at the outdoor market next to the testing site? And getting a rooibos tea and sitting in the sun while writing a paper about Shelley, Stoker, Orwell, Camus and the ties between plague literature and existential philosophy? As I type and sip my tea, I feel like a character in literary cross between a Heller novel and a Sartre play: I'll be spiritually damned if I stay in my flat and wallow in my solitude, and yet I could be legally condemned if I break the nebulous self-quarantine rules by choosing an on-site testing provider from a government-approved list.

The silver lining of my catch-22 quarantine is that I've accomplished a lot of things that would have been impossible under normal circumstances.

First off, I've consumed gallons of herbal tea. I've compulsively hit the trigger on the kettle to keep myself occupied in my studio apartment while I'm not typing or liking random stuff on Twitter.

Next, I surprised the government official who knocked on the door on day four to find me actually self-isolating and wearing a mask to boot. Apparently Big Brother is still alive and well—but conducting in-person, not remote, surveillance.

On the plus side for British manners is that the nice chap asked me politely if I needed "any support" after handing back my passport. *Yes, please*, I thought, *I'd like lots of support*. Company, conversation, and more groceries from the local Sainsburys than my handbag could contain when I last shopped on the way back from my day-two Covid test. And, while you're at it, get me a piping hot espresso-based beverage (with almond, not cow's milk). As much as I love the peculiar U.K. cultural ritual of reanimating the freeze-dried capsules of Nescafé instant coffee with tap water boiled by my oldest British friend, the plastic electric kettle, it's high time for a *grande* American-style latte. *Pronto*.

What I actually say is, "Thank you, sir," as if I'm a clueless character in a Wildean comedy of manners, unaware of the absurdity of my social predicament as the last vaccinated woman under lockdown abroad. After all, I could be fined up to ten thousand pounds if I am caught breaking the redundant rules of self-isolation before I, fully vaccinated, inevitably test out on day five. And I'm pretty sure Notre Dame would not cover that expense.

What I keep telling myself, on a loop—as I sit alone in my studio and write a paper on Shelley's impact on postapocalyptic, existential, and dystopian literature, film, and painting, for five days straight—is that some things in life (and academic research) are worth the risk despite the hardships they entail. At the Hertfordshire archives, I'll see the personal correspondence of the Member of Parliament Bulwer-Lytton, including letters from Mary Shelley's father, the political philosopher William Godwin, as well as the artist John Martin, who began the first major painting based on her pandemic novel in 1826 and exhibited it at the Royal Academy in 1849.[3] At the Weston Library, I'll read five unpublished letters of Bulwer-Lytton to Mary Shelley. I'll visit the British Library to study the history of the production of editions of *The Last Man*. In the rare books and manuscripts department, I'll take a look at a copy of a recently discovered (and still unpublished) 1828 letter of Mary Shelley to the Benthamite and *Westminster Review* editor John Bowring, as well as the original journals of her sister Claire Clairmont, who lived with her and Percy for most of their brief yet epic eight years together.[4]

At the Bodleian Library, I have the astonishing opportunity to examine Mary Shelley's journals, a treasure of British literature, in their original material form. I also have the chance to see her understudied translation of Sophocles's tragedy born of the Peloponnesian War and the Plague of Athens, *Oedipus Rex*.[5] Both of these plague narratives—or stories of disaster and other extreme personal and political hardships—shaped her writing of *The Last Man*.

Thursday, 10 June 2021
Oxford

It feels surreal to have held in my hands the journals that Shelley filled with her private thoughts.[6] The five extant volumes chronicle her emotional and philosophical journey through the sorrow of losing her husband Percy and five children whom she bore, cared for, fostered, or adopted while in a complicated (and open) romantic relationship with him (and her sister Claire, among other women) between 1814 and 1822. Less than eight months after eloping with Percy, Mary gave birth to their premature daughter, Clara, who died two weeks later. Upon seeing the words "find my baby dead" written in her hand in the first volume of her journals, I felt my spiritual connection with Shelley rekindled.[7]

What originally drew me to study her life and writings was her devastating string of experiences with child loss and miscarriage. For I know the pain of miscarriage. And worse, I have shared my parents' nearly unbearable bereavement when my younger brother Kevin died in a fire in 1995.

I was at Cambridge when the news of his death at age twenty-two reached me. I knew something was wrong as soon as I saw my boyfriend waiting for me outside in the public space of the Sidgwick Site as I exited my classical philosophy exam. Since we worked with different faculties toward different degrees, our academic paths had never crossed before. Looking at the sad blankness of his eyes, I could see that the crossroads had somehow found us—like Oedipus on the way to Thebes.

Earlier that morning, I had awakened alone—staring at the low arch of the ceiling in my sixteenth-century college room—haunted by an absolute sense of loss, as if the vast emptiness of the night air had seeped through the open windows and filled me overnight. Something was wrong, but what it was, I could not yet place. A few hours later, when I heard my boyfriend utter the muffled words, as if spoken from afar—*Your brother Kevin is dead*—I felt as though my mind had levitated above my body. I looked down to see myself crumple at the feet of the messenger: staring at myself, wailing. From the relative safety of that fragile mental distance, I could almost grasp the tragedy as it unfolded in two places at once. Only hours earlier in Maine, an old gas stove had exploded and incinerated my brother and his friend while they slept, intoxicated, after partying late into the night. At Cambridge, I fell to the concrete that tied together the brutalist architecture of the Sidgwick Site. I began to absorb the fact that the first morning of my final exams in philosophy would also be my last.

Sitting at a desk at Oxford more than twenty-five years later, I thought of Shelley bravely putting four stark words on paper—*find my baby dead*—on the very same paper I had the privilege to touch. She wrote these four words just hours after she lost her firstborn daughter. In stark contrast, it had taken me over a quarter century to produce this incipit for the story of my brother's death and its enduring impact on my psyche and my family.

With a chain of losses behind her that stood at the border of incomprehension, Shelley's resilience as a writer grew stronger. While she lived with Percy in Italy between 1818 and 1822, she lost four more children and a pregnancy. Fever and dysentery took their one-year-old daughter Clara, near Venice in September 1818. Malaria struck down their three-year-old son William, in Rome in June 1819. About a year later, they learned of the death of baby Elena Adelaide, the infant girl that Percy had arranged for them to adopt and place in the care of a foster family in Naples in early 1819. Almost two years passed before the Shelleys were bereaved of another child whom they helped to care for. Typhus robbed her sister Claire of her five-year-old daughter, Allegra Byron, who died in a Venetian convent in April 1822.

Just a few weeks later, Mary suffered a late-term miscarriage, which would have killed her from the hemorrhaging had not Percy stopped the flow of blood with ice. Tragedy soon hit her again: Percy died in a sailing accident off the coast of Tuscany in July of that year, at the peak of his creative powers—only age twenty-nine. When Percy's body washed onto shore, his friend Edward Trelawny would claim in 1858, the poet's lifeless hand still clutched a copy of Sophocles's tragedies.[8]

I too knew what it was like to lose a young man to the ocean. On the warm and sunny Labor Day weekend of 1999, I was on my way home from presenting a chapter of my dissertation on Shelley's mother Wollstonecraft during my first trip to the annual meeting of the American Political Science Association. As I waited to board the plane with my friend Patricia at the Atlanta airport, I picked up the black handle of a pay phone bolted to the wall. Using my prepaid phone card, I dialed the number for the summer home of my boyfriend Tad's family on Cape Cod. I felt a bit guilty that I had forgotten to call him in all the excitement and activity of the conference. I had been thinking of him and wanted to let him know I was safe and on my way back to Connecticut.

I knew it was too late as soon as I heard the oddly toneless voice of his brother on the other side of the line: *Tad was dead*, at age twenty-eight. The afternoon before, he fell into the shallow water near Nauset beach, in sight of his mother, one of his older brothers, a three-year-old nephew, and a random medical doctor who valiantly tried to revive him. The coroner would later record his death by coronary failure and drowning. His premature heart disease had surfaced as a teenager at boarding school, where he had a long spell of untreated pneumonia after a sailing competition. The resultant infection caused the calcification of his aorta, and permanent damage to his heart.

When I heard of Tad's death through the impersonal medium of an airport payphone, I fell to my knees on the floor. With flashbacks of the loss of my brother racing through my mind, I thought: *It can't be happening again. I can't survive this twice.* My friend knelt beside me and asked me what I needed as I sobbed. With a bleak sense of the absurdity of my situation, I asked for a priest. A chaplain, quite miraculously, appeared. The kind old Black Baptist minister held my hand, looked into my eyes, and prayed for me.

Then he contacted the priest at Yale who had introduced me to Tad at a graduate student retreat, just eighteen months before.

As I boarded the plane with my friend, she gave me a valium to calm me down. Once buckled into my seat, I stared out the window at the bright blue sky dotted with cumulus clouds, wondering how I could have the strength to tell all my friends and family of his death. By the time I returned to New Haven, everyone knew what had happened, but few, including myself, would ever speak of it.

Uncannily, the night before Tad died, I found myself staring at a postcard of Edouard Fournier's famous 1889 painting of Percy Shelley's funeral pyre on the beach at Viareggio. It was on the desk of the young adjunct English professor from Emory who had generously hosted me and my friend during our inaugural political science conference. The professor reminded me that Percy's heart was thought to have been extracted from his blackened corpse by his friend Edward Trelawny.[9] Over two decades would pass before I realized that Percy's heart may have survived the flames due to the same condition—the calcification or hardening of the aorta—that brought Tad to an early grave.

Looking at that postcard, on the evening of 3 September 1999, I felt an eerie and unforgettable sense of déjà vu. I knew then that I would someday write about the Shelleys and their tragedies. Little did I know that I would only begin to do so, almost two decades later, with my unique experiences of personal and familial loss looming far—yet feeling close—in the background.

As I stand at the tail end of my pandemic year, looking back at the Shelleys, I have been given the chance to turn my research on them inside out. After a busy and sometimes overwhelming fifteen months of working from home, teaching on Zoom, and living in seemingly endless quarantine, waiting for a vaccine, it has ironically taken one last and absolute stretch of social isolation to feel a profound emotional connection to my work. In the quiet of my days of monastic study in self-quarantine in London and at the Bodleian Library at Oxford, I finally took the time to confront—in words and with words—the strange parallels between Mary Shelley's life, her plagues, and mine.

Monday, 14 June 2021
Bournemouth

I have arrived, at last, to see the final resting place of Mary Shelley, Mary Wollstonecraft, William Godwin, Percy Florence Shelley, Jane Shelley, and the heart of Percy Bysshe Shelley. I sit down here, in the sun-dappled churchyard, to write. Though the Victorian gothic church sits close to a busy road that leads to the southern seashore, the sheltering trees create a space for solitude, punctuated by cheerful birdsong. I sit on a stairwell, open my laptop, and type with the grave in my view.

For years I had planned this trip. I always balked at the last minute, making up some lame excuse, like: *It's too far, it's too expensive, it'll take too much time away from more important research.* Deep down, however, I felt the poignancy of going to meet this writing family at their grave: so much so that it almost scared me to do it alone.[10]

And yet, today, that's just what I did. I began my journey at the original resting place of the Godwins at Old Saint Pancras churchyard in London. Google maps took me on a circuitous northern route from North Gower Street through Camden Town and back down to Somers Town and the surprisingly leafy area surrounding the Saint Pancras train station: I almost thought I'd never get there to attend morning communion at the chapel.

Once in that picturesque churchyard, I walked past where Wollstonecraft was buried by her husband of five months, the anarchist William Godwin. In the chapel, Mary and William had been quietly married in the spring of 1797, after their secretive courtship of about a year. Both of these radical political thinkers had written publicly about their distrust of the contemporary institution of marriage—in her first novel, *Mary, a Fiction*, and his major political treatise, *An Enquiry Concerning Political Justice.*

A mother with a toddler who had written the most famous work on the future liberation of women in the wake of the French Revolution—*A Vindication of the Rights of Woman*—Wollstonecraft had recently emerged from a devastating breakup with her common-law husband, the American trader Gilbert Imlay. It drove her to attempt suicide twice in the summer of 1795. Most people assumed she was still married to Imlay, because she published a romantic travelogue—based on their final months of correspondence—in early 1796.[11] The fact was that the couple had never formally exchanged vows after they met and fell in love in Paris in the spring of 1793.

And so, when the news broke of the Godwins' nuptials, London society sniggered. Then a real tragedy struck the young family. Wollstonecraft died of a childbirth infection in September 1797. The child survived.

Things eventually came full circle. In July of 1814, that surviving child—Mary Wollstonecraft Godwin—eloped with the married poet Percy Bysshe Shelley after a clandestine meeting at the grave of her mother at Old Saint

Pancras. That surviving child would go on to write *Frankenstein; or, the Modern Prometheus* in 1818 and *The Last Man* in 1826: the twin founding texts of modern political science fiction. After Percy died, Mary kept the remains of his heart, saved from the burnt corpse on the beach in Tuscany. She pressed the "embrowned ashes, now shrunk and withered" in the pages of the Pisa manuscript of Percy's 1821 elegy for John Keats, "Adonais."[12] She wrapped this two-fold poetic relic in a silken shroud and stored it in her writing desk. A year after she died in 1851, it was found by her son and daughter-in-law along with her journals.[13]

Myth has it that Mary wished to be interred with Percy's heart along with the remains of her parents. But the fact is that she requested to be buried with Wollstonecraft and Godwin at Bournemouth, near where her son Percy and his wife built a country home. Accordingly, her parents were removed from the Old Saint Pancras gravesite to be with their daughter after her death from brain cancer. After Mary's sole surviving child Percy Florence died in 1889, he and the residue of his father's heart were buried together in the growing Wollstonecraft-Godwin-Shelley grave by the sea.[14]

A decade later, Lady Jane Shelley was the last woman to join this circle of gothic figures in the churchyard at Bournemouth. In 1893, she had bequeathed the massive collection of papers, artworks, and cultural artifacts of this legendary literary family to major repositories such as the Bodleian Library at Oxford, which received—with a host of limiting conditions—the "original diary kept by Mrs. Shelley."[15] Upon Lady Jane's death in 1899, her estate gave the National Portrait Gallery in London the last portrait of Mary Wollstonecraft done from a live sitting.[16] It was painted by her friend John Opie in the summer of 1797, when she was pregnant with the child who would become an author even more renowned than her parents: Mary Wollstonecraft Godwin Shelley.

It was Jane and Percy Florence's adopted daughter Bessie Florence Gibson who had the final claim to the title of the last woman of the Shelley clan. Her portion of the family papers passed to Lord Abinger and ultimately to the Bodleian Library.[17] Mary Shelley's journals, in my estimation, are the most profound among them.

Examining volume one of the journals at Oxford, I noticed how Mary's handwriting was tight and controlled until she felt overwhelmed with grief and rage at Percy's suspected infidelity with her sister Claire, during the spring of 1815, after the death of their premature baby Clara in March. Mary's words turned loose and unruly, as if they were racing off the page, as she rushed to fill the volume. She wrote as if the intensity of her prose could put an end to the story of her lover and her sister's affair.

We don't know if Claire had a child with Percy, but biographers suspect that she was forced to abort it or to give up the baby for adoption.[18] What we do know is that Mary finished volume one of her journals in a dramatic fashion. With her handwriting growing ever larger, in loops of wild cursive, she brought the record of the tumultuous first year of her elopement with Percy to an abrupt end. Inscribed before eight blank pages, her final words were "I begin a new journal with our regeneration."[19]

Like Frankenstein's Creature, reanimated from the parts of dead bodies, the Shelleys regenerated their relationship from the losses they suffered in the earliest chapter of their short life together. In the summer of 1815, they found a blissful retreat near Windsor Castle, separated from Claire. This part of Mary's journals is now lost—and thought by many to be destroyed by the author herself.[20]

But Mary revived this lost chapter of her journals in fictional form in *The Last Man*. In this roman à clef, she represented Windsor Castle—the home of Adrian, Verney and their court circle—as an enchanted Garden of Eden set in the late twenty-first century. For the bulk of the novel, Shelley depicted the pastoral setting of Windsor Castle as safe from the encroachment of plague, as if Adrian's charismatic leadership and Verney's steadfast friendship could fend off the corrosion of their domestic and political idyll. So, in writing *The Last Man*, Mary returned, full circle, to the place where she had regenerated her love for Percy and bore their beloved son William. She regenerated happiness from loss and betrayal. From this suffering she built a great work of existential and plague literature. During the novel coronavirus pandemic, this neglected novel has been brought back to life by many readers who sought hope in its story of survival during an interminable time of personal and political disaster.

I was one of those readers. Since late February 2020, when I began to write an op-ed on *The Last Man* as an allegory for humane survival of losses of tremendous magnitude, Mary Shelley modeled a way of writing that transforms sorrow into hope.[21] This was her posthumous gift to me, as I honed my own strange and often disorienting sense of existential consciousness in response to Covid-19.

I entered this plague year panicked for the safety of myself and my family, then passed into long stretches of lonely isolation, anger, and despair. Midwinter, I knew I had to make a change: to find hope in what lay beyond the short-term horizon of the present pandemic. Writing a grant proposal and going on this trip was a result of that change.

On the walk to this sunlit grave from the Bournemouth train station, I had an epiphany that almost stopped me in my tracks: *I am not alone anymore*. Over the past year and more, reading Mary Shelley's journals and plague novel as forms of existential philosophy taught me how to feel alive and connected to others again.[22] From her I learned to regenerate myself from the scattered remains of the past into the unknown vista of the future, like the sea shining by the southern shore of England on a hot June afternoon.

NOTES

Preface

Note to Preface: The Preface was originally published as "Mary Shelley Created 'Frankenstein,' and Then a Pandemic" *New York Times*, Opinion, 13 March 2020, accessed 25 May 2023, https://www.nytimes.com/2020/03/13/opinion/mary-shelley-sc-fi-pandemic-novel.html.

1. Peter Daszak, "We Knew Disease X Was Coming: It's Here Now," *New York Times*, 27 February 2020, accessed 10 March 2023, https://www.nytimes.com/2020/02/27/opinion/coronavirus-pandemics.html.

2. Hilary Strang, "Common Life, Animal Life, Equality: 'The Last Man,'" *ELH* 78, no. 2 (2011): 409–31.

Introduction

1. Daphne Gottlieb, *Final Girl* (Soft Skull Press, 2003); Kris Rose, *The Final Girl: How Horror Movies Made Me a Better Feminist* (Portland, OR: Microcosm, 2021); *Scream*, directed by Wes Craven and written by Kevin Williamson (1996; Dimension Films); *Invisible Man*, directed and written by Leigh Whannell (2020; Universal Pictures); *Scream*, directed by Radio Silence and written by James Vanderbilt and Guy Busick (2022; Paramount). See Chapter 3 for my extended analysis of Shelley's legacies for the "final girl" and "invisible man" tropes in horror film and existential literature.

2. Wollstonecraft's husband Godwin noted her death at "20 minutes before 8" on 10 September 1797, then drew four lines of dashes in his diary to mark unspeakable grief. William Godwin, *Diary*, ed. Mark Philp, Bodleian Library, Oxford University, accessed 25 May 2022, http://godwindiary.bodleian.ox.ac.uk/diary/1797-09-10.html.

3. Mary Shelley, *The Journals of Mary Shelley*, ed. Paula R. Feldman and Diana Scott-Kilvert (Baltimore: Johns Hopkins University Press, [1987] 1995), 6; Mary Shelley, *Journals*, vol. I, 1814–15, MS. Abinger d. 27, Bodleian Library, Oxford University. When I cite the original, 1987, two-volume Oxford University Press edition of her *Journals*, I distinguish it from the single-volume 1995 paperback by citing the volume number.

4. Shelley read or recorded Percy reading (sometimes aloud) these classics of epidemic literature and history between 1815 and 1821. See Shelley, *Journals*, 93, 99, 100, 267, 294, 324–25, 325 note 3, 332–43, 341, 347, 350–51. For the couple's "collaborative literary relationship" built on reading thematically connected works alongside one another, see Anna Mercer, *The Collaborative Literary Relationship of Percy Bysshe Shelley and Mary Wollstonecraft Shelley* (London: Routledge, 2019).

5. In addition to their reading of classics of epidemic literature and history, the Shelleys tried yet failed to learn from medical doctors how to treat malaria and dysentery, the infectious diseases that killed their firstborn son William and second-born daughter Clara. They had their

second baby son Percy Florence "vaccined" (probably for smallpox) in 1820, after the devastating losses of their two toddlers during their first year in Italy in 1818–19. See Shelley, *Journals*, 227, 227 note 1, 278, 315.

6. For the story of the children and their deaths, see Chapter 1.

7. [Mary Shelley and Percy Shelley], *History of a Six Weeks' Tour through a part of France, Switzerland, and Holland* (London: T. Hookham and C. and J. Ollier, 1817), 19. Mary Shelley largely rewrote the multisource account of their 1814 elopement journey, based on the first journal volume that she kept with Percy, and to a lesser degree her stepsister Claire's journal. See Jeanne Moskal, ed., "Introductory note," in *The Novels and Selected Works of Mary Shelley*, vol. 8 (London: W. Pickering, 1996), 1–3.

8. Shelley, *Journals*, 433, 440, 452, 456, 497–98.

9. Ibid.

10. Ibid. Word-searching the digital edition of Morton D. Paley's Oxford World's Classics paperback of *The Last Man* yields seven uses of the term "strife" in Shelley's novel. She escalates the word's use as the novel reaches its climax, wherein the solitary narrator Lionel Verney looks back and writes his "History of the Last Man," or his account of how the world seemingly came to be populated by one person. Mary Shelley, *The Last Man*, ed. Morton D. Paley (Oxford: Oxford University Press, [1994] 2008), 81, 285, 358, 371, 376, 381, 403.

11. Mary Shelley, "Principal causes of Misery," MS. Abinger c. 65, folders 12–13, Bodleian Library, Oxford University.

12. Ibid.

13. Almafi-based paper maker Fratelli Galdieri used an undated triple fleur-de-lis, in a sunlike circle, as a watermark, circa 1846. An identical undated watermark can be seen on the first page of "Principal causes of Misery," along with a signature countermark of "FG" enclosed in a diamond shape on the second page. Fleur-de-lis watermarks were common in continental European and Italian papermaking after 1800. See Theo Laurentius and Frans Laurentius, *Italian Watermarks, 1750–1860*, Library of the Written Word 50, The Handpress World 37, series editor Andrew Pettegree (London: Brill, 2016), 20, 126; E. J. Barre, ed., *Dictionary and Encyclopedia of Paper and Paper-Making* (Oxford: Oxford University Press, 1952), 340–46. To rule out that "Principal causes of Misery" is from after 1846, I checked it against the Bodleian's collection of Italian correspondence to Shelley after that year. None of the letters she received from Italy after 1846, including from Lady Mount Cashell's descendants, had similar watermarking. This fact, plus the manuscript's Italian paper and watermarking, allowed me to confidently date "Principal causes of Misery" to the Shelleys' time in Italy. As the expert on Shelleyan watermarks Bruce Barker-Benfield pointed out in "Shelleyan Writing-Materials in the Bodleian Library: A Catalogue of Formats, Papers and Watermarks": "The presence of an Italian watermark in a Shelleyan notebook or loose sheet at once indicates a date later than March 1818." See Tatsuo Tokoo and Bruce Barker-Benfield, eds., *The Bodleian Shelley Manuscripts*, vol. 23 (New York: Routledge, 2004), 13 (hereafter cited as BSM).

14. BSM 23, 13.

15. I compared the handwriting of "Principal causes of Misery" with all five volumes of Mary Shelley's journals (1814–44), her "Greek Studies" notebook (c. 1820–39), and all Bodleian examples of her writing and correspondence from her final year in Italy (1822–23). The most unusual element of the handwriting in "Principal causes of Misery" is its uppercase lettering, but I found many examples of overlap with Shelley's use of capital letters from this period of mourning (including the capital M in her standard signature and the capital M in "Misery"). I also compared the anonymous manuscript with the handwriting of her correspondents from 1822–23. Even Lady Mount Cashell, whose handwriting has some commonalities with the writer of "Principal causes of Misery," did not prove to show as much overlap in lettering (capital or lower case) as the widowed Shelley. I concluded that the text quite possibly is in the distinctive,

grieving hand of Shelley—as in, reflective of her "mental exhaustion" and "desperate" situation as a widow without "any prospect of financial support from Sir Timothy Shelley." See Alan M. Weinberg, "Introduction," BSM 22, part ii, 39–40.

16. Lady Mount Cashell (Margaret Mason), a medical doctor, used the term "mental health" in a letter to the grieving Shelley, dated 17 November 18[22]. See MS. Abinger c. 46, folders 24–25, Bodleian Library, Oxford University.

17. Janet Todd, *Daughters of Ireland: The Rebellious Kingsborough Sisters and the Making of a Modern Nation* (New York: Penguin, 2005).

18. Eileen Hunt Botting, "An Introduction to *Original Stories*, or, Wollstonecraft between *Emile* and *Frankenstein*," for the *Women in Print* series/ShE-book digital edition of Mary Wollstonecraft's *Original Stories from Real Life* (1791), with illustrations by William Blake (Urbana-Champaign: University of Illinois Press, 2016), v–lvi.

19. Lady Mount Cashell (Margaret Mason), *Advice to Young Mothers on the Physical Education of Children, by a Grandmother* (London: Longman, Hurst, Rees, Orme, and Brown, 1823).

20. Margaret Mason to Mary Shelley, 17 November 1822, MS. Abinger c. 46, fols. 24–25.

21. Margaret Mason to Mary Shelley, 25 February 1823, MS. Abinger c. 46, fols. 50–51.

22. MS. Abinger c. 65, fols. 12–13.

23. See Chapter 2 for an extended study of the movement of her Italian papers to England in 1823.

24. Shelley, *Journals*, 428, 433.

25. MS. Abinger c. 65, fols. 12–13.

26. Mary Shelley, "List of books and quotes from Cicero and Goethe," MS. Abinger c. 65, fol. 10.

27. The Bodleian holds the following black-edged letters from Shelley to her friends: Mary Shelley to Maria Gisborne, 17–20 September 1822 (MS. Shelley c. 1, fol. 527–28) and 3–6 May 1823 (MS. Shelley adds. c. 6, fol. 7–8); Mary Shelley to Edward Trelawny, 31 January 1823, 5 April 1823, and 10 May 1823 (MS. Shelley adds. c. 6, fols. 3–4, 5–6, 9–10), and 22 March 1824 (MS. Shelley adds. c. 6); Mary Shelley to Jane Williams, 19–20 February 1823, 7 March 1823, 10 April 1823, and 31 May 1823 (MS. Abinger c. 46, fols. 44–45, 56–57, 65–66, 80–81); Mary Shelley to Leigh Hunt, 29 July 1824 and 22 August 1824 (MS. Shelley adds. c. 6, fols. 27–28, 29–30); Mary Shelley to Marianne Hunt, 10 October 1824 (MS. Shelley adds. c. 6, fols. 31–32). Shelley appears to have used mourning stationery acquired in Italy from September 1822 to May 1823 with her close friends and fellow mourners of Percy, Maria Gisborne, Jane Williams, and Edward Trelawny, then resumed the practice from March 1824 to October 1824 with Trelawny and the Hunts while in London. The mourning stationery that she used in London had a similar style of dusted-black edges, but was of a thicker stock than the typically thinner Italian paper. Bruce Barker-Benfield pointed out in "Shelleyan Writing-Materials in the Bodleian Library" that "some of those [papers] used by MWS for letters during the year after PBS's death have black edges, evidently as a sign of mourning . . . not the broad mourning-borders familiar in Victorian letters, but just the extreme edges, very easy to miss, where the black pigment will have been applied around a block or ream of loose paper before its sale as bilfolia." See BSM 23, 13. The BSM editors did not look beyond Mary Shelley's time in Italy (up to July 1823), so they did not record her black-edged letters to Trelawny and the Hunts from 1824, while she was living in London.

28. MS. Shelley c. 1, fol. 527–28.

29. MS. Shelley adds. c. 6, fols. 3–4, 5–6, 9–10.

30. Edward Dowden, *The Life of Percy Bysshe Shelley*, vol. 2 (London: Kegan Paul, [1886] 1887), 533–34.

31. Betty T. Bennett, ed., *The Letters of Mary Wollstonecraft Shelley*, vol. 1 (Baltimore: Johns Hopkins, 1980), 297. Hereafter cited as *Letters*.

32. William Godwin to Mary Shelley, 14–18 February 1823. MS. Abinger c. 46, fols. 42–43.

33. *Mounseer Nongtongpaw: or, The Discoveries of John Bull in a Trip to Paris, illustrated with Beautiful Copper Plates* (London: Published at the Juvenile Library, 41, Skinner Street, Snow Hill, 1808). Godwin reissued it in 1823. A copy of the 1823 edition is in the Stanford University Library. I examined the 1808 first edition at the British Library.

34. John Croker, "From the Quarterly Review (January 1818)" and "Edinburgh Review (March 1818)," in Mary Shelley, *Frankenstein: The 1818 Text, Contexts, Criticism*, ed. J. Paul Hunter, 2nd ed. (New York: W. W. Norton, 2012), 346–47; 351 (hereafter cited as *Frankenstein*).

35. [Mary Shelley], *Frankenstein, ou Le Prométhée moderne*, [trans. Jules Saladin] (Paris: Chez Corréard, Libraire, 1821).

36. Mary Wollstonecraft Shelley, *Frankenstein: or, the Modern Prometheus. In 2 Volumes. A New Edition* (London: G. and W. B. Whittaker, 1823).

37. Mary Wollstonecraft Shelley, *Mathilda*, ed. Elizabeth Nitchie, in *Studies in Philology* 56 (October 1959): i–104.

38. William Godwin to Mary Shelley, 14–18 February 1823, MS. Abinger c. 46, fols. 42–43.

39. As far as I am aware, no other scholar has cited this reference to "Nontonpaw" in Abinger c. 65, fol. 10, written in Mary Shelley's hand sometime after September 1822. Clustered with two of her other book titles, it suggests that the widowed Shelley considered it to be one of her own works and/or perhaps something she wanted to revise and reissue.

40. *Mounseer Nongtongpaw* (1808). The inner title page of the first edition held at the British Library has the subtitle "a new version." This Godwin-produced edition is entirely poetry, not prose. According to Jeanne Moskal, Shelley's juvenile "scribble"—which she surmises was in prose, contra Emily Sunstein who inferred it was in verse—probably shaped this new published poetic version based on Charles Dibdin's 1796 song "Mounseer Nongtongpaw." See *The Novels and Selected Works of Mary Shelley*, vol. 8, appendix 2, "'Mounseer Nongtongpaw': Verses Formerly Attributed to Mary Shelley."

41. Ibid.

42. Peter and Iona Opie, *A Nursery Companion* (Oxford: Oxford University Press, 1980). The Opies attributed *Nongtongpaw* to Mary Shelley based on a rediscovered letter of William Godwin in which he offered his daughter's "scribble" on Dibdin's 1796 song as a model to a writer commissioned to rewrite the verses for his children's press.

43. Shelley, *Journals*, 476–77, 486.

44. Ibid., 476–77.

45. Ibid., 486.

46. BSM 23, 13, 124–27.

47. BSM 23, 13.

48. MS. Shelley adds. c. 6, fols. 27–28, 29–30, 31–32.

49. John Franklin, *Narrative of a Journey to the Polar Sea* (London: J. Murray, 1823).

50. *Kent's Original Directory, 1823: Being an Alphabetical List of More Than 18,000 Merchants & Traders of London* (London: Henry-Kent Causton, 1823), 101.

51. As shown on a Fall 1825 letter from Claire Clairmont in Moscow to Jane Williams in London, in which she asks her friend to prompt her stepsister Shelley to reply to a recent letter, the address was "Chez Monsieur Lenhold, Marchand de Musique a Moscow." See Florence A. Thomas Marshall (Mrs. Julian Marshall), eds., *The Life and Letters of Mary Wollstonecraft Shelley*, vol. 2 (Frankfurt am Main: Outlook Verlag GmbH, [1889] 2020), 105.

52. Ibid.

53. Shelley, *Letters*, vol. 1, 504.

54. Shelley, *Journals*, 447. Mary Shelley, "Life of Shelley," BSM 22, part ii, 266–87; MS. Shelley adds. c. 5, fols. 113–18.

55. BSM 23, 13. All Italian papers in the Bodleian Shelley manuscripts are almost certainly from the period 1818–23 (unless part of a later, dated correspondence with friends in Italy).

Mary Shelley preserved some of her Italian papers (including "Principal causes of Misery" and her black-edged booklet on which she wrote "Last Man") and passed them down to her son Percy Florence and daughter-in-law Jane, who in turn arranged for their receipt by the Bodleian.

56. See the introduction in Eileen Hunt Botting, *Artificial Life after Frankenstein* (Philadelphia: University of Pennsylvania Press, 2021).

57. Judith Butler, *What World is This? A Pandemic Phenomenology* (New York: Columbia University Press, 2022), 26.

58. Mary Shelley, *The Last Man*, in *The Novels and Selected Works of Mary Shelley*, ed. Jane Blumberg with Nora Crook (London: Pickering & Chatto, [1996] 2001), vol. 4, 139. Hereafter cited as *The Last Man*. This was my standard edition for citation of the novel. When I cite the digitized Oxford World's Classics edition, I distinguish it by citing Paley as editor.

59. Ibid., 150–51.

60. Ibid., 183.

61. Octavia E. Butler, *Clay's Ark* (New York: Open Road Media, 2012); Octavia E. Butler, *Earthseed: The Complete Series* (New York: Open Road Media, 2017).

62. Ibid.

63. Uriel Abulof, *The Mortality and Morality of Nations* (Cambridge, 2015), 3, 23.

64. Ibid.

65. Ibid.

66. Ibid.

67. Ibid.

68. Shelley, *Journals*, 428.

69. Ibid., 430.

70. Ibid., 488.

71. MS. Abinger c. 65, fol. 10. Shelley, *Journals*, 486 note 2; Cicero, *De Finibus Bonorum et Malorum*, xiv. 46, trans. H. Rackham (Cambridge, MA: Loeb Classical Library 1961), 135.

72. Ibid.

73. Ibid.

74. Shelley, *Journals*, 486.

75. Ibid.

76. Ibid.

77. Ibid.

78. Ibid., 476.

79. Ibid., 487.

80. Ibid., 488. I have maintained the original spelling and style of her manuscripts without correction.

81. Ibid.

82. Ibid.

83. Ibid.

84. Ibid.

85. Ibid.

86. The original second journal book of Mary Shelley is missing (1815–16), probably due to either Mary Shelley or her heirs (Percy Florence and Jane Shelley) destroying it to protect the family from scandal related to information it may have contained pertaining to Percy's free-loving infidelities, including with her stepsister Claire, who may have been pregnant in 1815 with his child. The Bodleian Library has the five extant volumes in the Abinger papers: (I) 1814–15, Abinger d. 27; (II) 1816–1819, Abinger d. 28; (III) 1819–1822, Abinger d. 29; (IV) 1822–1826 ("The Journal of Sorrow"), Abinger d. 30; and (V) 1825/26–44, Abinger d. 31. Albert Camus, *La Peste*, Kindle edition (Éditions Feltrin, [1947] 2021).

87. Albert Camus, *The Plague* (New York: Knopf Doubleday, 2012); Albert Camus, *The Stranger* (New York: Knopf Doubleday, 2012).

88. Eileen Hunt Botting, "Mary Shelley's 'Romantic Spinozism,'" *History of European Ideas* 47, no.1 (2019): 1125–42; Shelley, *Journals*, 386, 386 note 2, 388.

89. See Chapter 2 for a study of her translation of *Oedipus Rex* and my redating of her use of her "Greek Studies" notebook in which it is written from late 1820 to 1839.

90. Mary Shelley, translation of Sophocles's *Oedipus* and *Philoctetes* in her "Greek Studies" notebook, c. 1820–39, MS. Abinger e. 52, and Mary Shelley, translation of Euripides's *Alcestis,* Shelley adds. c. 5, fols. 141–45, 138–40, Bodleian Library, Oxford University.

91. See Chapter 2.

92. Shelley, *Journals*, 452, 511.

93. Hunt Botting, "Introduction," *Artificial Life After Frankenstein.*

94. Mary Shelley, "The Invisible Girl," in *Mary Shelley: Collected Tales and Stories, with Original Engravings*, ed. Charles E. Robinson (Baltimore: Johns Hopkins University Press, 1976), 190–202.

95. For her eerie reminiscence of her conception of *Frankenstein* while having a waking nightmare at the Villa Diodati on the moonlit shore of Lake Geneva in June 1816, see Mary Shelley, "Introduction to *Frankenstein*, Third Edition (1831)," in Mary Shelley, *Frankenstein*, 267–75.

96. See volume 2, "Lived Experience," in Simone de Beauvoir, *The Second Sex*, trans. Constance Borde and Sheila Malovany-Chevallier (New York: Vintage, 2011), 276.

97. Shelley, *Journals*, 476.

98. Ibid., 476–77.

99. Shelley, *The Last Man*, 5.

100. Shelley, *Journals*, 242. MS. Abinger d. 28.

101. Shelley, *The Last Man*, 462.

102. H. G. Wells, *The War of the Worlds*, Kindle edition (Minneapolis, MN: First Avenue Editions, 2017); M. P. Shiel, *The Purple Cloud*, Kindle edition (Lulu.com, 2014); George Orwell, *Nineteen Eighty-Four*, ed. John Bowen (Oxford: Oxford University Press, 2021); Richard Matheson, *I Am Legend*, Kindle edition (New York: Rosetta Books, 2011).

103. Joanna Russ, *The Female Man*, Kindle edition (Open Road Media, 2018); Margaret Atwood, *The Handmaid's Tale and The Testaments Box Set* (Toronto: McClelland & Stewart, 2020); Butler, *Earthseed*; Margaret Atwood, *Oryx and Crake* (New York: Knopf Doubleday, 2004); Margaret Atwood, *The Year of the Flood* (New York: Anchor, 2010); Margaret Atwood, *MaddAddam*, vol. 3 (New York: Knopf Doubleday, 2013); Emily St. John Mandel, *Station Eleven* (New York: Knopf Doubleday, 2014); Emily St. John Mandel, *Sea of Tranquility* (New York: Knopf Doubleday, 2022); Sandra Newman, *The Men* (New York: Grove Atlantic, 2022).

104. See "The Literary Gazette and Journal of Belles Lettres, Arts, Sciences &c' (Feb. 1826)," *Romantic Circles* (blog), 1 March, 1998, http://romantic-circles.org/reference/chronologies/mschronology/reviews/lgrev.html.

105. William Godwin, *Morning Chronicle* review of *The Last Man*, 24 March 1826, MS. Abinger c. 31, fol. 68; "The Last Man!" *The Morning Chronicle* (London), 24 March 1826, page 1.

106. Godwin, *Diary*, 17 March 1826.

107. Ibid., 20 March 1826.

108. "The Last Man!" *The Morning Chronicle* (London).

109. Ibid.

110. Godwin, *Diary*, 10–13 January 1826.

111. "The Last Man!" *The Morning Chronicle* (London).

112. Ibid.

113. Ibid.

114. Godwin, *Diary*, 20–26 March 1826.

115. Sir Walter Scott, "From Blackwood's Edinburgh Magazine (March 1818)," in Shelley, *Frankenstein*, 348–66.

116. William Heath, artist, "The Last Woman," color cartoon and editorial commentary satirizing Mary Shelley's *The Last Man* in *The Northern Looking Glass*, vol. 1, no. 1, May 1826, 2–3.

117. Ibid.

118. Ibid.

119. Ibid.

120. Ibid.

121. Shelley, *Letters*, vol. 1, 416–17.

122. Shelley, *The Last Man*, 362–64.

123. Charles Robinson, "Introduction," in *Mary Shelley: Collected Tales and Stories, with Original Engravings*, ed. Charles E. Robinson (Baltimore: Johns Hopkins University Press, 1976), xii–xiii.

124. Mary W. Shelley, "The Invisible Girl," in *The Keepsake for 1833*, ed. Frederic Mansel Reynolds (London: Longman, Rees, Orme, Brown, Green, and Longman, 1832), 221.

125. Shelley, trans, *Alcestis*, MS. Shelley adds. c. 5, fols. 141–45, 138–40.

126. Shelley, *Journals*, 430–31.

127. Shelley, "Introduction to *Frankenstein*, Third Edition (1831)," 268.

128. Shelley, *Frankenstein*, 27–28.

129. John Croker, "From the Quarterly Review (January 1818)" and "Edinburgh Review (March 1818)," in Shelley, *Frankenstein*, 346–47; 351.

130. Mary W. Shelley, *Frankenstein*, 2 vols. (London: G. and W. B. Whittaker, 1823).

131. Shelley, "Introduction to *Frankenstein*, Third Edition (1831)," 268. *The Last Man* was semi-anonymously published by Henry Colburn in London in 1826 in two editions, as "by the author of *Frankenstein*" due to an ongoing financial conflict with her father-in-law who did not approve of her using the Shelley name in her publications. Another anonymous edition by the English-language publisher and bookseller in Paris, Galignani, appeared in 1826 with "the author of *Frankenstein*" on the title page. In 1827, an excerpt of the 1826 novel saw translation into French in Geneva. In 1833, a joint rerelease of *Frankenstein* and *The Last Man* by the Philadelphia publisher Carey, Lea & Blanchard had her name as "Mary W. Shelly" (sic) on the title pages, but also added "the author of *The Last Man*" to the former book and "the author of *Frankenstein*" to the latter book, which suggests that she was known internationally as the author of both groundbreaking works of scientific romance, and that their joint release would enhance sales of each of them. *Frankenstein* went on to be published in many editions and languages from its first foreign-language (French) edition of 1821, with "Mary W. Shelley," "Mary W. Shelly" (sic), or "Mary Wollstonecraft Shelley" as the author, while *The Last Man* was not reissued until the twentieth century. Muriel Spark introduced the first scholarly edition of Shelley's *The Last Man* for Falcon Press in London in 1954 but only a handful of review copies were printed before the press collapsed (one is held at Oxford [Bodleian 256 e.16843 (v.1)], with a handwritten note from the publisher, stating it is one of a half dozen copies). The University of Nebraska press produced the second scholarly edition of Shelley's *The Last Man* in 1965. See Chapter 3 for my analysis of Muriel Spark's recovery of Shelley's *The Last Man* as part of my tracing Shelley's legacies for "the last (wo)man" and "invisible girl" themes in feminist literature and film. For the early French translation history of Shelley's works, see Anne Rouhette, "Jules Saladin's 1821 Translation of *Frankenstein*," in *Mary Shelley and Europe: Essays in Honor of Jean de Palacio*, ed. Antonella Braida (Modern Humanities Research Association, 2020), 20.

132. Shelley, "Introduction to *Frankenstein*, Third Edition (1831)," 268.

133. See Chapter 3.

134. Richard Garnett, ed., *Tales and Stories by Mary Wollstonecraft Shelley—Now First Collected, with an Introduction by Richard Garnett* (London: William Paterson & Co., 1891), ix;

H. G. Wells, *The Invisible Man*, Kindle edition (New York: Atria Books, 2014); *The Invisible Man*, directed by James Whale and written by R.C. Sherriff (1933; Universal Pictures); Richard Wright, *The Man Who Lived Underground* (New York: HarperPerennial, 2021); Ralph Ellison, *Invisible Man* (New York: Vintage, 1995).

135. Muriel Spark, *Robinson* (New York: New Directions, 2003); Lorraine Hansberry, *A Raisin in the Sun*, Kindle edition (Tingle Books, [1959] 2021); Daphne Gottlieb, *Final Girl*; Kris Rose, "The Final Girl: How Horror Movies Made Me a Better Feminist"; *Scream* (1996); *Invisible Man* (2020); *Scream* (2022). See Chapter 3 for my extended analysis of Shelley's legacies for the "final girl" and "invisible man" tropes in film and existential literature.

136. Shelley referred to her own life as a "tale of horror and despair" in 1827. Shelley, *Journals*, 503.

137. The *New York Times* coronavirus tracker, summer 2022.

138. The director and translator Brian Doerries brought *Oedipus Rex*, *Philoctetes*, and other Greek tragedies to mass virtual audiences during the Covid-19 pandemic through innovative use of Zoom technology. See his introduction to Sophocles, *Oedipus Trilogy*, trans. Brian Doerries (New York: Vintage, 2021).

139. Henry R. Plomer, "Literature of the Plague," *The Library* 1-3, no. 1 (1 January 1891): 213, https://doi.org/10.1093/library/s1-3.1.209.

140. Ibid., 211.

141. Ibid.

142. Ibid., 221.

143. For her direct references to reading these sources in plague literature, see Shelley, *Journals*, 93, 99, 100, 267, 294, 324–25, 325 note 3, 332–43, 341, 347, 350–51. For some of her important literary allusions to these texts, see Shelley, *The Last Man*, 6 (Genesis), 176 (Thucydides, Lucretius, Ovid), 203 (Defoe, Brown), 209 (Boccaccio, Defoe, Brown), 261 (Wilson), 330 (Sophocles), 363 (Homer, Defoe).

144. Ibid.

145. Mary Shelley, "Boccaccio," in *Mary Shelley's 'Literary Lives' and Other Writings*, ed. Tilar J. Mazzeo, vol. 1 (London: Pickering & Chatto, 2002), 60; Mary Shelley, "Reviews and Essays: Giovanni Villani," in *The Novels and Selected Works of Mary Shelley*, vol. 2, *Matilda, Mythological Dramas, and Reviews & Essays*, ed. Pamela Clemit (London, England: Pickering & Chatto, 1996), 128–39.

146. Camus, *The Plague*.

147. René Girard, "The Plague in Literature and Myth," *Texas Studies in Literature and Language* 15, no. 5 (1974): 833–50.

148. Shelley, *The Last Man*, 183.

149. Justin Clemens, "Morbus Anglicus; or, Pandemic, Panic, Pandaemonium," *Crisis & Critique* 7, no. 3 (2020): 41–60; Shelley, *Journals*, 220.

150. Clemens, "Morbus Anglicus," 47–48.

151. Ibid., 43, 45.

152. Ibid., 50.

153. Ibid., 52.

154. Shelley, *The Last Man*, 183. In March 1820, Shelley noted Percy's reading Hobbes's *Leviathan*, sometimes, it seems, "aloud" to her. See Shelley, *Journals*, 311–13, 345. The epigraph for *Frankenstein* is drawn from Book 10 of Milton's *Paradise Lost*: "Did I request thee, Maker, from my clay/ To mould me man? Did I solicit thee/ From darkness to promote me?" Shelley, *Frankenstein*, 2.

155. Shelley, *Frankenstein*, 69, 102, 119.

156. Ibid., 35.

157. Shelley, *The Last Man*, 176.

158. Ibid.

159. Jean-Baptiste Cousin de Granville, *The Last Man*, trans. I. F. Clarke and M. Clarke (Middletown, CT: Wesleyan University Press, 2003).

160. Catherine Redford, "Friendship and Community in Last Man Literature, 1806–1833" (PhD diss., University of Bristol, 2013). Redford shows that the public debate over whether Campbell's "The Last Man" plagiarized Byron's "Darkness" peaked in British literary periodicals in 1825, the year that Mary Shelley was completing her novel *The Last Man* while living in London.

161. Shelley, *Letters*, vol. 3, 402.

162. Godwin, *Diary*, 10 January 1826.

163. See Chapter 3.

164. Shelley, *The Last Man*, 144.

165. Ibid., 183.

166. Ibid., 175.

167. Ibid., 250.

168. Ibid., 315.

169. Ibid., 144.

170. Ibid., 139.

171. Mike Davis, *The Monster Enters: COVID-19, Avian Flu, and the Plagues of Capitalism* (New York: OR Books, 2020).

172. Chris Baldick, *In Frankenstein's Shadow: Myth, Monstrosity, and Nineteenth-Century Writing* (Oxford: Clarendon Press, 1990), 132, 137.

173. Harold Bloom, *Take Arms Against a Sea of Troubles: The Power of the Reader's Mind over a Universe of Death* (New Haven: Yale University Press, 2020), 183.

174. Percy Bysshe Shelley, "The Mask of Anarchy" (1819), KNARF Project, University of Pennsylvania, accessed 28 November 2020, http://knarf.english.upenn.edu/PShelley/anarchy.html.

175. Ibid.

176. Elsie B. Michie, "Frankenstein and Marx's Theories" (1990), KNARF Project, University of Pennsylvania, accessed 28 November 2020, http://knarf.english.upenn.edu/Articles/michiel.html.

177. Shelley, *Frankenstein*, 31, 33, 34, 35, 36.

178. Michie, "Frankenstein and Marx's Theories."

179. Karl Marx, "The Fragment on Machines," *The Grundrisse* (1857–58), accessed 28 November 2020, 706, https://thenewobjectivity.com/pdf/marx.pdf.

180. Marshall Berman, *All That Is Solid Melts into Air: The Experience of Modernity* (London: Verso, 1983), 101.

181. Mike Davis, *The Monster at Our Door: The Global Threat of the Avian Flu* (New York: New Press, 2005); Mike Davis, *The Monster at Our Door: The Global Threat of the Avian Flu*, revised and expanded edition (New York: Macmillan, 2006).

182. Davis, *The Monster Enters*, 87–100.

183. Natalie Porter, *Viral Economies: Bird Flu Experiments in Vietnam* (Chicago: University of Chicago Press, 2019), 2.

184. Porter, *Viral Economies*, 1–2.; Davis, *The Monster Enters*, 120–23.

185. Ibid.

186. Davis, "Preface: *The Monster Enters*," *The Monster at Our Door*, 44–47.

187. John M. Barry, *The Great Influenza: The Story of the Deadliest Pandemic in History* (New York: Penguin, 2004), 171.

188. Ibid., 91. Centers for Disease Control and Prevention, "1918 Pandemic Influenza Historic Timeline," 18 April 2019, https://www.cdc.gov/flu/pandemic-resources/1918-commemoration/pandemic-timeline-1918.htm.

189. Davis, *The Monster Enters*, 53.

190. Daszak, "We Knew Disease X Was Coming." Davis cites Daszak's article with David Morens and Jeffery Taubenberger, "Escaping Pandora's Box: Another Novel Coronavirus," *New England Journal of Medicine* 382 (2 April 2020) in his introduction to *The Monster Enters*, 3, 181.

191. Davis, *The Monster Enters*, 180.

192. See the subtitle of Davis, *The Monster Enters: COVID-19, Avian Flu, and the Plagues of Capitalism*.

193. Davis, *The Monster Enters*, 119, 122.

194. Ibid.

195. Daniel Defoe, *A Journal of the Plague Year: Being Observations Or Memorials of the Most Remarkable Occurrences, as Well Publick as Private, Which Happened in London During the Last Great Visitation in 1665* (London: E. Nutt, 1722).

196. Donald M. Hassler and Clyde Wilcox, eds., *Political Science Fiction* (Columbia: University of South Carolina Press, 1997).

197. Yasmin Solomonescu reads the plague in *The Last Man* as both an "allegory" for the dangerous psychological contagion of "fascination" and a literal "cataclysm with far-reaching geopolitical implications—a symptom of Britain's colonial rule in an increasingly global economy of goods and diseases." See Solomonescu, "Mary Shelley's Fascinations: *The Last Man*," *Modern Philology* 114, no. 3 (2017): 707.

198. Shelley, *The Last Man*, 37, 183, 194, 247.

199. Ibid., 275.

200. Ibid., 37, 183, 194, 247.

201. "England–The Seaside—The Resting Place of Godwin—Mary Wollstonecraft and Mrs. Shelley," *National Anti-Slavery Standard* (New York), 3 October 1868. The correspondent based the description of Mary Shelley as a "nice-looking old lady" on contemporary remembrances of her in the Bournemouth region where she and her parents were buried and her son Percy Florence and his wife Jane still lived and entertained.

202. Muriel Spark, *Child of Light: A Reassessment of Mary Wollstonecraft Shelley* (Hadleigh: Tower Bridge, 1951), 195–230.

203. Harold Bloom, "Frankenstein, or the New Prometheus," *Partisan Review* 32, no. 4 (1965): 613–16; Harold Bloom, "Poets' Meeting in the Heyday of their Youth," *New York Times Book Review*, 15 February 1970: 281; Mary Shelley, *Frankenstein; or, the Modern Prometheus*, ed. Harold Bloom (New York: New American Library, 1965); Harold Bloom, "Editor's Note" and "Introduction" in *Mary Shelley*, ed. Harold Bloom (New York: Chelsea House, 1985), i, 1–10.

204. Hunt Botting, "Interlude," *Artificial Life After Frankenstein*.

205. Stephen King, *Danse Macabre* (London: Hodder, [1981] 2006), 65–67. Ralph Ellison alludes in the second sentence of the fictional prologue to *Invisible Man* to both Poe and Wells's version of the "Invisible Man" made famous at the movies.

206. Thomas Edison's studio produced a short silent film based on *Frankenstein* in 1910. For Wollstonecraft's international reception in art and literature since the late eighteenth century, see Eileen Hunt Botting, ed., *Portraits of Wollstonecraft*, 2 vols. (London: Bloomsbury, 2021).

207. For the ongoing reception of *Frankenstein* in the popular press on technology and politics, see Hunt Botting, *Artificial Life After Frankenstein*. See also Elizabeth Young's *Black Frankenstein: The Making of an American Metaphor* (New York: NYU Press, 2008).

208. Atwood, *MaddAddam*, 265.

209. Alison McQueen, *Political Realism in Apocalyptic Times* (Cambridge: Cambridge University Press, 2018), 195–97.

210. Douglas Adams, *Life, the Universe and Everything* (London: Pan, 1982).

Chapter 1

1. Shelley, *Journals*, 68. Ellen Moers drew attention to this passage in Shelley's first journal book and made its exegesis a central feature of feminist literary criticism on the psychological origins of *Frankenstein*. See Ellen Moers, *Literary Women* (New York: Doubleday, 1976).

2. Shelley, *Journals*, 226–27.

3. Ibid., 293.

4. Ibid., 443.

5. Leigh Hunt to M. W. Shelley, [25–27] July 1819, in *Shelley and His Circle, 1773–1822*, edited by Donald H. Reiman (Cambridge: Harvard University Press, 1973), vol. 6, 845. For Hunt in the context of British Romanticism, see Greg Kucich, "Keats, Shelley, Byron, and the Hunt Circle," in *The Cambridge Companion to English Literature, 1740–1830*, eds. Thomas Keymer and Jon Mee (Cambridge: Cambridge University Press, 2004), 263–79.

6. Leigh Hunt to M. W. Shelley, [25–27] July 1819; Shelley, *Journals*, 503.

7. Shelley to Leigh Hunt, 24 September 1819, *Letters*, vol. 1, 108.

8. Shelley, *Journals*, 249 note 3.

9. Ibid., 409 note 4.

10. Ibid., 412 note 1, 429.

11. Ibid., 432.

12. See Chapter 2.

13. MS. Abinger e. 52, 3.

14. Shelley, *The Last Man*, 183.

15. William Godwin, *Enquiry Concerning Political Justice, and Its Influence on Morals and Happiness* (London: G. G. and J. Robinson, 1798), 186, 189, 272; Mary Wollstonecraft, *An Historical and Moral View of the Origin and Progress of the French Revolution: And the Effect It Has Produced in Europe, Volume the First* (London: J. Johnson, 1795), 69, 296, 487; Leigh Hunt to M. W. Shelley, [25-27] July 1819.

16. Sophie Smith, "The Language of 'Political Science' in Early Modern Europe," *Journal of the History of Ideas* 80, no. 2 (April 2019): 203–26.

17. Mary Wollstonecraft, *A Vindication of the Rights of Woman*, ed. Eileen Hunt Botting (New Haven, CT: Yale University Press, 2014), 31, 43; Godwin, *Enquiry Concerning Political Justice*, 4, 106, 108.

18. Shelley, *Journals*, 85–102.

19. Christopher Brooke, "The Last Man in Lisbon," *The Political Science Reviewer* 46, no. 2 (2022): 364–76.

20. Jean-Jacques Rousseau, "Lettre à Voltaire sur la Providence" (1756), Wikisource, accessed 23 November 2020, https://fr.wikisource.org/wiki/Lettre_%C3%A0_Voltaire_sur_la_Providence.

21. Eric Nelson, *The Theology of Liberalism: Political Philosophy and the Justice of God* (Cambridge, MA: Belknap, 2019), 6.

22. "Ami, tu as vaincu. Je ne suis point à l'épreuve de tant d'amour; ma résistance es épuisée" (part 3, letter 15). Jean-Jacques Rousseau, *Julie, ou La nouvelle Héloïse*, ed. Michel Launay (Paris: Garnier-Flammarion, 1967), 245.

23. Shelley, *Journals*, 90, 96, 100, 109–10.

24. Shelley, *Letters*, vol. 1, 1 note 1.

25. Mika Aaltola, *Understanding the Politics of Pandemic Scares: An Introduction to Global Politosomatics* (London: Routledge, 2012); Bill Gates, *How to Prevent the Next Pandemic* (New York: Knopf, 2022), ch. 2; and the preface in Danielle Allen, *Democracy in the Time of Coronavirus* (Chicago: University of Chicago Press, 2022).

26. Shelley, *Journals*, 226–27; Shelley to Maria Gisborne, [13] September 1818, *Letters*, vol. 1, 79.

27. Shelley to Leigh Hunt, 6 April 1819; Shelley to Maria Gisborne, 11 May 1819; Shelley to Maria Gisborne, 30 May 1819; and with Claire Clairmont, Shelley to Maria Gisborne, 3–5 June 1819, *Letters*, vol. 1, 91, 97–100; Shelley, *Journals*, 264–65.

28. Shelley to to Leigh Hunt, 6 April 1819 and Shelley to Maria Gisborne, 26 April 1819, *Letters*, vol. 1, 91, 94.

29. Shelley to Maria Gisborne, 9 April 1819 and Shelley to Maria Gisborne, 26 April 1819, *Letters*, vol. 1, 93, 94.

30. Shelley to Maria Gisborne, 9 April 1819, *Letters*, vol. 1, 93.

31. Shelley to Marianne Hunt, 29 June 1819, *Letters*, vol. 1, 101.

32. Ibid.

33. Ibid., 13.

34. Ibid.

35. Ibid.

36. [Mary Shelley and Percy Shelley], *History of a Six Weeks' Tour*, 19.

37. Shelley, *Journals*, 27.

38. *Journals of Claire Clairmont*, MS 394 (vol. 1), British Library.

39. Shelley, *Journals*, 93.

40. Ibid., 91.

41. Ibid., 303.

42. Homer, *Iliad, Volume I: Books 1–12*, trans. A. T. Murray, revised by William F. Wyatt, Loeb Classical Library 170 (Cambridge, MA: Harvard University Press, 1924), book 1, line 61.

43. Thucydides, *The Peloponnesian War*, trans. Martin Hammond, ed. P. J. Rhodes (Oxford: Oxford University Press, 2009), book 2, 96–104.

44. Shelley, *The Last Man*, 176.

45. Percy Shelley, "The Revolt of Islam," canto 10, stanza 14, lines 1–2, KNARF Project, University of Pennsylvania, accessed 23 February 2023, http://knarf.english.upenn.edu/PShelley/islamtp.html.

46. Walter Graham, "Percy Shelley and the Empire of the Nairs," *PMLA* 40, no. 4 (December 1925): 889.

47. Percy Bysshe Shelley, *The Revolt of Islam; a Poem, in Twelve Cantos* (London: C. and J. Ollier, 1818), 227. Shelley, *The Last Man*, ed. Paley, 76, 223, 269, 381, 406.

48. Shelley, *The Last Man*, ed. Paley, 259.

49. Richard Garnett, "Alms for Oblivion," *The Cornhill Magazine*, New Series, vol. 13 (London: Smith, Elder & Co., July–December 1902), 497.

50. Shelley, *Journals*, 89.

51. Ibid., 99.

52. Ibid., 226–27; Mary Shelley's translation of Sophocles's *Oedipus Rex* in "Greek Studies" notebook (n.d., beyond "August 26th" written in her hand at the top of the first, ripped out, page, but see Chapter 2 for my dating of its use from at least late 1820 to 1839), MS. Abinger e. 52; Sophocles, *Ajax. Electra. Oedipus Tyrannus*, ed. and trans. Hugh Lloyd-Jones, Loeb Classical Library 20, online edition (Cambridge, MA: Harvard University Press, 1994), 528; Maria Schoina, "Grubbing at 'Greek Roots': Mary Shelley's Greek Learning," *The Keats-Shelley Review* 33, no. 1 (2 January 2019): 96–109.

53. Shelley, *Letters*, vol. 1, 90–101; Shelley, *Journals,* 262–64; Robert P. Gaynes, *Germ Theory: Medical Pioneers in Infectious Diseases* (Washington, DC: Wiley and ASM Press, 2011), 235.

54. Shelley, *Journals*, 493.

55. Ibid., 324.

56. See Chapter 2.

57. Shelley, *Journals*, 332–33, 342–43, 347.

58. Shelley, "Giovanni Villani," *The Novels and Selected Works of Mary Shelley*, vol. 2, 134.

59. Shelley, "Boccaccio," *Literary Lives*, vol. 1, 60.

60. Hunt Botting, *Artificial Life After Frankenstein*, ch. 3.

61. Shelley, *Journals*, 304. James Giles, "Introduction," *French Existentialism: Consciousness, Ethics, and Relations with Others* (Amsterdam: Editions Rodopi, 2021), 10.

62. Shelley, *Journals*, 435.

63. Ibid., 433.

64. Ibid.

65. Percy Bysshe Shelley to Leigh Hunt, 15 August 1819, *The Letters of Percy Bysshe Shelley*, ed. F. L. Jones, vol. 2 (Oxford: Clarendon Press, 1964), 109.

66. Shelley, *Journals*, 452; MS. Abinger c. 65, fol. 12.

67. MS. Abinger c. 65, fol. 12.

68. Shelley, *Journals*, 452; MS. Abinger c. 65, fol. 12.

69. Shelley, *Journals*, 452.

70. Ibid.

71. Ibid.

72. Ibid., 453.

73. Angela Wright, *Mary Shelley*, Gothic Authors: Critical Revisions (Cardiff: University of Wales Press, 2018), 90.

74. Shelley, *Letters*, vol. 1, 393.

75. Mary Shelley, "On Ghosts," *Novels and Selected Works*, vol. 2, 113, 142.

76. Ibid.

77. Ibid.

78. Ibid.

79. Ibid. William Shakespeare, *Romeo and Juliet*, act 2, scene 3, lines 9–14; Lucan's *Pharsalia*, trans. Nicholas Rowe in *The British Poets*, vol. 99, *Lucan*, vol. 2 (Chiswick: C. Whittingham, 1822), 163; Isaiah 26:19. Susan J. Wolfson provides a wider background for understanding Shelley's melancholy in the Romantic culture of women's writing in which Wollstonecraft, who also drew heavily from Shakespeare, was a central figure. See Wolfson, "Romanticism & Gender & Melancholy," *Studies in Romanticism* 53, no. 3 (Fall 2014): 435–56.

80. Shelley, "On Ghosts," 143.

81. Ibid.

82. Shelley, *Journals*, 452.

83. Ibid., 217–21.

84. BSM 23, 57.

85. Dowden, *The Life of Percy Bysshe Shelley*, vol. 2, 533–34.

86. Percy Bysshe Shelley, *Essays, Letters from Abroad, Translations and Fragments*, ed. Mrs. Shelley (London: Edward Moxon, [1839] 1840). Mary Shelley's transcription of Percy Shelley's translation of "Plato's Banquet," in MS. Shelley adds. d. 8, Bodleian Library.

87. MS. Shelley adds. d. 8.

88. Shelley, *Journals*, 451. Shelley would have encountered John's mystical account of Jesus as the Alpha and Omega in the King James Version, Revelation 22:13, "I am the Alpha and the Omega, the Beginning and the End, the First and the Last," in the standard Bible of the Church of England and the Book of Common Prayer.

89. Shelley, *Journals*, 433, 440, 443, 451.

90. Ibid., 399.

91. MS. Shelley adds. d. 8.

92. Hunt Botting, *Artificial Life After Frankenstein*, ch. 3.

93. Shelley, *The Last Man*, ed. Paley, 398.

94. Ibid., 398–99. Percy Shelley, "Queen Mab," canto 6, line 198, in *Shelley's Poetry and Prose*, ed. Donald H. Reiman and Neil Fraistat, 2nd ed (New York: Norton, 2002), 52: "Necessity! thou mother of the World!"

95. Shelley, *The Last Man*, ed. Paley, 463.

96. Ibid.

97. Ibid., 399.

98. Andrea Haslanger, "The Last Animal: Cosmopolitanism in *The Last Man*," *European Romantic Review* 27, no. 5 (2016): 659–78.

99. Shelley, *Journals*, 486.

100. Ibid., 241.

101. William H. F. Altman, "Tullia's Secret Shrine: Birth and Death in Cicero's *De Finibus*," *Ancient Philosophy* 28 (2008): 1.

102. Shelley, *Journals*, 486.

103. Ibid.

104. Ibid., 487.

105. Ibid., 443.

106. Ibid., 447.

107. MS. Abinger c. 65, fol. 12.

108. Martha C. Nussbaum, *The Fragility of Goodness*, revised edition (Cambridge: Cambridge University Press, [1986] 2001).

109. Shelley, *Journals*, 447.

110. Shelley, *The Last Man*, ed. Paley, 274.

111. Ibid.

112. Shelley, *Journals*, 446.

113. Ibid.

114. Ibid.

115. Shelley, *The Last Man*, ed. Paley, 420.

116. Ibid.

117. Ibid., 478 (Paley's note).

118. Ibid.

119. *Words of Haydn's oratorio of the Creation: to be performed by the Enfield Musical Society* (Enfield, CT: J. H. Meyers, 1868).

120. Shelley, *The Last Man*, ed. Paley, 420.

121. Eileen Hunt Botting, *Family Feuds: Wollstonecraft, Burke, and Rousseau on the Transformation of the Family* (Albany, NY: SUNY Press, 2006), ch. 4; Wollstonecraft, *Rights of Woman*, 3–4.

122. Rousseau, "Lettre à Voltaire sur la Providence."

123. Wollstonecraft, *Rights of Woman*, 3. See also Sylvana Tomaselli on Wollstonecraft's optimistic views of God's providence and her progressive yet largely anticlerical views on institutionalized Christian religion. Sylvana Tomaselli, *Wollstonecraft: Philosophy, Passion, Politics* (Princeton, NJ: Princeton University Press, 2020), 207.

124. Rousseau, "Lettre à Voltaire sur la Providence."

125. Orianne Smith, "Rational Dissent" and Emily Dumler-Winckler, "Theology and Religion," in *The Wollstonecraftian Mind*, ed. Sandrine Bergès, Eileen Hunt Botting, and Alan Coffee (New York: Routledge, 2019), chs. 4 and 23.

126. Hunt Botting, *Family Feuds*, ch. 4.

127. Shelley, *Frankenstein*, 158.

128. Hunt Botting, "Mary Shelley's 'Romantic Spinozism.'" See also MS. Abinger c. 31, fol. 77 for William Godwin's memoir of his early seminary training: "Till 1782 I believed in the doctrines of Calvin, that is, that the majority of mankind were objects of divine condemnation, to that their punishment would be everlasting." He concluded the one-page manuscript by saying "I remember having entertained doubts in 1785, when I corresponded with D[r.] Priestley. But I was not a complete unbeliever till 1787, after about twelve months."

129. Shelley, *Journals*, 152 note 1.

130. Ibid., 196–97 note 5.

131. Ibid., 397 note 1.

132. Ibid., 386 note 2, 388, 399, 400. See also Shelley, *Letters*, vol. 1, 213–14, for evidence that she was alert to her atheistic circle's judgment and skepticism of her churchgoing.

133. Shelley, *Journals*, 315.

134. Mary Shelley to Jane Williams, 31 May 1823, *Letters*, vol. 1, 340.

135. Shelley, *The Last Man*, 361.

136. Ibid., 362.

137. Ibid.

138. Ibid.

139. Ibid.

140. Slavoj Žižek, *Pandemic!: COVID-19 Shakes the World* (New York: OR Books, 2020), 135. To his credit as a communist, Žižek donated all royalties from the publication of this book to Médecins Sans Frontières.

141. Ibid., 129.

142. Ibid., 130.

143. Ibid.

144. Natalie Proulx, "12 Ideas for Writing Through the Pandemic with *The New York Times*," *New York Times*, 15 April 2020.

145. Shelley, *The Last Man*, 182. Not everyone dies of the plague in the novel, but human failure to contain it leads to other forms of death. Lionel's son Evelyn, for example, dies of typhus near the end of the third volume.

146. Ibid., 183, 362.

147. Ibid., 183.

148. Ibid.

149. Ibid.

150. Ibid.

151. Ibid.

152. Lord Byron (George Gordon), "Darkness," Poetry Foundation, accessed 25 November 2020, https://www.poetryfoundation.org/, https://www.poetryfoundation.org/poems/43825/darkness-56d222aeeee1b.

153. Shelley, *Journals*, 428.

154. Shelley, *The Last Man*, 139, 315.

155. Shelley, *Journals*, 476.

156. Ibid.

157. Shelley, *Journals*, 430.

158. Ibid.

159. Rebecca Barr, "Pandemic and the Horrors of Solitude," *Solitudes: Past and Present* (blog), 9 April 2020, https://solitudes.qmul.ac.uk/blog/pandemic-and-the-horrors-of-absolute-solitude/.

160. Claire Connolly, "The Power of Literature in a Time of Plague," *Irish Times*, 14 July 2020.

161. Mrs. Mason to Mary Shelley, 17 November 1822, MS. Abinger c. 46, fols. 24–25.

Chapter 2

1. Mary Shelley, trans., "Oedipus," in her "Greek Studies" notebook, MS. Abinger e. 52, Bodleian Library, Oxford University, 2. To confirm the accuracy, I read her transcription of the Ancient Greek alongside the play in Sophocles, *Ajax. Electra. Oedipus Tyrannus*, ed. and trans. Hugh Lloyd-Jones, Loeb Classical Library 20, online edition (Cambridge, MA: Harvard University Press, 1994), 528. See also the first systematic study of Shelley's "Greek Studies" notebook: Maria Schoina, "Grubbing at 'Greek Roots': Mary Shelley's Greek Learning," *The Keats-Shelley Review* 33, no. 1 (January 2019): 96–109. As Schoina notes, Shelley changed the "syntax" to "facilitate translation" and "grammatical analysis," and her handwriting and lettering in Greek is often difficult to decipher, so for ease of reading and comparison I have transcribed the Greek letters and accents as they appear in the Loeb edition while preserving the word order and literary form of the transcription and translation exactly as Shelley gave the passage in her notebook. I use Schoina's numbering system for citing MS. Abinger e. 52.

2. MS. Abinger e. 52, 2. There have been two previous article-length studies involving, to varying degrees, the Greek text and material form of Shelley's "Greek Studies" notebook, which was deposited in the Abinger papers at the Bodleian Library in 2004: Schoina, "Grubbing at 'Greek Roots;'" and Will Bowers, "On First Looking into Mary Shelley's Homer," *The Review of English Studies* 69, no. 290 (2018): 510–31.

3. MS. Abinger e. 52, 3. These quotations are drawn from the first three (unnumbered) manuscript pages. Schoina shared her photos of the manuscript with me in December 2020, before I had the chance to visit the Bodleian to study the originals in June, August, and December 2021, and in summer 2022. Beyond the first three pages of MS. Abinger e. 52, I use Schoina's verso-recto numbering system for the remainder of the notebook to pinpoint the locations of my quotations from it.

4. Shelley, *Letters*, vol. 2, 183.

5. Adrienne Rich, *Diving into the Wreck, Poems 1971–1972* (New York: Norton, 2013).

6. In their co-kept journal from 1814–15, Percy records Mary's "first lesson in greek" on 18 September 1814. Percy also tutored her stepsister in the language. Claire Clairmont states in her journal "Write and learn the Philoctetes" and "Write Greek again" on 21 September 1814. Shelley, *Journals*, 27; MS. Abinger d. 27: Mary Shelley's Journals, vol. I, 1814–15, Bodleian Library; Journals of Claire Clairmont, MS. 394 (vol. 1), British Library.

7. Schoina, "Grubbing at 'Greek Roots,'" 99–100. In a letter sent to Maria Gisborne at Livorno from 18 June 1820, Shelley wrote, "have the kindness to ask Peacock four [for] Schrevelius's lexicon Jones's Greek grammar—& the Greek exercises Hogg used to do—&bring them with you." By 19 July 1820 she wrote to Gisborne in Livorno again, "I have now very seriously begun Greek." On 21 February 1821, she wrote to Gisborne in Pisa, "Be so kind as to send the Sophocles . . . I work hard at Greek & shd get on were it not for the intolerable grammar." Shelley, *Letters*, vol. 1, 148, 155, 184.

8. Shelley, *Journals*, 347.

9. Pisa "had a small but vibrant Greek diaspora" circa 1819. See Mark Mazower, *The Greek Revolution* (New York: Penguin, 2021), 95.

10. To make these findings, I compared the original manuscripts of her journals (MS. Abinger d. 27–31) and her "Greek Studies" notebook (MS. Abinger e. 52) with the encyclopedic research contained in *The Bodleian Shelley Manuscripts*, ed. Donald H. Reiman, Irving Massey, P. M. S. Dawson, E. B. Murray, Carlene A. Adamson, Charles E. Robinson, and Betty T. Bennett et al., 23 vols. (New York: Routledge, 1986–2002), especially vol. 22, part ii, 44–49, 70; vol. 23, 28, 48, 77, 131–37 (cited as BSM).

11. BSM 23, 28, 48; Shelley, *Letters*, vol. 1, 128–29.

12. R. Glynn Grylls, *Mary Shelley: A Biography* (New York: Haskell House, [1938] 1969), 132. Grylls transcribed this passage from the 21 March 1821 letter from Shelley to Maria Gisborne in the Abinger collection. She was one, if not the first, of the twentieth-century scholars to gain access to these papers not on deposit yet at the Bodleian. See also Shelley, *Letters*, vol. 1, 183–85.

13. Stephen Hebron and Elizabeth Campbell Denlinger, *Shelley's Ghost: Reshaping the Image of a Literary Family* (Oxford: Bodleian Library, 2010), 24.

14. Timothy Webb, "Shelley's Sophocles: A Legend Re-Examined," *Keats-Shelley Memorial Bulletin* (1968): 47–52, note 1.

15. Stephen Hebron, "Shelley's Ghost—An Exhibition at the Bodleian Library, Oxford," *The Keats-Shelley Review* 25, no. 1 (2011): 10–12.

16. For Shelley's copy of Percy's translation of Plato's *Symposium*, see MS. Shelley adds. d. 8. There were at least two copies in circulation among her friends as of 1839, but only this manuscript remains. Shelley published Percy's translation of "The Banquet of Plato" (with her preface and in edited form) in her edition of *Essays, Letters from Abroad, Translations and Fragments by Percy Bysshe Shelley* (London: Edward Moxon, 1840), vol. 1, 70–163. BSM 20, 122–29.

17. BSM 23, 5.

18. For a complete guide to the Abinger collection, see the Bodleian's online catalogue: https://archives.bodleian.ox.ac.uk/repositories/2/resources/3190. In 1987, the Shelley scholars and editors Paula Feldman and Diana Scott-Kilvert published their complete edition of Shelley's *Journals* (MS. Abinger d. 27–31) in two volumes with Oxford University Press. In 1996, the Shelley scholar and editor Charles E. Robinson published the "Frankenstein" manuscripts (MS. Abinger c. 56, fols. i-ii, 1–64; MS. Abinger c. 56–7, fols. 1–94; and MS. Abinger c. 58, fols. 1–31) in *The Frankenstein Notebooks: A Facsimile Edition of Mary Shelley's Manuscript Novel, 1816–17*, 2 vols. (New York: Garland, 1996).

19. Lewis Patton, "The Shelley-Godwin Collection of Lord Abinger," *Library Notes* 27 (April 1953): 11–17. See also the history of the Abinger collection: https://archives.bodleian.ox.ac.uk/repositories/2/resources/3190.

20. Schoina noted that 2004 was the year of the deposit of the "Greek Studies" notebook (MS. Abinger e. 52) into the Bodleian in her 2019 article, "Grubbing at 'Greek Roots,'" 109 note 64. On 10 December 2003, the Bodleian announced that the "remaining third" of the Abinger collection, previously on "loan," would be purchased by the library. See Bruce C. Barker-Benfield, "Keeping Shelley MSS Together at the Bodleian," *Romantic Circles* (blog), 11 December 2003, https://romantic-circles.org/blog_rc/keeping-shelley-mss-together-bodleian.

21. Anthony John Harding, "Shelley, Mythology, and the Classical Tradition," in *The Oxford Handbook of Percy Bysshe Shelley*, eds. Michael O'Neill and Anthony Howe with Madeline Callaghan (Oxford: Oxford University Press, 2013), 432; Shelley, *Journals*, 27, 217–20.

22. Charles E. Robinson, "Shelley to the Editor of the 'Morning Chronicle': A Second New Letter of 5 April 1821," *Keats-Shelley Memorial Bulletin* 32 (1981): 55; Alan M. Weinberg, "Introduction," BSM 22, part ii (1997), 30–31; Bowers, "On First Looking into Mary Shelley's Homer," 523. Bowers demonstrates Shelley's steady though imperfect progress in translating Homer, by providing the first study of her 1820–21 notebook (held at the University of Iowa) that contains her translation of part of Book I of the *Odyssey*. Bowers ultimately concurs with Robinson and Weinberg, however, that Shelley's command of Ancient (or, presumably, Modern) Greek was not strong enough to solo-translate the short Greek independence manifesto "Cry of War to the Greeks" from (presumably) Modern Greek in April 1821, although the surviving manuscript is in her hand, with Percy's marginal corrections. In the section titled "The Plagues of Love and War," I argue that "Cry of War to the Greeks" was a most likely a collaborative translation of the Shelleys with the input of their Greek friend Mavrokordatos, but I do not extrapolate from this English-language document in Shelley's hand her abilities in translating Ancient Greek circa 1821.

Instead, I marshal a new constellation of textual, contextual, and material evidence to show the likelihood of her use and consultation of her "Greek Studies" notebook (MS. Abinger e. 52) from late 1820 to 1839.

23. Schoina, "Grubbing at 'Greek Roots,'" 107–8.

24. Ibid., 107. Schoina transcribed the prior 1824 letter from Hogg to Shelley from the Abinger collection.

25. Shelley, *Letters*, vol. 1, 449.

26. Ibid.

27. Ibid.

28. Shelley and her stepsister Claire Clairmont received tutoring from Percy in Greek, beginning in September 1814. Shelley's first lesson "in Greek" from Percy was on 18 September. Clairmont states in her journal "Write and learn the Philoctetes" and "Write Greek again" on 21 September. Shelley, *Journals*, 27; MS. Abinger d. 27; MS. 394 (vol. 1), British Library.

29. Neville Rogers, undated note, in MS. Abinger e. 52; Weinberg, BSM 22, part ii, 45.

30. Percy Bysshe Shelley and Mary Wollstonecraft Shelley, "Fragments: 'Notes on Shakespeare and Sophocles,'" MS. Shelley adds. d. 6, fols. 109–10, Bodleian Library; see also BSM 22, part i, 37–38, 256–59; Mary Shelley, "Editor's Note on 'Prometheus Unbound,'" in Percy Bysshe Shelley, *Poetical Works*, ed. Mary Wollstonecraft Shelley (London: Edward Moxon, 1839), 127; MS. Abinger e. 52, 65 verso, 66 recto.

31. Schoina, "Grubbing at 'Greek Roots,'" Rogers, undated note, in MS. Abinger e. 52; Weinberg, "Introduction," BSM 22, part ii (1997), 30–31.

32. Bowers, "On First Looking into Mary Shelley's Homer," 520 note 37.

33. Alan Weinberg, "Greek Exercises," BSM 22, part ii, 45–49.

34. Bowers, "On First Looking into Mary Shelley's Homer," 520 note 37; BSM 20, 122–29.

35. Barker-Benfield, "Shelleyan Writing-Materials in the Bodleian Library: A Catalogue of Formats, Papers and Watermarks," BSM 23, 12.

36. See "Shelley's Literary Incorporation of Oedipus" in this chapter. Also, Shelley, *Journals*, 81; MS. Abinger d. 27.

37. Rich, *Diving into the Wreck*; Eileen M. Hunt, "Mary Shelley's *The Last Man*: Existentialism and IR Meet the Post-Apocalyptic Pandemic Novel," in "Existentialism and IR," ed. Liane Hartnett, Andrew Hom, and Cian O'Driscoll, special issue, *Review of International Studies*, (June 2022): 1–23.

38. Alison Flood, "Margaret Atwood: Covid-19 Lockdown is Not a Dystopia," *The Guardian*, 16 April 2020. See also Matthew B. Hill, ed., *Dystopian States of America: Apocalyptic Visions and Warnings in Literature and Film* (Santa Barbara, CA: ABC-CLIO, 2022), which includes an entry on Shelley's *The Last Man*, 191–92.

39. Shelley, *Journals*, 326–77; Mazower, *The Greek Revolution*, 96, 99.

40. Neville Rogers speculated the beginning of her "Oedipus" translation in early 1821, based on her journals, in an undated note placed in MS. Abinger e. 52.

41. Shelley, *Journals*, 341.

42. Ibid., 341–44, 350–51, 356–72, 373. After Shelley noted in her journal that she met Mavrokordatos on 2 December 1820, almost every entry afterward in the year mentions Mavrokordatos or others in his Pisan circle of Greek expatriates. On 26 June, she records that Mavrokordatos "sails" to fight in the Greek revolution, which insurrection leaders such as Alexander Ypsilantis claimed began "on or around March 25, 1821." See Mazower, *The Greek Revolution*, 64.

43. Shelley, *Journals*, 341.

44. Mary Shelley, *Matilda*, in *The Novels and Selected Works of Mary Shelley*, vol. 2, 5.

45. Shelley, *Journals*, 350–51, 358.

46. Ibid., 325; see also Bowers, "On First Looking into Mary Shelley's Homer"; Shelley, *Letters*, vol. 1, 155.

47. See Hunt Botting, "Mary Shelley's 'Romantic Spinozism.'"

48. Shelley, *Journals*, 350–51, 356.

49. Ibid., 365–66.

50. Ibid., 366–72.

51. Ibid., 373.

52. [Alexander Mavrokordatos?], unsigned and undated Greek alphabet with inscription from *Philoctetes* (c. 1821), MS. Shelley adds. c. 5, Group "B," fol. 150a. For its dating via watermark, paper, and context, see BSM, vol. 22, part ii, 46.

53. Jennifer Tolbert Roberts, *The Plague of War: Athens, Sparta, and the Struggle for Ancient Greece* (Oxford: Oxford University Press, 2017), 83–98; Thucydides, *The Peloponnesian War*, ed. P. J. Rhodes, trans. Martin Hammond (Oxford: Oxford University Press, 2009), book 2, 96–104.

54. Shelley, *Journals*, 12; MS. Abinger d. 27. Mary's first entry in journal book one, which she kept with Percy, is 11 August, in which she names her sister Claire (Jane) as a companion on their elopement through the countryside of France, laid waste by the "Cossacs" (Austrian/Russian troops) during the end of the Napoleonic Wars earlier in 1814. For context, see Shelley, *Journals*, 12 note 1.

55. Charlotte Gordon, *Romantic Outlaws: The Extraordinary Lives of Mary Wollstonecraft and Mary Shelley* (New York: Random House, 2015), ch. 31.

56. Shelley, *Letters*, vol. 2, 215.

57. A. A. Kousoulis, K. P. Economopoulos, E. Poulakou-Rebelakou, G. Androutsos, and S. Tsiodras, "The Plague of Thebes, a Historical Dpidemic in Sophocles' *Oedipus Rex*," *Emerging Infectious Diseases* 18, no. 1 (2012): 153–57.

58. There has been a woman-centered shift in biographical writing about the Shelleys and their circle, in which Mary Shelley has gradually taken center stage as what Hegel would call a "world-historical" author-creator of ideas in her own right alongside Percy, Byron, and her mother Wollstonecraft. Most of these major biographies are by women and have appeared in this century, with a few by leading woman literary critics and Shelley scholars breaking new ground in the 1980s and 1990s, building on the foundational work of Muriel Spark, author of what some describe as the first modern scholarly biography of Mary Shelley, though she was in fact preceded by another woman biographer, Rosalie Glynn Grylls, who had unprecedented access to the Abinger papers. See R. Glynn Grylls, *Mary Shelley: A Biography* (Oxford: Oxford University Press, 1938); Muriel Spark, *Child of Light: A Reassessment of Mary Shelley* (London: Tower Bridge, 1951); Anne K. Mellor, *Mary Shelley: Her Life, Her Fiction, Her Monsters* (New York: Routledge, 1989); Betty T. Bennett, *Mary Wollstonecraft Shelley: An Introduction* (London: Pickering and Chatto, 1996); John Williams, *Mary Shelley: A Literary Life* (London: Macmillan, 2000); Miranda Seymour, *Mary Shelley* (New York: Grove Atlantic, 2002); Lyndall Gordon, *Vindication: A Life of Mary Wollstonecraft* (New York: HarperCollins, 2005); Daisy Hay, *Young Romantics: The Shelleys, Byron, and Other Tangled Lives* (New York: Farrar, Straus and Giroux, 2010); Charlotte Gordon, *Romantic Outlaws*; Rachel Feder, *Harvester of Hearts: Motherhood under the Sign of Frankenstein* (Evanston, IL: Northwestern University Press, 2018); Fiona Sampson, *In Search of Mary Shelley: The Girl Who Wrote Frankenstein* (New York: Pegasus, 2018). The famous Romantic biographer Richard Holmes, however, helped pave the way for the positive reception of this woman-centered turn in the historiography of the Shelleys and their circle by writing *Footsteps: Adventures of a Romantic Biographer* (New York: Vintage, 1985) in which he traced Shelley's mother Wollstonecraft's steps through revolutionary Paris, about ten years after he first published *Shelley: The Pursuit* (Quartet Books, 1976), in which he treated Percy as the center of British Romanticism. But even more important than Holmes's contribution to this woman-centered biographical turn was arguably the publication of the complete set of Shelley's *Journals*, edited by Paula R. Feldman and Diana Scott-Kilvert, by Oxford in 1987 and three volumes of Shelley's *Letters*, edited by Betty T. Bennett, by Johns Hopkins by 1988.

59. Weinberg, ed., "The Dating of the Copybook and Publication of its Contents," BSM 22, part i, 39–40. In addition to *Symposium*, Shelley copied and preserved Percy's "Notes on Xenophon," translation of and notes on Plato's *Ion*; translation of selections of Plato's *Republic*; "On the Athenians;" and his fragment on "Shakespeare and Sophocles." The notebook she used to copy some of these manuscripts, salvaged from the shipwreck of the Don Juan, is Italian and "has features in common with [her] Journal of Sorrow, a notebook which was begun in Genoa on 2 October 1822." Weinberg, BSM 22, part i, 39. Following Weinberg's method of comparing notebooks to help determine dating of Shelley's "Greek Studies" notebook, I noted physical similarities (e.g., brown leather binding and covers, English paper) between volume three of her journals (MS. Abinger d. 29), begun in 1819, and her "Greek Studies" notebook (MS. Abinger e. 52), likely begun in late 1820 (see the section on "Reconceptualizing and Redating").

60. MS. Shelley adds. c. 5, Group "B," fol. 150a. Transcription and translation is my own. Bowers was the first to identify the source of the quote as *Philoctetes* in "On First Looking into Mary Shelley's Homer" (2018), 523 note 61.

61. Mazower, *The Greek Revolution*, 259–60.

62. MS. Shelley adds. c. 5, Group "B," fol. 150a. Shelley, *Journals*, 226, 293, 428.

63. Shelley, *Journals*, 476–95.

64. Alessandro Manzoni, *The Betrothed* (New York: Penguin Classics, [1827] 1983). Shelley praised the author and his plague novel in an 1838 *Monthly Chronicle* review. See Mary Shelley, "Modern Italian Romances," in *Mary Shelley's Literary Lives and Other Writings*, eds. Pamela Clemit and A. A. Markley, vol. 4 (London: Routledge, [2002] 2020), 230.

65. Shelley, *The Last Man*, 64, 290.

66. The familial iteration of the rumor comes from William Godwin, who confided to Maria Gisborne on 4 July 1820 that Percy's romantic abandonment of Fanny Godwin in favor of Mary led to the older sister's suicide in October 1816 and other bitter intergenerational conflicts and sibling rivalries in the family: "Mr. G told me that the three girls were all equally in love with——and that the eldest put an end to her existence owing to the preference given to her younger sister." Maria Gisborne Journals, 2 May to 26 December, 1820, Ashley MS. 3262, British Library.

67. Shelley, *Journals*, 560. The editors Feldman and Scott-Kilvert noted that the phrase "as atonement claimed by fate for her death" was "heavily cancelled" in the manuscript of volume five of her journals, and that Lady Jane Shelley was the likely culprit (as she was known to purge Shelleyan manuscripts of evidence of scandal in the family). See Shelley, *Journals*, 560–61, note 4. For this reason, the editors left the text uncancelled in their edition of the *Journals*. Their uncovering of this important text is relevant for this study, given that the language of "atonement" and "fate" resonates with the passage on Oedipus from Aeschylus's *Seven Against Thebes* that, I argue in "Shelley's Literary Incorporation of Oedipus," Shelley likely wrote and adapted in Ancient Greek in the endpapers of the first volume of her journals.

68. Rachel Feder documents the lives and deaths of all of Mary Shelley's four biological children, plus a late-term miscarriage that nearly killed her on 16 June 1822, and the death of her beloved niece Clara Allegra Byron from typhus (12 January, 1817–19 April, 1822). Shelley's four biological children were: Clara Shelley (22 February, 1815–6 March, 1815) who probably died of a genetic disease, Clara Everina Shelley (2 September, 1817–24 September, 1818) who died from dysentery and fever, William Shelley (24 January, 1816–7 June, 1819) who died from malaria and fever, and Percy Florence Shelley (12 November, 1819–5 December, 1889) who survived her and, together with his wife Jane, preserved his parents' literary legacies with a major gift of their papers to the Bodleian. See Feder, *Harvester of Hearts*, 79, 139, 141 and Shelley, *Journals*, 412 note 1.

69. Gordon, *Romantic Outlaws*, 442.

70. Mazower, *The Greek Revolution*, 259–60.

71. Shelley, *Journals*, 473.

72. Because historians of ideas have often been trained to be averse to biography, especially the "tabloid school of biography" (a term condescendingly used by Edmund H. O'Neill to describe early twentieth-century American biographies of a "Freudian" or "sordid" quality that were ultimately superseded by what he called the "modern" scholarly biography), there is all the more reason to consider that histories of lives (however gleaned, through journals, letters, testimonies, literature, journalism, archives, or secondary sources) are one of the most important yet neglected dimensions of doing history of political thought thoroughly and well. This is doubly true for women, whose lives and ideas are systematically marginalized or even ignored in mainstream history, perhaps especially intellectual history, and the wider academy. See Edmund H. O'Neill, *A History of American Biography, 1800–1935* (Philadelphia: University of Pennsylvania Press, 1935), 11, 227, 349.

73. Sophocles, *Oedipus Tyrannus*, trans. Lloyd-Jones, 327–29, 346–47; MS. Abinger e. 52, 1–3, 12 verso, 13 recto.

74. An irony is that Elizabeth Nitchie made the groundbreaking literary discovery of the manuscript of Shelley's suppressed incest novella *Mathilda* (c. 1819–20) on the same microfilm that Shelley's "Greek Studies" notebook was preserved, but no one has studied the remarkable thematic connections between the two manuscripts, especially around the figure of Oedipus, until now. Nitchie, however, noted the allusion to *Oedipus at Colonus* on the first page of *Mathilda*, setting up future scholarship to explore the novella's incest theme in light of Sophocles. Shelley, *Mathilda*, ed. Nitchie, 81, note 4.

75. The closest predecessor for Shelley's *The Last Man* is Jean-Baptiste Cousin de Granville's long prose poem, *Le Dernier Homme* (1805), translated into English as *Omegarus and Syderia* (1806). See Introduction.

76. Schoina, "Grubbing at 'Greek Roots.'"

77. Ibid., 108–9.

78. Rogers, undated note, in MS. Abinger e. 52.

79. Mazower, *The Greek Revolution*, 96–97.

80. Bowers, "On First Looking into Mary Shelley's Homer," 522–23.

81. Ibid., 519–20. See also John Williams, who argues that the widowed Shelley as an "author sets about dealing with the trauma through the use of literary form," in *Mary Shelley: A Literary Life*, 90–91.

82. Schoina, "Grubbing at 'Greek Roots,'" 97 note 7; Bowers, "On First Looking into Mary Shelley's Homer," 520 note 37; Shelley, *Letters*, vol. 1, 567.

83. See BSM 22, part ii and Shelley adds. c. 5, 141–5, 138–40; 146–49. See also Schoina, "Grubbing at 'Greek Roots,'" 108. Shelley's transcript of lines 1–106 of Euripides's *Alcestis* (Shelley adds. c. 5, 141–45, 138–40) has an 1825 Hagar & Son (English) watermark (BSM 22, part ii, 69, figure 25). Her Greek exercises from this period (Shelley adds. c. 5, 146–49) have an 1826 Hagar & Son (English) watermark. Weinberg and Barker-Benfield pointed out that the Hagar watermark "reappears in almost exactly the same position, and in much the same paper, in a series of nine letters of Mary Wollstonecraft Shelley [dated 7 August to 17 September 1827 during her summer holiday to Sompting and Arundel] . . . which have very similar whole-sheet measurements to those estimated for the *Alcestis* transcript." See BSM 22, part ii, 47.

84. Shelley, *Letters*, vol. 2, 170.

85. Shelley, "Editor's Note to 'Prometheus Unbound,'" in *Poetical Works*, 127.

86. Bowers, "On First Looking into Mary Shelley's Homer," 520.

87. Schoina, "Grubbing at 'Greek Roots,'" 109 note 64.

88. BSM 22, part ii, 44–49; BSM 23, 131–37.

89. BSM 22, part ii, 70; BSM 23, 77.

90. Thomas L. Gravell and George Miller, *A Catalogue of Foreign Watermarks Found on Paper Used in America, 1700–1835*, Garland Reference Library of the Humanities 318 (New York: Garland, 1983), 53, 191, 237; BSM 22, part ii, 51–53, 70, figure 29; BSM 23, 78–79.

91. BSM 23, 28; Shelley, *Letters*, vol. 1, 128–29.

92. Ibid. See also Jean de Palacio, "Shelley's Library Catalogue," *Revue de Littérature Comparée* 36, issue 2 (1 April 1962): 270–76.

93. BSM 23, 48.

94. Shelley, *Journals*, 304–6, 339, 341, 347; Shelley, *Letters*, vol. 1, 155.

95. Shelley, *Journals*, 330.

96. Ibid.

97. Ibid., 330–33.

98. Shelley, *Journals*, 27; Journals of Claire Clairmont, MS. 394 (vol. 1), British Library.

99. Mary Shelley, "Introduction to *Frankenstein*, Third Edition (1831)," in *Frankenstein*, 165; Mary Poovey, *The Proper Lady and the Woman Writer: Ideology as Style in the Works of Mary Wollstonecraft, Mary Shelley, and Jane Austen* (Chicago: University of Chicago Press, 1984).

100. Shelley published some of Percy's Greek translations from Homer and Euripides in her edition, *Posthumous Poems of Percy Bysshe Shelley* (London: John and Henry L. Hunt, 1824).

101. John Dryden, "The Preface to Ovid's Epistles" (1680) as cited in Samuel Bray, "Form and Substance in the Fusion of Law and Equity," in *Philosophical Foundations of the Law of Equity*, ed. Dennis Klimchuk, Irit Samet, and Henry Smith (Oxford: Oxford University Press, 2018), 234.

102. Stephanie Nelson, "Shelley and Plato's Symposium: The Poet's Revenge," *International Journal of the Classical Tradition* 14, no.1/2 (Summer 2007): 100–129. Nelson notes that while the translation has tremendous literary and philosophical value, it is "flawed" due to Percy's "refusal to use a lexicon" (100).

103. Sophocles, *Oedipus Rex*, trans. Robert Fagles, in *The Three Theban Plays: Antigone, Oedipus the King, Oedipus at Colonus* (New York: Penguin, 1984), 172.

104. Sophocles, *Oedipus Tyrannus*, trans. Lloyd-Jones, 346–47 (lines 241–42); MS. Abinger e. 52, 12 verso, 13 recto. Shelley literally translates the phrase, "as being a pollution to us." In the Loeb edition, Lloyd-Jones translates the phrase more liberally as "since we are polluted."

105. Sophocles, *Oedipus Tyrannus*, trans. Lloyd-Jones, 327–29 (line 28), 346–47 (lines 241–42); MS. Abinger e. 52, 12 verso, 13 recto.

106. Robert Parker, "Pollution, the Greek concept of" (2016), *The Oxford Classical Dictionary*, 4th ed. (online); Larry May, "Homicide and Pollution," in *Ancient Legal Thought: Equity, Justice, and Humaneness From Hammurabi and the Pharaohs to Justinian and the Talmud* (Cambridge: Cambridge University Press, 2019), 321–38; Bernard Williams, *Shame and Necessity* (Berkeley: University of California Press, [1993] 2008), 60–71.

107. Sophocles, *Oedipus Tyrannus*, trans. Lloyd-Jones, 346–47 (lines 241–42); MS. Abinger e. 52, 12 verso, 13 recto. Shelley translates "εἷς" as "one" in the top right column of her crib. In her youth, Shelley would have had access to her father William Godwin's highly successful children's edition of the Greek and Roman myths, published as Edward Baldwin, *The Pantheon: or Ancient History of the Gods of Greece and Rome* (London: Thomas Hodgkins, 1806).

108. Jean Cocteau in his play *La Machine infernale* (Paris, 1934) makes a similar translation of Sophocles, describing Oedipus as the "polluting" agent, not the plague. Jean Cocteau, *The Infernal Machine and Other Plays* (New York: New Directions, 1963), 6.

109. Parker, "Pollution, the Greek concept of."

110. Mary Shelley likely first studied Aeschylus's *Seven Against Thebes* with Percy in 1814–15, as, I go on to argue in "Shelley's Literary Incorporation of Oedipus," there is an adapted Greek quotation from this play that is likely in her hand in the endpapers of volume one of her journals, co-kept with Percy. The editors of Shelley's *Journals*, Feldman and Scott-Kilvert, did not take a clear stand on who wrote the adapted quote. See Shelley, *Journals*, 81; MS. Abinger d. 27.

The couple's other shared passion in Attic tragedy was Sophocles, whose plays Percy read in 1817–18, and she read regularly from 1818 to 1821, according to her journals and other writings. Her journal first records Percy's regular reading of Euripides when they moved to Italy in the spring of 1818. Shelley, *Journals*, 81, 102, 209, 226, 350–51.

111. Shelley, *The Last Man*, 139, 183.

112. Sophocles, *Oedipus Tyrannus*, trans. Lloyd-Jones, 346–47 (lines 241–42).

113. Shelley, *Journals*, 417 note 1.

114. MS. Abinger e. 52, 1.

115. Ibid., 65 verso, 66 recto.

116. Percy Bysshe Shelley and Mary Wollstonecraft Shelley, "Fragments: Notes on Shakespeare and Sophocles," MS. Shelley adds. d. 6, fols. 109–10; see also BSM 22, part i, 37–38, 256–59; Shelley, "Editor's Note on 'Prometheus Unbound,'" in *Poetical Works*, 127.

117. Ibid.

118. MS. Abinger e. 52, 4 verso.

119. Ibid., 65 verso, 66 recto. Mary Shelley also corrected Percy's (unintentionally) comical description of Sophocles as the "geek Shakespeare" when he meant to write the "Greek Shakespeare." See her "Editor's Note to Prometheus Unbound," in *Poetical Works*, 127.

120. MS. Abinger e. 52, 65 verso, 66 recto.

121. Christopher Frayling, *Vampyres: Genesis and Resurrection* (London: Thames and Hudson, 2016), part 2, ch. 1.

122. Bowers, "On First Looking into Mary Shelley's Homer."

123. David E. Petrain, "An English Translation of John William Polidori's (1815) Medical Dissertation on Oneirodynia (Somnambulism)," *European Romantic Review* 21, no. 6 (2010): 775–88; D. L. Macdonald and Kathleen Scherf, eds., *The Vampyre and Ernestus Berchtold; or, The Modern Oedipus: Collected Fiction of John William Polidori* (Toronto: University of Toronto Press, 1994).

124. Miranda Seymour, *In Byron's Wake: The Turbulent Lives of Byron's Wife and Daughter: Annabella Milbanke and Ada Lovelace* (London: Pegasus, 2018), chs. 6–7.

125. Gordon, *Romantic Outlaws*, ch. 31.

126. Gillen D'Arcy Wood, *Tambora: The Eruption that Changed the World* (Princeton, NJ: Princeton University Press, 2015), 52.

127. Macdonald and Scherf, eds., *The Vampyre and Ernestus Berchtold*, 51. The original title of Bram Stoker's *Dracula* (1897) was either to be "The Dead Un-Dead" or "The Un-Dead." Either way, as David J. Skal points out in his biography *Something in the Blood: The Untold Story of Bram Stoker* (New York: Liveright, 2016), he coined a new and influential term for the modern vampire: the undead.

128. Frayling, *Vampyres*, part 2, ch. 2.

129. Lord Byron, *Giaour: A Fragment of a Turkish Tale* (London: John Murray, 1813), 23.

130. Frayling, *Vampyres*, part 1 and part 2, ch. 2.

131. William Michael Rossetti, ed., *The Diary of John William Polidori, 1816* (London: E. Matthews, 1911), 135–37. On 5 September 1816, Polidori records that he "threatened to shoot" Percy Shelley around the time of these quarrels about horses; it may have been a challenge to a duel. Polidori recalls that he had been visiting with "Mrs. Shelley" on 2 July, prior to the feuds with Percy and Bryon that propelled his dismissal from Byron's employment.

132. Frayling, *Vampyres*, part 1 and part 2, ch. 2.

133. Rossetti, ed., *The Diary of John William Polidori*, 4.

134. Shelley, *Journals*, 341–44, 350–51, 356–72, 373.

135. Roderick Beaton, *Byron's War: Romantic Rebellion, Greek Revolution* (Cambridge: Cambridge University Press, 2013), 69; Mazower, *The Greek Revolution*, 93–96.

136. Shelley, "Editor's Note to 'Hellas,'" in *Poetical Works*, 179.

137. Because we only have the English translation in Mary Shelley's hand, we can only speculate the original language from which she and others in her Pisan circle helped to translate "The Cry of War to the Greeks." For circumstantial evidence we may turn to the Ancient Greek syntax in her papers, which dates to her early 1821 tutoring sessions with Mavrokordatos. On the syntax manuscript, she attempts some translation of Ancient Greek into French. Perhaps her skills in French to English translation were as important as her skills in Greek to English translation in this international Pisan circle of philhellenes for whom French was quite literally a conversational and written lingua franca. No matter in what language the document was written—although Modern Greek is the most probable and assumed form—Shelley likely used her knowledge of French *and* Ancient Greek to help translate it. See Mary Shelley, "Elementary Greek Syntax, with additions by Alexander Mavrokordatos," MS. Abinger c. 63, fols. 40–1. For the political context for the translation, see Shelley, "Editor's Note on 'Hellas'" in *Poetical Works*, 180.

138. Mary Shelley [tr.(?)], "The Cry of War to the Greeks," in *Mary Shelley's Literary Lives and Other Writings*, vol. 4, 350–53.

139. Ibid., 350, 352.

140. Ibid., 350–53.

141. Emily W. Sunstein, *Mary Shelley: Romance and Reality* (Baltimore: Johns Hopkins University Press, 1991), 208.

142. "Portrait de Mme Shelley par le Comte de Metaxas," MS. Abinger c. 51.

143. Gordon, *Romantic Outlaws*, 376.

144. As discussed in Chapter 1, the most explicit evidence for her growing association of Percy with Oedipus is her entry concerning the death of their daughter Clara in September 1818, in which she reflects on how Percy read *Oedipus Rex* aloud to her while their daughter was ill, then expected Mary and the sick baby to travel to Venice, where the infant died as soon as they arrived. Shelley, *Journals*, 226–27. For further analysis of this passage, see "Shelley's Literary Incorporation of Oedipus."

145. *Letters from Harriet Shelley to Catherine Nugent* (London: privately printed, 1889), 59.

146. Shelley, *Journals*, 152, 152 note 1.

147. Shelley, *Frankenstein*, 36, 51.

148. Ibid., 141.

149. Ibid., 119. It is interesting to note that Victor Frankenstein worries that future generations will curse him as their "pest," as if the scientist who created the "scourge" (69) of the "monster" (36) is identical to the ever-multiplying "catastrophe" (35) he makes.

150. Shelley, *Journals*, 81.

151. Aeschylus, *Persians. Seven Against Thebes. Suppliants. Prometheus Bound*, ed. and trans. Alan H. Sommerstein, Loeb Classical Library 145, online (Cambridge, MA: Harvard University Press, 2009), 258–59 (lines 975–78).

152. MS. Abinger d. 27; Shelley, *Journals*, 81.

153. Ibid.

154. Paula R. Feldman and Diana Scott-Kilvert, "Mary Shelley's Use of Symbols," in Shelley, *Journals*, appendix 1, 579–81.

155. Shelley, *The Last Man*, 29.

156. Ibid.

157. Shelley, *Letters*, vol. 2, 215.

158. Sampson, *Mary Shelley*, 71.

159. MS. Abinger d. 27.

160. Sampson, *Mary Shelley*, 114.

161. Shelley, *Journals*, 79.

162. Ibid., 226–27. At the time of her infant Clara's feverish sickness and death from dysentery in September 1818, while Percy read *Oedipus Rex* aloud to her, Shelley also noted in her

journal that she was reading Alfieri's tragedies. She was apparently planning to translate his 1786 incest tragedy *Myrrha*, a project since lost. On the latter point, see William Veeder, "The Negative Oedipus: Father, *Frankenstein*, and the Shelleys," *Critical Inquiry* 12 (Winter 1986): 365–90, especially note 17.

163. Sampson, *Mary Shelley*, 172.

164. Shelley, *Journals*, 226.

165. Ibid., 428.

166. Ibid., 293.

167. Percy Shelley to Leigh Hunt, 15 August 1819, in *The Letters of Percy Bysshe Shelley*, ed. F. L. Jones, vol. 2 (Oxford: Clarendon, 1964), 109.

168. Mary Shelley, *Matilda*, ed. Pamela Clemit, in *The Novels and Selected Works of Mary Shelley*, vol. 2, 57.

169. Shelley, *Mathilda*, ed. Nitchie.

170. Shelley, *Matilda*, ed. Clemit, 5.

171. Ellen Moers influentially coined the term "female gothic" to describe a particular form of gothic-romantic literature, written by women and voicing women's concerns about their entrapment in men-dominant societies, which emerged in late eighteenth- and early nineteenth-century British literature. See Moers, *Literary Women* (New York: Doubleday, 1976).

172. Shelley, *The Last Man*, 330.

173. For her first direct allusion to *Oedipus at Colonus*, see Shelley, *Matilda*, ed. Clemit, 5. For her recording of her reading Sophocles's *Oedipus Rex* and *Antigone*—and the latter, it would appear from her journal, in "Greek" with "αμ" (Alexander Mavrokordatos)—in early 1821, see Shelley, *Journals*, 350–51, 358.

174. Aristotle's *Poetics* in Aristotle, Longinus, Demetrius, *Poetics. Longinus: On the Sublime. Demetris: On Style*, trans. Stephen Halliwell, Loeb Classical Library 199, online (Cambridge, MA: Harvard University Press, 1995), 64–65 (lines 30–34).

175. Shelley, *The Last Man*, 64.

176. Ibid., 290. The editors of *The Last Man* for volume 4 of *The Novels and Selected Works of Mary Shelley*, Jane Blumberg and Nora Crook, correctly identify this passage from *Oedipus at Colonus*, but incorrectly allude to the existence of Mary Shelley's translation of this play in the "Bodleian." That manuscript is in fact her translation of *Oedipus Rex*, in her "Greek Studies" notebook (MS. Abinger e. 52), which was only available on microfilm and not deposited in the Bodleian until 2004 (eight years after the publication of *The Novels and Selected Works of Mary Shelley*).

177. Shelley had submitted *The Last Man* to her publisher by November 1825. The last dated entry of her "Journal of Sorrow" is December 1825. At the back of her "Journal of Sorrow," she transcribed her inscription to Jane Williams in a first-edition copy of *The Last Man* that she gave to her friend and fellow widow in January 1826. Shelley, *Letters*, vol. 1, 503–4; Shelley, *Journals*, 495.

178. Mary Shelley, "The Fields of Fancy," in *Works of Mary Shelley*, vol. 2, appendix 1, 405.

179. Ibid. Shelley, *Matilda*, ed. Clemit, 5.

180. Louis Breger, *Freud: Darkness in the Midst of Vision* (New York: John Wiley & Sons, 2000), 27.

181. Richard Armstrong, "Oedipus as Evidence: The Theatrical Background to Freud's Oedipus Complex," *PsyArt* (1 January 1999), accessed 4 August 2021, https://psyartjournal.com/article/show/armstrong-oedipus_as_evidence_the_theatrical_backg.

182. Sigmund Freud, *The Interpretation of Dreams*, trans. A. A. Brill, revised ed., Kindle edition (Scotts Valley, CA: IAP, 2009), location 4252.

183. Ibid.

184. Peter Gay, *Freud: A Life for Our Time* (New York: Norton, 1988), 112.

185. Freud, *Interpretation of Dreams*, location 4232.

186. Ibid.

187. Ibid., location 4235.

188. Ibid., locations 4235, 113.

189. Ibid., location 113.

190. Ibid., location 3366.

191. Ibid.

192. Ibid., location 3362.

193. Ibid.

194. Letters from Sigmund Freud to Ernst Jones, 26 January 1920 and 11 March 1928. Quoted from the Sigmund Freud Papers, Manuscript Division, Library of Congress, Washington, DC. As cited in the "Freud and Pandemic: 1920/2020" exhibit at the Freud Museum, London, June 2021.

195. Sigmund Freud, "The Ego and the Id" (1923), trans. Joan Riviere, reprinted in *Texas Association for Counseling and Development* 17, no. 1 (1989): 5–22.

196. Bowers, "On First Looking into Mary Shelley's Homer."

197. Schoina, "Grubbing at 'Greek Roots.'"

198. Shelley, *Journals*, 476–77.

199. Beyond Philoctetes, Shelley also identified with the most famous modern literary figure to be stranded on a remote island, Robinson Crusoe. She read Defoe's 1719 novel before writing her own version of its epic story of solitary survival in *The Last Man*. In 1838, she confided in her journal that she was "sunk . . . in a state of loneliness no other human being ever before I beleive ever endured—Except Robinson Crusoe." Shelley, *Journals*, 515–18, 555.

200. Shelley, *Journals*, 431–32.

201. Nussbaum, "Preface," *The Fragility of Goodness*, 385.

202. Sophocles, *Oedipus Trilogy*, trans. Brian Doerries (New York: Vintage, 2021), xi.

203. Shelley, *The Last Man*, 183.

204. Ibid., 41.

205. Thomas W. Laqueur, "The Queen Caroline Affair: Politics as Art in the Reign of George IV," *The Journal of Modern History* 54, no. 2 (September 1982): 441; Samuel Gladden, "Shelley's Agenda Writ Large: Reconsidering *Oedipus Tyrannus; or, Swellfoot the Tyrant*," in *Romantic Circles* (blog), Praxis Series, "Reading Shelley's Interventionist Poetry, 1819–1820," May 2001; Dana Van Kooy, "The Queen Caroline Affair as a Theatrical and Dramatic Spectacle," Horace Walpole Library, Yale University, accessed 20 November 2021, https://walpole.library.yale.edu/sites/default/files/files/Van%20Kooy.pdf.

206. Gladden, "Shelley's Agenda Writ Large."

207. Van Krooy, "The Queen Caroline Affair."

208. Shelley, *Journals*, 554. Shelley, *Letters*, vol. 2, 259. See also her contributions to *The Liberal: Verse and Prose from "The South"* (London: John Hunt, 1822–23).

209. Shelley, *Letters*, vol. 2, 183.

210. Mary Wollstonecraft to Joseph Johnson, 26 December 1792, in *The Collected Letters of Mary Wollstonecraft*, ed. Janet Todd (New York: Columbia University Press, 2004), 216; Wollstonecraft, *An Historical and Moral View of the Origin and Progress of the French Revolution*.

211. MS. Abinger c. 65, folders 12–13. See Introduction.

212. Rich, *Diving into the Wreck*.

213. Weinberg, ed., "The Dating of the Copybook and Publication of its Contents," BSM 22, part i, 39–40. See also Shelley, *Letters*, vol. 1, 296, for her December 1822 record of copying the partial translation of Plato's *Republic* from Percy's Greek studies salvaged from the shipwreck of the *Don Juan*. To support the inference that Percy's translation of Plato's *Symposium* was among the Greek studies manuscripts recovered from the ship that sank between 4 July and 8 July 1822,

one of Percy's last letters, dated 4 July 1822, says "I have found the translation of the Symposium." See Percy Shelley, *Letters*, vol. 2, 444. See also Weinberg, BSM 22, part i, 24.

214. Clemens, "Morbus Anglicus," 41–60.

215. Hunt Botting, "Mary Shelley's 'Romantic Spinozism.'"

216. Shelley, *The Last Man*, 362–64.

217. Ibid.

218. R. H. Hill, *The Shelley Correspondence in the Bodleian Library* (Oxford: John Johnson, 1926), 46.

Chapter 3

1. Patricia Owens and Katharina Rietzler, *Women's International Thought: A New History* (Cambridge: Cambridge University Press, 2021); Samuel Moyn, *Humane: How the United States Abandoned Peace and Reinvented War* (New York: Farrar, Straus and Giroux, 2021); Duncan Bell, "J. G. Ballard's Surrealist Liberalism," *Political Theory* 49, no. 6 (2021): 934–67; Duncan Bell, *Dreamworlds of Race: Empire and the Utopian Destiny of Anglo-America* (Princeton, NJ: Princeton University Press, 2020); Liane Hartnett, "Love as a Practice of Peace: The Political Theologies of Tolstoy, Gandhi and King," in *Theology and World Politics: International Political Theory*, ed. Vassilios Paipais (London: Palgrave Macmillan, 2020); Eileen Hunt Botting, *Artificial Life After Frankenstein* (Philadelphia: University of Pennsylvania Press, 2020), especially ch. 2 and "Coda"; Duncan Bell, "Pragmatism and Prophecy: H. G. Wells and the Metaphysics of Socialism," *American Political Science Review* 112, no. 2 (2018): 409–22; Duncan Bell, "Founding the World State: H. G. Wells on Empire and the English-Speaking Peoples," *International Studies Quarterly* 62, no. 4 (2018): 867–79; Eileen Hunt Botting, *Mary Shelley and the Rights of the Child: Political Philosophy in "Frankenstein"* (Philadelphia: University of Pennsylvania Press, 2017), especially chs. 2–4; Emma Planinc, "Catching up with Wells: The Political Theory of H. G. Wells's Science Fiction," *Political Theory* 45, no. 5 (2017): 637–58; Kate McLoughlin, *Authoring War: The Literary Representation of War from the Iliad to Iraq* (Cambridge: Cambridge University Press, 2011); James Dawes, *The Language of War: Literature and Culture in the U.S. from the Civil War through World War II* (Cambridge, MA: Harvard University Press, 2009); Paul Sheeran, *Literature and International Relations: Stories in the Art of Diplomacy* (London: Routledge, 2007); Paul Fussell, *Abroad: British Literary Traveling between the Wars* (Oxford: Oxford University Press, 1982).

2. Liane Hartnett argued in her 2018 international relations dissertation that "liminal" literature (written by now-canonized thinkers such as Tolstoy, Tagore, and Camus) has been a productive site for fresh and rebellious, pacific and anti-imperial ideas on the role of love in international relations. See Liane Hartnett, "Love in a Time of Empire: An Engagement with the Political Thought of Tolstoy, Tagore, and Camus" (PhD diss., London School of Economics, 2018). See also Hartnett, "Love as a Practice of Peace: The Political Theologies of Tolstoy, Gandhi and King"; Liane Hartnett and Or Rosenboim, "Historical International Relations and International Political Thought," in *Routledge Handbook of Historical International Relations*, ed. Benjamin de Carvalho, Julia Costa Lopez, and Halvard Leira (London: Routledge, 2021); Maša Mrovlje, "Beyond Nussbaum's Ethics of Reading: Camus, Arendt and the Political Significance of Narrative Imagination," *The European Legacy* 24, no. 2 (2019): 162–80; Maša Mrovlje, *Rethinking Political Judgement: Arendt and Existentialism* (Edinburgh: Edinburgh University Press, 2019).

3. Bell, *Dreamworlds of Race*; Sungju Park-Kang, *Fictional International Relations: Gender, Pain, and Truth* (London: Routledge, 2019); Julia Welland, "Joy and War: Reading Pleasure in Wartime Experience," *Review of International Studies* 44, no. 3 (2018), 438–55; Elizabeth

Dauphinee, *The Politics of Exile: Interventions* (London: Routledge, 2013); Maja Zehfuss, *Wounds of Memory: The Politics of War in Germany* (Cambridge: Cambridge University Press, 2011); Annick T. R. Wibben, *Feminist Security Studies: A Narrative Approach* (London: Routledge, 2011); Emma Hutchison, "Unsettling Stories: Jeanette Winterson and the Cultivation of Political Contingency," *Global Society* 24, no. 3 (2010): 351–68; Roland Bleiker, *Aesthetics and World Politics* (London: Palgrave Macmillan, 2009).

4. Émile Cammaerts, "Literature and International Relations," *Journal of the Royal Society of Arts* 70, no. 3608 (1922): 166–67.

5. Hunt Botting, *Artificial Life After Frankenstein*, 2–5; Gary Westfahl, *Cosmic Engineers: A Study of Hard Science Fiction* (Westport, CT: Greenwood Press, 1996).

6. Westfahl, *Cosmic Engineers*, 21.

7. Shelley, *Frankenstein*, 33.

8. Shelley, *The Last Man*, 362.

9. Hunt Botting, *Artificial Life After Frankenstein*, 3.

10. Shelley, *Frankenstein*, 69, 119; Shelley, *The Last Man*, 176.

11. Shelley, *The Last Man*, 183, 362.

12. Hunt Botting, *Artificial Life After Frankenstein*, 4, 43; Philip Ball, *The Modern Myths: Adventures in the Machinery of the Popular Imagination* (Chicago: University of Chicago Press, 2021), 70.

13. Peter Melville, *Romantic Hospitality and the Resistance to Accommodation* (Waterloo, Canada: Wilfrid Laurier University Press, 2007), 155–56.

14. Thomas More, *Utopia*, ed. George Logan and Robert Adams (Cambridge: Cambridge University Press, 2002).

15. Flood, "Margaret Atwood: Covid-19 Lockdown is Not a Dystopia."

16. Shelley, *The Last Man*, 190.

17. Orwell, *Nineteen Eighty-Four*; Atwood, *The Handmaid's Tale and The Testaments*.

18. Dennis Glover, *The Last Man in Europe* (Melbourne, Australia: Black Inc., 2017); Orwell, *Nineteen Eighty-Four*, 212.

19. George Orwell, "Review of English Diaries of the Nineteenth Century," *Manchester Evening News*, 28 July 1944.

20. Margaret Atwood, *Speeches for Doctor Frankenstein* (Bloomfield Hills, MI: Cranbrook Academy of Art, 1966).

21. "Survivor—Eye of the Tiger Lyrics," Lyrics, accessed 27 October 2021, https://www.lyrics.com/lyric/958332/Survivor/Eye+of+the+Tiger.

22. Shiel, *The Purple Cloud*; Matheson, *I Am Legend*.

23. Aram Goudsouzian, *Sidney Poitier: Man, Actor, Icon* (Chapel Hill: University of North Carolina Press, 2011); American Film Institute, *The American Film Institute Catalog of Motion Pictures Produced in the United States* (Berkeley: University of California Press, 1997); Amy J. Ransom, *I Am Legend as American Myth: Race and Masculinity in the Novel and Its Film Adaptations* (Jefferson, NC: McFarland & Company, 2018).

24. Matheson, *I Am Legend*, location 988.

25. Ransom, *I Am Legend as American Myth*.

26. Hunt Botting, *Artificial Life After Frankenstein*; Eileen Hunt Botting, "Mary Shelley Created 'Frankenstein,' and Then a Pandemic," *New York Times*, 13 March 2020; Anjuli Fatima Raza Kolb, "Paravictorianism: Mary Shelley and Viral Sovereignty," *Victorian Studies* 62, no. 3 (2020): 446–59; Kate Singer, "It's the End of the World as We Know It and I Feel Queer: Mary Shelley, Queer Affect, and Shapeshifting Through *The Last Man*," in *Material Transgressions: Beyond Romantic Bodies, Genders, Things*, ed. Kate Singer, Ashley Cross, and Suzanne L. Barnett (Liverpool: Liverpool University Press, 2020), 213–30; Serena Baiesi, "Mary Shelley and the Anthropocene: An Eco-feminist Reading of *The Last Man*," *Textus* 34, no. 3 (2021): 49–67;

Omar F. Miranda, ed., "Mary Shelley's The Last Man: Abridged Edition," *Romantic Circles* (blog), February 2022, https://romantic-circles.org; Stefania Maria Maci, "'Pestilence is the Enemy We Fly': Metaphors for the Pandemic in Mary Shelley's *The Last Man*," in *Translation and Interpretation: Practicing the Knowledge of Literature*, ed. Raul Calzoni, Francesca Di Blasio, and Greta Perletti (Göttingen: Vandenhoeck & Ruprecht Verlage, 2022), 157–66; Diana Rose Newby, "Race, Vitalism, and the Contingency of Contagion in Mary Shelley's *The Last Man*," *ELH* 89, no. 3 (2022): 689–718; Sarottama Majumdar, "Mary Shelley's *The Last Man*: Dystopian Fiction and Pandemics," in *Literary Representations of Pandemics, Epidemics and Pestilence*, ed. Nishi Pulugurtha (New York: Routledge, 2022), 63–71; Chris Washington, ed., *Mary Shelley's The Last Man: A Norton Critical Edition* (New York: W. W. Norton, 2023).

27. McQueen, *Political Realism in Apocalyptic Times*, 23; Hunt Botting, *Artificial Life After Frankenstein*, 54.

28. Joanna Russ, *The Female Man*, Kindle edition (New York: Open Road, 1975), 93.

29. David Armitage, *Civil Wars: A History in Ideas* (New Haven, CT: Yale University Press, 2017).

30. Hunt Botting, *Mary Shelley and the Rights of the Child.*

31. Mary Shelley, *The Journals of Mary Shelley, 1814–1844*, eds. Paula R. Feldman and Diana Scott-Kilvert (Oxford: Clarendon Press, 1987), vol. 1, 93.

32. [Mary Shelley and Percy Shelley], *History of a Six Weeks' Tour.*

33. Thucydides, *The Peloponnesian War*; Shelley, *The Last Man*, 176.

34. Chris Mackie, "Thucydides and the Plague of Athens—What It Can Teach Us Now," *The Conversation*, 19 March 2020; Eileen Hunt Botting, "The Politics of Epidemics, from Thucydides to Mary Shelley to COVID-19," *Current History* 120, no. 822 (1 January 2021): 35–37.

35. Defoe, *A Journal of the Plague Year.*

36. Jacques Derrida, *Specters of Marx: The State of the Debt, the Work of Mourning and the New International* (New York: Routledge, 2012); Barbara Johnson, "The Last Man" [1980], *A Life with Mary Shelley*, with foreword by Cathy Caruth, introduction by Mary Wilson Carpenter, and essays by Judith Butler and Shoshana Felman (Stanford, CA: Stanford University Press, 2014), 3–14.

37. Shelley, *The Last Man*, 139.

38. Melville, *Romantic Hospitality and the Resistance to Accommodation*; Shelley, *The Last Man*, 183.

39. Hunt Botting, *Artificial Life After Frankenstein*, 51.

40. Strang, "Common Life, Animal Life, Equality: 'The Last Man.'"

41. Shelley, *The Last Man*, 362.

42. Hunt Botting, *Mary Shelley and the Rights of the Child.*

43. Johann Gottlieb Buhle, *Histoire de la philosophie moderne, depuis la renaissance des lettres jusquà Kant* (Paris: F. I. Fournier, 1816); "Manuscript Lists of Books from the Library of Percy Bysshe Shelley," Archives and Manuscripts, New York Public Library, accessed 1 December 2021, https://archives.nypl.org/cps/22404.

44. Emer de Vattel, *The Law of Nations: Or, Principles of the Law of Nature, Applied to the Conduct and Affairs of Nations and Sovereigns* (Philadelphia: T. & J. W. Johnson, 1844).

45. Vattel, *The Law of Nations*, 452–500; Simone Zurbuchen, "Vattel's Law of Nations and Just War Theory," *History of European Ideas* 35, no. 4 (1 December 2009): 408–17; David Armitage, "The Contagion of Sovereignty: Declarations of Independence since 1776," *South African Historical Journal* 52, no. 1 (1 January 2005): 1–18; David Armitage, *The Declaration of Independence: A Global History* (Cambridge, MA: Harvard University Press, 2007).

46. Richard H. Helmholz, "Use of the Civil Law in Post-Revolutionary American Jurisprudence," *Tulane Law Review* 66 (1992): 1649–84; Ben Holland, "The Moral Person of the State: Emer de Vattel and the Foundations of International Legal Order," *History of European Ideas* 37, no. 4

(2011): 438–45; F. S. Ruddy, "International Law and the Enlightenment: Vattel and the 18th Century," *International Lawyer* 3, no. 4 (1 January 1969): 839–58; Isaac Nakhimovsky, "Vattel's Theory of the International Order: Commerce and the Balance of Power in the Law of Nations," *History of European Ideas* 33, no. 2 (1 June 2007): 157–73.

47. Vattel, *The Law of Nations*, 452–500; Shelley, *The Last Man*, 31.

48. Shelley, *The Last Man*, 31.

49. Ibid.

50. Gordon, *Romantic Outlaws*, 376; Beaton, *Byron's War: Romantic Rebellion, Greek Revolution*, 70.

51. Vattel, *The Law of Nations*, 139.

52. Shelley, *The Last Man*, 26.

53. Buhle, *Histoire de la philosophie moderne*, vol. 6, 216–19.

54. Immanuel Kant, *Political Writings*, ed. Hans Reiss, trans. H. B. Nisbet (Cambridge: Cambridge University Press, 1991), 106.

55. Ibid., 106, 126.

56. Ibid., 103, 105.

57. Shelley, *Journals*, vol. 1, 37, 76, 94.

58. George Keate, *Ferney: An Epistle to Monsr. de Voltaire* (London: J. Dodsley, 1768); "History of Voltaire's Château," Château de Voltaire, Centre des monuments nationaux, accessed 28 October 2021, https://www.chateau-ferney-voltaire.fr/en/Explore/Chateau-de-Voltaire/History-of-Voltaire-s-Chateau.

59. Voltaire, *Candide, ou, L'optimisme* (Paris: Delarue, 1877); Shelley, *The Last Man*, 310.

60. Ruddy, "International Law and the Enlightenment."

61. Catherine Redford, "'The till Now Unseen Object of My Mad Idolatry': The Presence of Jane Williams in Mary Shelley's *The Last Man*," *Romanticism* 19, no. 1 (2013): 89–99; Paley, "Introduction," in Shelley, *The Last Man*, ed. Paley, xxi.

62. Percy Bysshe Shelley, *Shelley's Declaration of Rights* (Whittingham and Wilkins, 1868); Percy Bysshe Shelley, *The Masque of Anarchy: A Poem* (London: Shelley Society, 1892); Percy Bysshe Shelley, *A Philosophical View of Reform . . . with an Introduction and Appendix by T. W. Rolleston* (London: H. Milford, 1920).

63. Vattel, *The Law of Nations*, 134.

64. Ibid., 132.

65. Ibid., 138.

66. Shelley, *The Last Man*, ed. Paley, 336.

67. Ibid., 469.

68. Ruddy, "International Law and the Enlightenment," 845, 858.

69. Shelley, *The Last Man*, 362.

70. David Armitage, *Foundations of Modern International Thought* (Cambridge: Cambridge University Press, 2012), 165–66.

71. Shelley, *The Last Man*, 176, 278–79, 319.

72. Edmund Burke, *Reflections on the Revolution in France*, 7th ed. (London: Printed for J. Dodsley, 1790), 68; William Godwin, *Enquiry Concerning Political Justice* (G. G. and J. Robinson, 1798).

73. Mark Philp, ed., *Godwin's Political Justice* (Ithaca, NY: Cornell University Press, 1986), 2, 23, 48.

74. Thomas Hobbes, *Leviathan*, ed. Richard Tuck (Cambridge: Cambridge University Press, 1996).

75. John Locke, *Two Treatises of Government*, ed. Peter Laslett (Cambridge: Cambridge University Press, 1988); Godwin, *Enquiry Concerning Political Justice*.

76. Shelley, *The Last Man*, ed. Paley, 320–21.

77. MS. Abinger c. 65, fols. 12–13.

78. Shelley, *Journals*, vol. 1, 215.

79. David Hume, "The History of England, vol. 5," *Online Library of Liberty*, accessed 28 October 2021, https://oll.libertyfund.org/title/hume-the-history-of-england-vol-5.

80. Ralph Verney, *Verney Papers: Notes of Proceedings in the Long Parliament* (London: Camden Society, 1845).

81. "Verney Estate—East & Botolph Claydon Village," The Claydons, accessed 28 October 2021, https://www.theclaydons.org/verney-estate.

82. Holland, "The Moral Person of the State"; Jennifer Pitts, *Boundaries of the International: Law and Empire* (Cambridge, MA: Harvard University Press, 2018), 79–84.

83. John Wilson, *The City of the Plague: And Other Poems* (G. Ramsay, 1816); Svetlana Evdokimova, *Alexander Pushkin's Little Tragedies: The Poetics of Brevity* (Madison: University of Wisconsin Press, 2003).

84. Fyodor Dostoevsky, *Notes from Underground* (New York: Knopf Doubleday, 2011).

85. Dostoevsky, *Notes from Underground*; Friedrich Nietzsche, *Thus Spoke Zarathustra* (New York: Penguin, 1974); Byron, "Darkness." For trenchant commentary on Byron's "Darkness" alongside Shelley's *The Last Man*, see Chris Washington, *Romantic Revelations: Visions of Post-Apocalyptic Life and Hope in the Anthropocene* (Toronto: University of Toronto Press, 2019), 66, 71, 73.

86. Jeff Love and Jeffrey Metzger, eds., *Nietzsche and Dostoevsky: Philosophy, Morality, Tragedy* (Evanston, IL: Northwestern University Press, 2016).

87. Friedrich Nietzsche, *Beyond Good & Evil: Prelude to a Philosophy of the Future* (New York: Knopf Doubleday, 2010), 89.

88. Nietzsche, *Thus Spoke Zarathustra*, 124–30.

89. Ibid.

90. Nina Amstutz, *Caspar David Friedrich: Nature and the Self* (New Haven, CT: Yale University Press, 2020).

91. Catherine Redford, "Friendship and Community in Last Man Literature, 1806–1833" (PhD diss., University of Bristol, 2013).

92. Ibid.

93. Barbara C. Morden, *John Martin: Apocalypse Now!* (Newcastle Upon Tyne, UK: Northumbria University Press, 2010).

94. William Feaver, *The Art of John Martin* (Oxford: Clarendon Press, 1975), 184–87.

95. Max Adams, *The Prometheans: John Martin and the Generation that Stole the Future* (London: Quercus, 2010), 4.

96. Feaver, *The Art of John Martin*, 184–87. I confirmed Feaver's finding by visiting Hertfordshire Archives and Local Studies to read two letters from John Martin to Edward Bulwer-Lytton in 1849 (ref. DE/K/C11/33-4).

97. Feaver, *The Art of John Martin*, 185–86, 234 note 124.

98. Thomas Campbell to Edward Bulwer-Lytton, 24 October 1842, in the Bulwer-Lytton letter book at Hertfordshire Archives and Local Studies.

99. Redford, "Friendship and Community in Last Man Literature, 1806–1833."

100. Shelley, *Journals*, vol. 1, 118.

101. Gillen D'Arcy Wood, *Tambora: The Eruption That Changed the World* (Princeton, NJ: Princeton University Press, 2015).

102. Shelley, *Journals*, vol. 2, 477.

103. Redford, "Friendship and Community in Last Man Literature, 1806–1833."

104. Ibid.

105. Jonathan Jones, "Frankenstein and the Gory Gang: How the Novel Blazed a Trail for High Art Horrors," *The Guardian*, 31 October 2018.

106. "One of Twenty Vignettes—The Last Man," National Galleries of Scotland, accessed 29 October 2021, https://www.nationalgalleries.org/art-and-artists/19265; Thomas Campbell, *The Poetical Works of Thomas Campbell: A New and Improved Edition, With a Portrait, Etc* (Oliver & Boyd, 1837).

107. William Hutchins Callcott and Thomas Campbell, *The Last Man* (London: Addison & Hodson, 1844); William Hutchins Callcott and Thomas Campbell, *The Last Man* (London: Addison & Lucas, 1850); William Hutchins Callcott and Thomas Campbell, *The Last Man* (New York: Firth, Pond & Co., 1850); William Hutchins Callcott and Thomas Campbell, *The Last Man*, Sweet Songs for Sabbath Evenings (Boston: Oliver Ditson & Co., 1857); William Hutchins Callcott and Thomas Campbell, *The Last Man* (New York: Wm. A. Pond & Co., 1863–77).

108. Callcott and Campbell, *The Last Man* (1857).

109. Ibid.

110. "Robert George Kelly, Painter," Library Ireland, accessed 29 October 2021, https://www.libraryireland.com/irishartists/robert-george-kelly.php; Walter Strickland, *A Dictionary of Irish Artists* (Cambridge: Cambridge University Press, 2012).

111. I thank Andy Hom and Cian O'Driscoll for this insight.

112. Bram Stoker, *Dracula*, ed. Roger Luckhurst (Oxford: Oxford University Press, 2011); Wilkinson & Hodge Sotheby, *Catalogue of Valuable Printed Books, Autograph Letters, and Illuminated and Other Manuscripts Including the Library of the Late Bram Stoker, Esq., and Other Properties: Monday, the 7th of July, 1913, and Following Day* (London: Dryden Press, 1913).

113. Eileen M. Hunt, "'Dracula's Daughter': The Rediscovery of a Love Poem for George Orwell," *Times Literary Supplement*, 4 June 2021.

114. David Ryan, *George Orwell on Screen: Adaptations, Documentaries and Docudramas on Film and Television* (Jefferson, NC: McFarland, 2018), 76; Claire Tomalin, *The Young H. G. Wells: Changing the World* (New York: Penguin, 2021), 1.

115. Wells, *The War of the Worlds*; Thomas Hood, "The Last Man," *Romantic Circles* (blog), 1 October 1997, accessed 5 December 2021, https://romantic-circles.org/editions/mws/lastman/hood.htm; Lee Sterrenburg, "The Last Man: Anatomy of Failed Revolutions," *Nineteenth-Century Fiction* 33, no. 3 (1978): 324–47.

116. Hunt Botting, *Artificial Life After Frankenstein*, 125–26.

117. Don G. Smith, "Shelley's 'Frankenstein': A Possible Source for Poe's 'MS. Found in a Bottle,'" *Poe Studies/Dark Romanticism* 25, no. 1/2 (1992): 37–38.

118. Mary Shelley, *The Last Man* (Philadelphia: Carey, Lea and Blanchard, 1833); *Frankenstein, or, The Modern Prometheus* (Philadelphia: Carey, Lea and Blanchard, 1833). Hunt Botting, *Artificial Life After Frankenstein*, 39–40.

119. George Orwell, *The Complete Works of George Orwell*, eds. Peter Davison and Ian Angus, vol. 10 (London: Secker and Warburg, 1986), 195.

120. Orwell, "Review of English Diaries of the Nineteenth Century"; Glover, *The Last Man in Europe*.

121. Orwell, *Nineteen Eighty-Four*, 212.

122. Shelley, *Journals*, vol. 2, 477; James Aitken, ed., *English Diaries of the Nineteenth Century* (London: Penguin, 1944), 31–33.

123. Aitken, *English Diaries of the Nineteenth Century*, 31–33.

124. Orwell, *Nineteen Eighty-Four*, 212; email correspondence from L. J. Hurst to the author, 5 December 2021.

125. Malcolm Pittock, "*The Last Man* and *Nineteen Eighty-Four*," *English Language Notes* 35, issue 3 (1998): 67–73. While Pittock underscored Alfred Noyes's 1940 novel *The Last Man* as a probable source for *Nineteen Eighty-Four*, there were many other "Last Man" novels in the early twentieth century, as the concept of being (actually or figuratively) the last man (or the last woman) became a popular trope across science fiction, westerns, romances, and crime novels after

the success of M. P. Shiel's 1901 novel *The Purple Cloud*. Some of the most influential of the sf novels were by Olaf Stapledon: *Last and First Men* (1930) and *Last Men in London* (1932). But at the time of writing, I am unable to establish Shelley as a source for Stapledon in the way I have done for Orwell. For this reason, I omit Stapledon from my genealogy of Shelleyan "Last (wo) man" narratives of the twentieth century, despite his status as one of the great authors of "political science fiction" after her. Duncan Bell is presently writing a study of Stapledon in the context of futuristic thought of the early twentieth century that will undoubtedly reveal more. I thank Bell and David Armitage for introducing me to the work of Stapledon. See Olaf Stapledon, *Last and First Men / Last Men in London* (London: Penguin Classics, 1972).

126. Alfred Noyes, *The Last Man*, 2nd ed. (London: Catholic Book Club, 1941), 5–6, 8–9.

127. Ibid., 5–6.

128. Ibid.

129. George Orwell, *As I Please, 1943–1946* (Boston: David R. Godine Publisher, 2000), 144.

130. Ibid., 99.

131. Sylvia Topp, *Eileen: The Making of George Orwell*, Kindle edition (Unbound Publishing, 2020), locations 1472, 1828.

132. Eileen O'Shaughnessy, "End of the Century 1984," in *The Chronicle of the Girls of Sunderland High School*, no. 54 (Printed for Private Circulation, June 1934), 81; Sally Coniam, "Orwell and the Origins of *Nineteen Eighty-Four*, with a transcript of Eileen O'Shaughnessy's 'End of the Century 1984,'" *Times Literary Supplement* 5047, 31 December 1999, 14.

133. Orwell, *Nineteen Eighty-Four*, 1.

134. Ibid; O'Shaughnessy, "End of the Century 1984."

135. Orwell, *Nineteen Eighty-Four*, 27.

136. Matthew Lamb, "The Meeting That Never Was," *Los Angeles Review of Books*, 13 March 2015, https://lareviewofbooks.org/article/meeting-never/.

137. Camus, *The Plague*; Camus, *The Stranger*.

138. Mary Shelley, *Frankenstein: Annotated for Scientists, Engineers, and Creators of All Kinds*, ed. David H. Guston, Ed Finn, and Jason Scott Robert (Cambridge, MA: MIT Press, 2017), 80.

139. Hartnett, "Love in a Time of Empire: An Engagement with the Political Thought of Tolstoy, Tagore, and Camus."

140. Albert Camus, *The First Man* (New York: Knopf Doubleday, 2012).

141. Dostoevsky, *Notes from the Underground*, 40.

142. Dostoevsky, *Notes from Underground*; Nietzsche, *Thus Spoke Zarathustra*; Camus, *The Stranger*.

143. Defoe, *A Journal of the Plague Year*.

144. Albert Camus, *The Myth of Sisyphus and Other Essays* (New York: Knopf Doubleday, 2012).

145. Adam Potkay, "*Frankenstein* in the History of Happiness: From Ancient Ethics to Richard Wright," *The Keats-Shelley Review* 34, no. 1 (2020): 35–45; Charlotte Gordon, *Mary Shelley: A Very Short Introduction* (Oxford: Oxford University Press, 2022), 97.

146. Richard Wright, *The Man Who Lived Underground: A Novel* (New York: Harper Perennial, 2021), 222.

147. Ibid., 177, 205. The memoir is titled "Memories of my Grandmother," published for the first time in 2021 alongside *The Man Who Lived Underground*.

148. Ibid., 224.

149. Ralph Ellison, *Invisible Man* (New York: Vintage, [1947] 1980), 2.

150. W. E. B. Du Bois, *The Souls of Black Folk* [1903], Kindle edition (Seattle: Amazon Classics, n.d.), 23.

151. Ellison, *Invisible Man*, 573.

152. Ibid., 3.

153. See introduction and this chapter.

154. Matheson, *I Am Legend*.

155. Shiel, *The Purple Cloud*.

156. Shiel, *The Purple Cloud*, 2; Shelley, *The Last Man*, ed. Paley, 6.

157. Matheson, *I Am Legend*, location 2343.

158. Bruce Peabody and Gloria Pastorino, *Beyond the Living Dead: Essays on the Romero Legacy* (Jefferson, NC: McFarland, 2021); Ransom, *I Am Legend as American Myth*.

159. Shiel, *Purple Cloud*, 11.

160. Michael Ashley, ed., *The End of the World and Other Catastrophes* (London: British Library, 2019), 30–35, 330.

161. Meryl Altman, "Beauvoir and Blackness," in *Beauvoir in Time*, Value Inquiry Book Series 348 (Boston: Brill, 2020), 237–46.

162. Simone de Beauvoir, *The Second Sex*, trans. Constance Borde and Sheila Malovany-Chevallier, with an introduction by Judith Thurman (New York: Vintage, 2010), 4, 311, 736.

163. See introduction.

164. Martin Stannard, *Muriel Spark: The Biography* (New York: Norton, 2010), 115, 142, 158.

165. Muriel Spark, *Robinson*, 9.

166. Lorraine Hansberry, *A Raisin in the Sun*, 127.

167. Hunt Botting, *Artificial Life After Frankenstein*, interlude.

168. All allusions and quotations drawn from the Lorraine Hansberry papers at the Schomburg Center for Research in Black Culture at the New York Public Library. See also Eileen M. Hunt, "Wollstonecraft: A Daring Experiment," *Times Literary Supplement*, Footnotes to Plato online series, November 2022.

169. Ibid. See also William Godwin, *Memoirs* (1798).

170. Charles J. Shields, *Lorraine Hansberry: The Life Behind 'A Raisin in the Sun'* (New York: Henry Holt, 2022).

171. Russ, *The Female Man*, 213. Russ alludes to the late 1930s/1940s genre of "*Spicy Western Stories*" in the final lines of the novel, coyly implying that *The Female Man* is both descended from and destined to become a pulp erotic classic. For "last man" narratives in mid-century pulp erotic fiction, see Randy Salem, *Man among Women* (Beacon, 1960); Trudy Starling, *World without Men* (New York: Domino, 1965); Marise Querlin, *World without Men* (London: Mayflower-Dell, 1965).

172. Russ, *The Female Man*, 93.

173. Margaret Atwood, "My Hero: George Orwell," *The Guardian*, 18 January 2013; Atwood, *Speeches for Doctor Frankenstein*.

174. Atwood, *The Handmaid's Tale and The Testaments*; *Oryx and Crake*; Atwood, *MaddAddam*; Margaret Atwood, "Margaret Atwood on *The Year of the Flood*," Penguin Random House Canada, YouTube video, 19 August 2010, https://www.youtube.com/watch?v=npamsWwWu_0&list=PLMPkmRDc0CwMp3BowPTWPGyYy2XS2_8hR&index=2&t=0s.

175. Samuel R. Delany, "Racism and Science Fiction," *New York Review of Science Fiction*, August 1998, https://www.nyrsf.com/racism-and-science-fiction-.html.

176. Butler, *Clay's Ark*.

177. Erin Blakemore, "Human-Pig Hybrid Created in the Lab—Here Are the Facts," *Science*, 26 January 2017; Atwood, *MaddAddam*.

178. Atwood, *Oryx and Crake*.

179. Atwood, "Margaret Atwood on *The Year of the Flood*."

180. Butler, *Earthseed*.

181. Ibid.

182. Jean-Paul Sartre and Albert Camus, *No Exit and Three Other Plays* (New York: Knopf Doubleday, 2015); Mandel, *Station Eleven*, 48, 144, 148.

183. Gottlieb, *Final Girl*.

184. Jill Owens, "The Powells.Com Interview with Margaret Atwood," *Powell's Books* (blog), 6 October 2009, https://www.powells.com/post/interviews/the-powellscom-interview-with-margaret-atwood.

185. Jordan Williams, "Station Eleven by Emily St. John Mandel," *American Microreviews & Interviews* (blog), accessed 8 February 2021, http://www.americanmicroreviews.com/station-eleven-by-emily-st-john-mandel.

186. "The Literary Gazette and Journal of Belles Lettres, Arts, Sciences, &c. (Feb. 1826)."

187. Jeanne Morefield, "Women's International Thought: Toward a Counter-Archival Transformation of Global Power–Knowledge," *International Politics Reviews*, 26 October 2021. For two classic works of feminist political theory that have reread the canon of political thought through the lenses of both women's perspectives and masculinist gender biases, see Susan Moller Okin, *Women in Western Political Thought* (Princeton, NJ: Princeton University Press, 1979) and Nancy J. Hirschmann, *Gender, Class, and Freedom in Modern Political Theory* (Princeton, NJ: Princeton University Press, 2007). Much work remains to be done, however, to create a feminist counter-archive of political science fiction that can be used to critically reevaluate the canons of political philosophy and literature for their blind spots, biases, and omissions. This book is one small step toward fulfilling that objective.

Postface

1. Shelley, *The Last Man*, 139, 362. The first time she used the term "PLAGUE" and the second and third time she used the term "LAST MAN" in her pandemic novel, Shelley used "all caps" to underscore, perhaps in a self-consciously melodramatic way, that they were the primary catalysts of action (and reaction) in the narrative.

2. Edward Bulwer-Lytton, *Paul Clifford* (London: Colburn and Bentley, 1830), 1.

3. Feaver, *The Art of John Martin*, 185–86. Feaver references the John Martin letters to Edward Bulwer-Lytton held by Hertfordshire Archives and Local Studies (one letter from 1842, DE/K/C1/46 and two letters from 1849, DE/K/C11/33-4).

4. Mary Shelley, "Autograph letter signed to Sir John Bowring, an editor of the 'Westminster Review,' asking for help with the publishing of a book by her stepbrother Charles Clairmont, 25 November [1828]," 4 Jul 2013, RP 10112, British Library. Original letter held by the Pforzheimer Collection of Shelley and His Circle, MWS 0416, New York Public Library.

5. Schoina, "Grubbing at 'Greek Roots'"; Bowers, "On First Looking into Mary Shelley's Homer." MS. Abinger c. 63, fols. 40–1; MS. Abinger e. 52.

6. MS. Abinger d. 27–31.

7. Shelley, *Journals*, 68.

8. E. Flügel, "Shelley's Sophocles," *Anglia* (Tübingen), no. 24 (1901); Timothy Webb, "Shelley's Sophocles: A Legend Re-Examined," *Keats-Shelley Memorial Bulletin* 19 (1968): 47–52.

9. Dowden, *The Life of Percy Bysshe Shelley*, vol. 2, 533–34.

10. Julie A. Carlson, *England's First Family of Writers: Mary Wollstonecraft, William Godwin, Mary Shelley* (Baltimore: Johns Hopkins University Press, 2007).

11. Mary Wollstonecraft, *Letters Written during a Short Residence in Sweden, Norway and Denmark* (London: Joseph Johnson, 1796). William Godwin would publish heavily edited versions of Wollstonecraft's original letters to Imlay in his edition of her *Posthumous Works*, released with his *Memoirs of the Author of A Vindication of the Rights of Woman* (London: Joseph Johnson, 1798).

12. Dowden, *Life of Percy Bysshe Shelley*, vol. 2, 534.

13. Lady Jane Shelley went on to edit the journals of Mary and Percy Shelley for the limited edition and privately printed *Shelley and Mary* (1882), which served as the basis for all published

selections from the journals until Paula R. Feldman and Diana Scott-Kilvert produced the first comprehensive scholarly edition of Mary Shelley's *Journals* in 1987 from the five extant manuscript volumes, which were given to the Bodleian Library by their owner, Lord Abinger, in 1974. See Feldman and Scott-Kilvert, "Publication History," in Shelley, *Journals*, xxv–xxvi.

14. Hermione Lee, *Virginia Woolf's Nose: Essays in Biography* (Princeton, NJ: Princeton University Press, 2005), 25.

15. "The Shelley Collection in the Bodleian," *The Academy, 1869-1902, 0269-333X*, no. 1109 (1893): 112–13.

16. Hunt Botting, ed., *Portraits of Wollstonecraft*, vol. 1, 36.

17. Feldman and Scott-Kilvert, "Publication History," in Shelley, *Journals*, xxvi.

18. Seymour, *Mary Shelley*, 150; Gordon, *Romantic Outlaws*, 140.

19. Shelley, *Journals*, 79.

20. Feldman and Scott-Kilvert, "Introduction," in Shelley, *Journals*, xix. The editors suggest that either Mary Shelley or Lady Jane Shelley tore out thirty-nine pages of the surviving five volumes of the journals. One entire volume, from May 1815 to July 1816, is presumed missing or destroyed by Shelley herself.

21. Hunt Botting, "Mary Shelley Created *Frankenstein*, and Then a Pandemic."

22. Hunt Botting, "Journals of Sorrow: Mary Shelley's Visions of Contagion," *Times Literary Supplement*, 8 May 2020.

INDEX

Note: Page numbers in italic type indicate illustrations.

ACKNOWLEDGMENTS

Or, Coming Full Circle

Without quite realizing it, I began work on *The First Last Man* in February 2020. Though full of trepidation for catching the novel coronavirus, I flew to New York City late that month to complete a long-planned research trip to the New York Public Library to consult the papers of Mary Shelley and Mary Wollstonecraft in The Carl Pforzheimer Collection of Shelley and His Circle as well as the papers of Lorraine Hansberry in the Schomburg Center for the Study of Black Culture. During a visit with Doron Weber at the nearby Sloan Foundation, which generously supported the publication of my book *Artificial Life After Frankenstein,* he encouraged me to consider writing an opinion piece relating Mary Shelley's *The Last Man* to the nascent Covid-19 pandemic.

The morning after my son's school shut down in the first week of March, I submitted the essay to The Stone, the philosophy series at the *New York Times.* A slightly revised version of this op-ed appears as the preface to this book, as it marks the beginning of a long and unexpected, surprising yet strangely fulfilling journey of studying Mary Shelley through the lenses of plague literature, international political theory, and existential philosophy. It also gave me the perfect postapocalyptic image for the cover art, by the artist Isabel Selinger.

Especially during the precarious research period of the Covid-19 pandemic, I am indebted to my university, Notre Dame, and three of its research institutes—the Nanovic Institute for European Studies, the Kroc Institute for International Peace Studies, and The Institute for Scholarship in the Liberal Arts—for their support of my archival work on Mary Shelley, her family, and her friends at the Bodleian Library and the British Library in 2021–22. In Summer 2022, I was honored to have received the

Carr-Thomas-Ovenden Fellowship in English Literature at the Bodleian Library to continue my study of the papers of "Mary Shelley and Her Circle," to borrow a brilliant feminist revisionary term coined by the late Barbara Johnson in 2009.

The pandemic inspired in me a sense of obligation to share my arguments on Shelley's relevance for the ethics of public health. A flurry of public-facing writing ensued, in excellent venues such as the *Times Literary Supplement, Chicago Tribune, Public Seminar, Current History*, the *CBC Ideas* radio podcast, and *Ideology Theory Practice*, the blog of *The Journal of Political Ideologies*. Several academic journals also supported peer-reviewed development of the experimental and envelope-pushing arguments for this book: *History of European Ideas, Frontiers in Sociology, Digital Defoe*, and *The Review of International Studies*. A version of Chapter 3 was published open access in June 2022 as "Mary Shelley's *The Last Man*: Existentialism and IR Meet the Post-Apocalyptic Pandemic Novel," in a special issue of *The Review of International Studies* on "Existentialism and IR," guest edited by Liane Hartnett, Andrew Hom, and Cian O'Driscoll. I am grateful to the guest editors for encouraging me to write this paper, welcoming me into the international studies community, and inviting me to present the arguments on panels at the British International Studies Association (BISA) conference in 2021, 2022, and 2023.

Beyond the online BISA meeting in June 2021, I have benefited from presenting aspects of this book at various other virtual conferences and seminar series during the ongoing pandemic. A writing group with my fellow editors of *The Wollstonecraftian Mind* (2019), Sandrine Bergès and Alan Coffee, provided a friendly philosophical forum in which to test my ideas and interpretations. In April 2021, Paul Nugent arranged for me to give a talk to the Southeastern Connecticut World Affairs Council on "The Politics of Epidemics, from Thucydides to Mary Shelley to Covid-19," which shaped Chapter 1. In November 2021, Maria Schoina hosted me for the Aristotle University of Thessaloniki's "Problematics Seminar" in the Department of English. My talk, "We make the plague: Mary Shelley's translation of *Oedipus Rex*," became the basis of Chapter 2. In the summer of 2022, participating in two online seminars helped me to crystallize the scope and form of the book. Laura Kirkley and her U.K.-based "Gothic Women Adaptations Seminar" invited me to speak on the topic "From *Frankenstein* to *Dracula* to Big Brother: Stoker's Gothic Adaptation of Shelley and its Impact on Orwellian Dystopian Literature," which informs Chapter 3. I also presented an overview of the introduction to the "International Relations Seminar" at Australian National University, hosted by Cian O'Driscoll.

Since the Covid-spurred lockdowns of early 2020, the silver lining of relying more on Zoom and Teams technology, not to mention Twitter, has been to connect with scholars and make new friends around the world. However virtual, these bonds have been real. Just one example of a truly generous form of digital scholarship was Maria Schoina's gift of sending me her scans of Mary Shelley's translation of *Oedipus Rex* just after Christmas of 2020. The Orwell Society's online "George Talks" have been an ongoing source of inspiration, support, and research community. Again and again, my students at Notre Dame proved to me that they are the best I could ever teach, whether they are sitting around a seminar table, or represented in a virtual table on Zoom. My research apprentice Serena Melonio, as a sophomore political science major and recent transfer from Holy Cross College, stepped into editing this project near the end but enabled me to finish it with confidence. Although I have never met her in person, my editor at Penn Press, Jenny Tan, shepherded this improbable book, conceived during Covid, through the review process to be read by two experts whose reports were the most generous and detailed that I have ever received. Another scholar I have not met, David Luljak, not only indexed the book, but also proofread it with care and expertise.

Meanwhile, at home and in person, my son Jacob gave me daily inspiration to write this book. He has grown from infancy to second grade since I began this UPenn Press trilogy on Mary Shelley and political philosophy in 2015. Our shared passion for postapocalyptic art has led to mutual appreciation of the finer points of the film *Godzilla vs. Kong* (2021), as well as two children's book series, *The Last Kids on Earth* (2015–) and *The Bad Guys* (2015–).

Lastly: I could never enumerate all the people who made this book possible during a very challenging time for humanity as a whole, and so I can only make a general dedication. This book is for everyone who has suffered isolation and despair.

Mary Shelley shows us the way out.